Stews

200 Earthy, Delicious Recipes

Jenna Holst

Macmillan • USA

For my mother

MACMILLAN
A Simon & Schuster Macmillan Company
1633 Broadway
New York, NY 10019-6785

Macmillan Publishing books may be purchased for business
or sales promotional use. For information please write:
Special Markets Department, Macmillan Publishing USA,
1633 Broadway, New York, NY 10019.

Library of Congress Cataloging-in-Publication Data

Holst, Jenna.
    Stews: 200 earthy, delicious recipes / by Jenna Holst.
        p.   cm.
    Includes index.
    ISBN: 0-02-861848-3
    1. Stews.   2. Cookery, International.   I. Title.
TX693.H65   1998
641.8'23—dc21   98–15174
                                    CIP

Designed by Amy Trombat

Manufactured in the United States of America
10 9 8 7 6 5 4 3 2

contents

Acknowledgments

With gratitude to: my brother, Jim, for his quiet, yet steadfast reassurance; Annabel Davis-Goff, Julia della Croce, David Burke, Amy Cotler, Lori Longbotham, Nick Malgieri, Mary Cleaver, Tamara Holt, Ali Barker, Emily Aronson, and Burt Wolf for their guidance and encouragement; Bruce Holst, Katie Nilsen, Ansa Halgryn, Robert Wichtendahl, and Nicole Larkey for their friendship, tastebuds, and culinary skills; Dirk Rodenburg, my butcher; Jane Dystel, my agent, for her support throughout the project; Jennifer Griffin, my editor; and to all the wonderful cooks and authors who preceded me.

INTRODUCTION

Stews are one of man's oldest and most adored culinary accomplishments, with scores of representatives from all nations and cultures. A good stew, whether ladled from a three-legged cast iron pot set over an open fire or a Dutch oven set upon a sleek modern stovetop, is a cherished centerpiece of the most casual supper or most elegant repast.

Nothing compares to the smell of a stew slowly simmering to perfection. Unpretentious, homespun fare as well as an honest, time-honored tradition, stews are the ultimate comfort food. Their aroma evokes fond recollections; sometimes after the first bite, I think perhaps Proust was right—our taste buds awaken us and transport us through time. Each stew embodies memories of the past and is a catalyst for those yet to come.

This is a book for people who cook at home. It was written to be browsed, read, and relaxed with, as well as to inspire pleasurable dinners. Surprisingly easy to prepare and always pleasing to the palate, stews let the cook get out of the kitchen for a while, mingle with friends, do another chore, or take five. Modern lives are often overbooked, so any extra time is more than welcome. Although cooking time for many stews is long, preparation is relatively fast. Except for fish stews, these dishes have fuller flavor upon reheating, so many of the recipes can be made ahead, frozen, reheated and then taken to work for a microwave lunch or eaten later in the week for a convenient dinner.

This book is not a "how-to" science manual—I have not written instructions that must be followed to the nth degree. When I taught cooking, my students would follow a textbook recipe that said, "Cook until tender, about 15 minutes." They would set their electronic watches for the exact time and wonder why the food was not yet tender or was already overcooked. They had to learn to taste and check things as they went along. In the recipes, the time a stew takes to cook or a bread takes to bake once it is prepped is accurate within the specified time range. However, it is important to taste the stews to insure they are just right.

What I call "time warps" can occur in the prep phase. If a recipe says, "Cook the onions until tender, about 10 minutes," check them a bit earlier—perhaps this time it will take 9 minutes and next time 12. Not every vegetable is the same size or has the same water content; not every piece of meat has the same density or fat content; or the size you cut things may not be exactly the same the size that I cut it.

Raw ingredients will vary slightly—so blame Mother Nature and remember those elementary school rules: read the directions before you begin, pay attention, and check your work as you go along. And have fun. Open all your senses and notice things—how the smell changes, how the sounds vary, how the visual appearance of each dish alters as it cooks.

It's stew, not astrophysics, and in the overall scheme of things, very little can go wrong. Stews are among the most forgiving dishes you can make. If what you make is a flop or you hate it, laugh and order pizza. Although cooking and entertaining can be stressful, try to remember that it's only dinner, and the important part of dinner is the company you're sharing the meal with.

Many years ago, I went to a dinner party at a chic Hudson River estate. The Georgian-style house, set high on a hill, had sweeping verandas overlooking splendid gardens and gently rolling fields leading down to the riverbank. Over drinks on the veranda we watched a breathtaking sunset—a palate of pinks, reds, and lavenders dancing on the mountains across the Hudson.

Inside, the dining room seemed to be the size of a football field. Four large silver candelabras graced the enormous polished mahogany table, which could comfortably seat twenty-four. At each place, there was a salad-size plate with three artfully arranged and garnished jumbo shrimp in a flavorful vinaigrette. Wine was poured. Warm rolls were served. Everyone was jovial. The plates for the first course were cleared.

The kitchen door opened and a large silver platter entered; the host was holding it above his head. It contained mounds of perfect, bright green string beans garnished with fresh herbs and tomato concassé. The host set the platter down at the end of the table, and then left only to return with another platter containing more green beans, which he placed at the opposite end of the table. He disappeared into the kitchen, returning once again with another platter, which he graciously placed in the center of the table. The guests began laughing—this too, had green beans.

Apparently, there had been a disaster in the kitchen—the rest of the food had been ruined while the host was having drinks with his guests. (Obviously, he hadn't made stew.) There were plenty of green beans though, and we ate a lot of them. For dessert, we had fresh raspberries and cream. No one asked what the host had intended to serve. We ate, talked, made new friends, and had a wonderful time.

Cooking is part work, part play. It is also common sense, and can be a form of self-expression. Recipes bear the mark of the person making them, not just of the person writing them. These stews are meant to be eaten, loved, changed, and passed down from person to person so they will be adapted and

A BIT ABOUT MAKING STEWS

Stews can be prepared on the stovetop, in the oven, or over a fire. Feel free to prepare oven stews on the stovetop, or vice versa; however you may need to adjust the cooking time and you'll have to watch carefully toward the end. Taste for tenderness and add more liquid if necessary.

At one time, I thought all stews required you to flour the meat, brown the meat, add liquid and vegetables, and then simmer over low heat for a couple of hours. I have since learned that just as the use of spices and herbs changes from place to place, so does the method of stewmaking.

Flouring prior to browning is popular in many European and American stews—the flour helps thicken the sauce. However, in Belgium, Spain, and Italy, ground nuts or bread crumbs sometimes replace the flour as a thickening agent. This technique extends to Mexico and Africa where root or pureed vegetables may also be used to thicken stews. In some countries, the sauce is rather soupy and unthickened.

Sometimes meat or poultry is browned, sometimes it is cooked just until the color changes, and sometimes it is simply immersed in a gently bubbling broth or in the juices of the vegetables. For fish, vegetable, and fruit stews, the technique is most often to simmer in a flavored liquid. In Malaysia and Indonesia, unbrowned meat or poultry is often simmered in coconut milk or in vinegar and sugar; in South Africa, unfloured meat or poultry is simmered in vinegar and sugar or in the juices from vegetables; in India, it is simmered in tomatoes, or coconut milk or broth, or the juices from

continued

ix

vegetables; in the Caribbean, it is simmered in coconut milk or broth or the juices from fruits and vegetables.

Each technique grew out of its own culture, and its evolution is linked to the local ingredients, the amount and type of cooking fuel, and the type of pots. Today, many countries share similar fuel sources and cooking utensils, and even ingredients are increasingly becoming more "standard" or at least readily obtainable. However, the culinary traditions remain.

savored. I hope that you will feel the freedom to experiment a little or even a lot with them.

INGREDIENTS AND SUBSTITUTIONS

If you don't like an ingredient, try using something that is cut the same size and that has a similar texture. For example, the recipe calls for cubed parsnips but you can't stand parsnips, try carrots; if the recipe calls for Swiss chard, use spinach or escarole. If you turn your nose up at okra or marjoram, leave it out. Sure the stew will taste different, but it's better than having a meal you can't stomach.

Meat

Whether you are making a beef, veal, venison, pork or lamb stew, avoid prepackaged meat labeled "stew meat," which is often low-quality or includes scraps. Instead, purchase the cuts specified in the recipes. Except for oxtail and short ribs, all the meat called for is boneless.

Although it is popular to cut back on fat, some fat is required to make a good stew. Fat gives flavor and helps the meat stay moist and tender. Meat should be trimmed of visible fat, leaving the natural marbling. If too much fat is removed, the meat will be tasteless and can turn stringy. Once I was served a beef in red wine made with the leanest beef. While the stew was cooking, it smelled divine, and we looked forward to dinner with great anticipation. Unfortunately, the meal was a disappointment. The meat was somewhat tough, never acquiring that "melt in your mouth" consistency.

Following is a quick guide to suggested cuts of meat:

Beef: bottom round, chuck, or round

Veal: shoulder

Venison: shoulder

Pork: shoulder, Boston butt, or fresh ham from leg

Lamb: shoulder or leg

Poultry

I know a man who will not eat poultry. He grew up on chicken fricassee, dislikes stewed chicken skin, and has taken it to the extreme by banning all poultry from his diet. I too am not fond of stewed skin, so I did an informal survey. It seems that many Americans do not like stewed skin; that, combined with an increased awareness of the effect of dietary fat, means that many of us no longer eat the skin. Even when well browned, poultry skin softens when simmered in liquid and makes the sauce more fatty. Consequently, none of my recipes call for poultry with the skin on. Cooked without skin, the meat absorbs the flavor of the sauce.

I also prefer boneless stew that can be eaten easily, especially for a buffet. Some of the chicken recipes call for skinless, boneless breasts, but many call for skinless, boneless thighs, which have more character. The use of skinless, boneless poultry may depart from some fine culinary tradition; to prevent any potential loss of taste, I make a rich, flavorful broth and use it in the recipes.

Seafood

The success of any seafood dish is in the quality of the seafood, and that means fresh. Old fish and shellfish will ruin the dish. Always buy the freshest fish or shellfish from a reputable purveyor. Many commercial fisheries now freeze products immediately, and these are preferable to "fresh" seafood that is of questionable quality. Fish and shellfish should not have an unpleasantly strong odor.

TURNING STEWS INTO FABULOUS MEALS

Menu planning is actually simple. Often a loaf of bread and a tossed salad is enough to turn a stew into sumptuous meal. However that combination does not work well with some recipes, or you might prefer something special for entertaining. With the broad availability of ingredients from around the world and our vast exposure to the food of many cultures, it becomes trickier to devise a menu that creates the right blend of flavors, variation of color, and a nutritional balance. I've cross-referenced the recipes in the book, so that you can easily plan menus that work. This is a mix-and-match process, which gives you several choices of side dishes.

xi

Legumes

Sometimes small pebbles and chunks of dirt find their way into a package of legumes, and some beans shrivel in the container. To avoid the possible cracked tooth or unpleasant taste, always rinse and pick over the legumes for extraneous particles and discolored or withered beans before using. Legumes can become mealy if frozen; although stews containing legumes are best eaten fresh, I do sometimes freeze certain dishes that contain them, such as chili.

Broth

Freshly made or homemade is ideal; recipes for broth are in Chapter 9. However, in the real world, there isn't always time. I choose either a fresh store-bought broth or a low-sodium canned version or "doctorit." (See page 281: Faking It: The Doctored-Up Canned Broth.) Always taste for salt before adding the amount recommended in the recipe. Some canned broth, even low-sodium ones, can taste quite salty. I don't recommend cubes except when absolutely nothing else is available; these are most often extremely high in sodium.

Tomatoes

When beautiful fresh tomatoes are available, I use them in my cooking. When tomatoes are out of season, pithy, or extremely expensive, I substitute canned. I generally remove the skin and seeds from fresh tomatoes; however, when using canned, I leave the seeds in for they can be annoying to extract. Therefore, in many recipes I give both the number of tomatoes and the cup measurement equivalent of chopped tomatoes. When using fresh tomatoes, one medium tomato is approximately 1/3 to 1/2 cup when seeded and chopped; Italian or plum tomatoes are between 1/4 and 1/3 cup when seeded and chopped.

Note that Italian or plum tomatoes are sweeter than regular medium tomatoes, which have a higher acid content. The two types are not always interchangeable, particularly in Indian recipes where the acidity of the tomato

is needed for balance. But unless specified, you can use either.

Chilis

Whether fresh or dried, chilis need to be handled with care. They can burn your eyes, nose, lips, fingertips, and any skin they touch, and their sting can last up to several days. Trust me when I tell you that this is an extremely painful sensation.

To prevent skin irritation, you can wear thin rubber gloves when handling the chilis. If you choose not to wear gloves, always wash your hands well after touching the chilis or its seeds. And keep your fingers away from your face and eyes.

Chilis are an acquired taste; use the amount you are comfortable with. If you like only a hint of chili, use less than the recipes call for. Also, there are numerous types of chilis. Although, I frequently use jalapeños, cayenne, or serranos, you can certainly use chilis that you are familiar with and prefer, or those that are more readily available where you live.

The potency of chilis, even of a particular type, can vary. I've had some jalapeños that were extremely hot and others that were moderate. You might want to taste a tiny sliver to determine how much you use. (Warning— never take a taste of a habanero, also known as Scotch Bonnet, as these are the most potent of all chilis.) To cut back on the chili's heat, remove the ribs, and the seeds. You'll see that in many recipes, I offer a range, such as "1 to 2 jalapeños," to compensate for natural fluctuation in spiciness.

Fresh chilis can be found in most produce sections. Dried chipotle (also called smoked jalapeño), pasilla, and guajillo chilis are available in most supermarkets or in specialty stores.

Sambal Ulek

Sambal ulek or oelek, is bottled ground fresh chilis, often imported from Thailand, Indonesia, or the Netherlands, and can be found in Asian groceries and in the ethnic sections of supermarkets and specialty stores. It must be refrigerated after opening. It's easy to make your own—follow the recipe in Chapter 9 (page 276).

Unusual Ingredients

All of these ingredients are available in Asian groceries and in the ethnic sections of supermarkets and specialty stores.

Lime leaves are from the makrud tree; they are available fresh or dried and are sometimes sold as Kaffir lime leaves. Fresh leaves can be frozen in a plastic bag. Their potency will diminish once frozen or dried, so double the amount called for in a recipe.

Lemon grass stalks are available fresh or dried. I use fresh lemon grass, but 1 stalk is roughly equivalent to 2 tablespoons chopped. If dried, use 1 tablespoon.

The Herb Garden

I prefer to use fresh herbs, and I have an herb garden. Many dried herbs, especially sage, chervil, mint, cilantro, and dill, lack the character of their fresh counterparts. Once you have tried fresh, you will notice the difference. Fortunately, supermarkets and greengrocers have responded to the increased demand for fresh herbs.

To store herbs in the refrigerator, wrap them gently in a damp—not wet—paper towel. Place the wrapped herbs in a plastic bag or a sealable plastic container, or wrap them loosely in plastic wrap. Parsley should always be used fresh; store it in the refrigerator with its stems in a small cup of water.

If you have too much of a fresh herb after making a recipe, dry your own so it won't go to waste. It will still be fresher than commercial dried herbs. Leave them out to air-dry, which will take only a day or two, and then remove the leaves from the stalks and crush. Store them in a covered container. Basil leaves, can be frozen in a plastic bag, but the potency will diminish.

When it comes to bay leaves, feel free to use dried. If using dried thyme, only use dried thyme leaves, not ground thyme, for recipes in this book. Freeze-dried and frozen chives are acceptable, but fresh is always best. Always use fresh herbs for garnish.

xiii

𝒯HE SPICE SHELF

Buy spices in small quantities as you need them, unless you use a particular one often. Ground spices will diminish in strength from the moment they are opened, and last only four to six months at the desired potency.

Spices should be stored in a sealed container in a cabinet away from heat; preferably not above the stove. If you have the space, store them on their own or with canned goods. Some foods, such as chocolate or rice, can take on the flavor of the spices. Unless you are careful, you may end up with chocolate that tastes like curry and rice that tastes like chili powder.

You can grind whole spices in a mini food processor or small coffee mill. Designate that appliance as your spice grinder; otherwise food and coffee will pick up the flavor of the spices.

Fish sauce is imported from Thailand and adds a salty flavor.

Coconut milk, canned and unsweetened, is imported from the Caribbean or Thailand. Recipes using coconut milk cannot be frozen. Do not substitute sweetened coconut milk used for making pina coladas.

Garlic and Ginger

I always use fresh ginger and fresh garlic in the recipes. The dried version is no substitute. Note the following measurement equivalents:

1 clove garlic, minced = 1/2 teaspoon minced fresh garlic

1-inch piece ginger, minced = 1 tablespoon minced fresh ginger

Salt

In cooking, I prefer kosher salt with a medium-coarse grain. You can substitute a medium-coarse sea salt. However, in baking, I always use common table salt, which is finely ground.

Vegetable or Olive Oils

For vegetable oil, I use peanut or canola oil. If olive oil is called for, there really is no substitute for the flavor, so try to use it. You don't have to use extra virgin olive oil for general cooking, unless specifically called for. It has a stronger flavor and should be reserved for salad dressings, sauces, and garnishing. Unless stated otherwise, use virgin olive oil.

Cutting Back on Fat

Although I have reduced the fat in these recipes when compared to traditional recipes, you might want to cut the fat even further. Here are a few hints:

- If you have a nonstick pan, you can use a little less oil or butter when you sauté.

- A trick for using less cooking oil in a nonstick pan is to make a Fat Mister: put the olive or other vegetable oil in a plastic plant sprayer. Heat the pot; then spray the pot with the oil. It works just like any commercial nonstick spray.

- Trim meat and poultry of excess fat, but don't overtrim. Stews require some fat.

- Substitute nonfat sour cream for regular sour cream.

- When milk is called for, use 1% or 2% milk (if you do this, realize that the sauce will not have the same velvety consistency).

- When cream is called for, use half cream and half milk.

- There is no suitable substitute for coconut milk.

REHEATING

Most stews (except fish stews), benefit if left to sit for a few hours or overnight before serving. The flavors have additional time to blend fully.

Stovetop

Reheat over medium-low to medium heat and stir often. You may need to add a little liquid to prevent the stew from scorching. I often use a small amount of whatever liquid was used in preparing the stew, such as water, broth, or milk. I do not add extra wine or liquor.

Microwave

Use a microwave-proof container. Since the wattage of microwave ovens varies, consult the manufacturer's instructions for timing.

THE FAT QUESTION: BUTTER VERSUS MARGARINE?

I use butter for the flavor, and because I don't like hydrogenated fat. You may substitute margarine, if that is what you prefer.

FREEZING

Most stews, except for those made with fish and coconut milk, freeze well. Some stews that contain root vegetables (such as potatoes) or legumes (such as black beans or chickpeas) are best eaten within a few days of having been made. Root vegetables and legumes can get mealy if frozen. Here are a few freezer tips:

- Always use a freezer-proof container or freezer bag. Remove excess air and seal the container well. To prevent freezer spills, I sometimes double-bag a stew, first removing the excess air and sealing one bag and then placing it in a second bag, removing the excess air, and sealing it.

- Label and date containers so you know what is in them and how old they are.

- If you have a refrigerator with a separate freezer compartment, try to use everything within two to three months of being frozen. If you have a separate deep freezer that you don't open often, food can stay a month or two longer.

- If an item has serious freezer burn, discard it. It may have thawed if the door was left ajar or the power went off.

- Never refreeze an item that has been thawed.

MEASURING CORRECTLY FOR BREAD AND PIE CRUSTS

To insure good results when making the bread and pie crust recipes, measure accurately. Here are a few tips:

Flour

Measuring flour is the only real tricky spot for some people. Before measuring, lightly stir the flour, which settles in the bag or canister. Then spoon the flour into the measuring cup or spoon, and sweep the top of the cup or spoon with a butter knife or spatula so that it is flush with the top. If you dip the cup into the bag, you will invariably get a lot more than is called for and the result will be a heavy bread or pie crust. All of the bread and crust recipes were designed with the stir, spoon, and sweep method.

Eggs

All of the eggs called for in the recipes are large eggs. This is important as the recipes will not work as well with jumbo, extra large, or medium eggs. There will be too much or too little liquid.

THE RIGHT POTS

A stewpot, or Dutch oven as it is often called, is a pot that has a thick bottom and thick walls and is fairly heavy. Ideally it should have a tight-fitting lid and ovenproof handles. The capacity should be between $4^1/2$ to $6^1/2$ quarts. I have a rondeau, a double-handled stainless-steel-lined aluminum $4^1/2$-quart pot that is 10 inches across and 4 inches deep, and an enameled cast iron $6^1/2$-quart stewpot, both of which I use frequently. Years ago, cast iron was the material of choice in many lands; in my opinion, enameled cast iron is really the best. Acidic food such as tomatoes reacts with the plain cast iron and can discolor the food.

A good pot is an investment; like mine, yours will pass an endurance test of several decades. When you buy a stewpot, consider how easy it will be for you to lift it when it is full of food. If you feel that enameled cast iron is too heavy, choose another type of pot, such as a stainless-steel-lined aluminum pot or a heavy stainless pot with a layer of aluminum sandwiched between two layers of stainless steel. Plain aluminum has the same disadvantage as cast iron—acidic foods can react with it. A thick aluminum core in the base and walls conducts the heat evenly, while the stainless steel lining acts like the enamel coating—preserving the color and taste of the food.

Another good feature of stainless-steellined or enamel-coated pots is that you can cool the stew in the pot before putting it away. You can't do this with aluminum and cast iron because they can impart an unpleasant taste to the food. If you are like me, you might choose to put the covered pot directly into the fridge, and deal with storing leftovers in airtight containers in the morning.

one

BEEF, VEAL, & VENISON

Beef

Balinese Beef

Flemish Farmer's Carbonades

Quebec Maple Beef Stew

Cape Town Mafrew

Vienna Waltz Beef

Provençal Beef Stew

Beef Rendang

Beef Goulash

Kentucky Burgoo

Malmö Meatballs

Tangy Beef Stroganoff

Oxtail with Fennel & Tomatoes

World War II Bride's Ragu

Wine-Marinated Beef Stew

All-Beef Chili

Curried Ground Beef

Marjory's Beef Horseradish

Root Cellar Beef Stew

Veal

Venison

Additional Recipes (Chapter Six)

beef
Balinese Beef

I HAVE ALWAYS LOVED the intricate layering of spices found in Indonesian and Malaysian cuisine. Stews from this region prove that stews need not be made only when the frost is on the pumpkin, but can be enjoyed throughout the year. This marvelous dish has always gotten rave reviews.

2

serves 6

2 tablespoons vegetable oil

2¹/4 pounds beef round, cut into 1-inch cubes

8 scallions, white part only, thinly sliced; ¹/3 of green part, thinly sliced and reserved

2-inch piece fresh ginger, minced

4 cloves garlic, minced

1 to 2 jalapeños or serranos, seeded and diced

¹/4 teaspoon ground cumin

¹/4 teaspoon cayenne

3 tablespoons dark brown sugar

2 tablespoons soy sauce

2 tablespoons fresh lime juice

2¹/2 cups peeled, seeded, and chopped tomatoes (about 6 medium tomatoes)

2 green bell peppers, seeded and sliced

¹/4 pound mushrooms, sliced

chopped fresh mint leaves for garnish, optional

sambal ulek or crushed red chili flakes

1 In a stewpot over medium heat, heat the vegetable oil. Working in batches, brown each piece of beef on all sides. Add the white part of the scallions, the ginger, garlic, jalapeño, cumin, and cayenne. Cook, stirring often, for 2 minutes.

2 Add the brown sugar, soy sauce, lime juice, tomatoes, and bell peppers, and stir to combine.

3 Reduce the heat to medium-low. Cover and simmer until the meat is tender, about 1¹/2 to 2 hours. Stir in the mushrooms and cook, uncovered, for 10 to 15 minutes longer.

4 Garnish with the reserved green part of the scallions and mint. Serve the sambal ulek on the side, so each diner can add a personal touch of additional heat.

note *This dish can be made ahead, and it reheats well. It can be frozen for 2 to 3 months.*

serve with any of the following:

starch   white, basmati, or Texamati rice; or Spiced Rice, *page 244*

salad   Spicy Green Bean Sambal, *page 254*; or Cucumber Tomato Salsa, *page 261*

dessert   Pineapple in Coconut Milk, *page 208*

3

Flemish Farmer's Carbonades

MANY YEARS AGO, I was in Belgium completing high school. On Sundays, we sometimes went to a farm outside Brussels in a Flemish-speaking area of the country, where I first tasted this dish and learned how to make it. When I returned to the United States, I ordered Carbonnades (the French spelling) in a restaurant and was surprised at how it lacked the character of what I had come to know on the Flemish farm.

4

In the United States and elsewhere, the French-style stew, thickened with a flour roux, is commonplace. I prefer this farmer's version, made with dark beer and thickened with pumpernickel bread. It's a delicious way to use up stale bread and flat beer.

serves 6

2^1/2 cups moderately strong dark beer (Belgian or other good imported dark beer, or Samuel Adams Dark), preferably flat

2 tablespoons butter or vegetable oil or a combination

2^1/2 pounds beef bottom round or chuck, cut into 1^1/2- inch cubes

3 medium onions, sliced

3 cloves garlic, chopped

1^1/2 tablespoons sugar

1 teaspoon salt

^{1}/4 teaspoon freshly ground black pepper

4 medium carrots, cut into 1-inch pieces

1 To prepare the beer flat: Open the beer and let it stand for a minimum of 3 hours or overnight. Preheat the oven to 350°. In an ovenproof stewpot over medium heat, melt 1 tablespoon of the butter. Working in batches, brown each piece of beef on all sides. Transfer the meat to a plate and set aside.

2 In the same pot, melt the remaining butter over medium heat. Add the onions and cook, stirring occasionally, until they are tender, about 10 minutes. Add the garlic and continue cooking, stirring often, for 2 more minutes. Stir in the sugar, salt, and pepper. Return the browned beef to the pot and stir to mix evenly. Add the beer and carrots.

3 Spread each slice of bread with ¹/₂ teaspoon of the mustard and cut the slices into quarters. Place the bread in the stewpot, stirring to submerge it and to let it crumble in the liquid.

4 Cover and bake until the meat is tender, about 1¹/₂ to 2 hours. Just before serving stir in the chives.

note *If you don't have the time or forget to let the beer get flat, don't fret—make the dish anyway. It will still be quite good. This dish can be made ahead, and it reheats well. It can be frozen for 2 to 3 months.*

4 slices pumpernickel bread
2 teaspoons Dijon mustard
2 tablespoons chopped fresh parsley or chives

5

serve with any of the following:

starch   pumpernickel bread; or Mashed Turnips & Apples, *page 238*; or Creamy Potato Gratin, *page 233*   salad   Pickled Cucumber Salad for savory dishes with dill, *page 258*; or Pickled Beets, *page 259*

Quebec Maple Beef Stew

IN THE PROVINCE OF QUEBEC, maple is a flavoring used in just about everything, including this hearty stew. The winter vegetables cook down, forming one of the best gravies going. My family lived briefly on the Saguenay Peninsula in Quebec. The weather, even in August, can be quite chilly, down to the thirties at night. This stew is perfect for cool-weather dining, especially if you are eating in front of a lit fireplace.

6

serves 6

2 tablespoons vegetable oil

2 1/2 pounds beef round or chuck, cut into 1 1/2-inch cubes

2 medium leeks, white part only, thinly sliced

1 cup pure maple syrup

12 ounces sweet potatoes or butter-nut squash, peeled and cut into 1-inch cubes, about 2 cups

12 ounces rutabaga (yellow turnips) or turnips, peeled and cut into 1-inch cubes, about 2 cups

2 1/2 cups beef broth

1 1/2 teaspoons fresh thyme leaves or 3/4 teaspoon dried thyme leaves

3/4 teaspoon salt

1/4 teaspoon freshly ground black pepper

1 In a stewpot over medium heat, heat the vegetable oil. Working in batches, brown each piece of beef on all sides. Return all the beef to the pot. Add the leeks and cook, stirring occasionally, for 5 minutes.

2 Pour in the maple syrup and stir to combine thoroughly. Add the sweet potatoes, rutabaga, broth, thyme, salt, and pepper and stir to mix well.

3 Reduce the heat to medium-low. Simmer, partially covered, until the meat is tender, about 1 1/2 to 2 hours.

VARIATION
For a change or if you don't like or can't find rutabagas or turnips, use 2 cups peeled, sliced parsnips.

note *This stew can be made ahead, and it reheats well. It can be frozen for 2 to 3 months.*

7

serve with any of the following:

starch Herbed Dijon Beer Bread, *page 218*; or Buttermilk Cornbread, *page 219*; or Biscuits Any Which Way, *page 230*   **salad** Tomato & Sautéed Mushroom Salad *page 250*; or Colorful Crunchy Slaw, *page 253*   **dessert** Spiced Apples in Cider & Brandy, *page 211*

Cape Town Mafrew

I FIRST TASTED THIS EXTRAORDINARY STEW at the home of a Cape Malay friend who lives in Cape Town, South Africa. She is an excellent cook. Sharing food with friends and neighbors is a way of life among the Cape Malays, and their hospitality is unparalleled. Mafrew was one of several dishes she prepared for a "simple" meal. Guests went home with the leftovers, and much to my good fortune Mafrew went home with me. The unusual blend of spices in this stew won my palate, and now I make it every chance I get.

8

serves 6

2 1/2 tablespoons vegetable oil

2 medium onions, chopped

1 cup peeled, seeded, and chopped tomatoes

3 cloves garlic, minced

1-inch piece fresh ginger, minced

2 cinnamon sticks

1 tablespoon good quality curry powder, such as Madras brand

1 1/2 teaspoons ground coriander

1 1/2 teaspoons ground cumin

1 1/2 teaspoons fennel seed

3/4 teaspoon ground cardamom

1/4 to 1/2 teaspoon cayenne, or to your taste

2 1/2 pounds beef round, cut into 1 1/2-inch cubes

1/2 cup water

3/4 teaspoon salt

2 medium potatoes, peeled and cubed

1   In a stewpot over medium heat, heat the vegetable oil. Add the onions and cook, stirring occasionally, until they are translucent, about 5 minutes. Add the tomatoes, garlic, and ginger and cook for 1 minute. Add the cinnamon sticks, curry powder, coriander, cumin, fennel seed, cardamom, and cayenne and stir. Continue cooking, stirring often, until the aroma of the spices is very strong, about 5 minutes.

2   Add the beef, water, and salt. Reduce heat to between low and medium-low, or barely above low on your stove's dial. Cover and simmer for 1 hour or until the beef is almost tender.

3   Add the potatoes and stir to combine. Cover and simmer until the beef and potatoes are tender, about 30 to 40 minutes longer.

note This dish can be made ahead, and it reheats well. It can be frozen for 2 months.

serve with any of the following:

starch   white, basmati, or Texamati rice; or Spiced Rice or Yellow Spiced Rice variation, *page 244*   salad   Carrot Orange Sambal, *page 256*; or Avocado Salad, *page 260*   condiment   Fresh Mango Chutney, *page 270*

9

Vienna Waltz Beef

YEARS AGO, I WAS AN ACTRESS in New York City. It is no secret that show-biz people love to eat. At the end of a project we would have a "wrap" party. This dish not only satisfied the appetites of the tired and hungry masses, but also was a savory way to say thank you and bid a fond farewell. Like a waltz, this stew is easy to do and always pleasing.

10

serves 6

2 tablespoons vegetable oil

2 pounds beef round, cut into 1^{1}/2-inch cubes

2 pounds onions, thinly sliced

3 cloves garlic, minced

5 tablespoons Hungarian sweet paprika

1 teaspoon Hungarian hot paprika or ^{1}/4 to ^{1}/2 teaspoon cayenne

2 teaspoons caraway seeds

1^{1}/2 cups beef broth or water

^{3}/4 teaspoon salt

^{1}/4 teaspoon white pepper

chopped fresh parsley for garnish

1 In a stewpot over medium heat, heat the vegetable oil. Working in batches, brown each piece of beef on all sides. Remove the beef from the pot and set aside.

2 Add the onions to the pot and cook until they are tender, about 10 minutes. Add the garlic and cook, stirring often, for 2 minutes. Add the sweet paprika, hot paprika or cayenne, and caraway seeds and cook, stirring constantly, for 1 to 2 minutes.

3 Return the beef to the pot. Pour in the broth. Add the salt and pepper. Reduce the heat to medium-low. Cover and simmer until the meat is tender, about 1^{1}/2 to 2 hours. Garnish with chopped parsley.

note   *This dish can be made ahead, and it reheats well. It can be frozen for 2 to 3 months.*

serve with any of the following:

starch   broad noodles or Great Potato Pancakes, *page 232*; or Round Country Loaf, *page 224*; or Lemon Scallion Soda Bread, *page 217*   salad   Make-Ahead Herbed Garden Salad, *page 263*; or Herbed Vegetable Slaw, *page 252*; or Pickled Beets, *page 259*

11

Provençal Beef Stew

THIS FRAGRANT STEW from southern France is magnificent—the blessed marriage of beef, tomatoes, garlic, orange, parsley, and thyme. It is the kind of dish that seconds are required, with a light gravy that just begs for bread to be dunked in it.

When I was a child, my mother told me the person who got the bay leaf in her bowl would have good luck. Consequently, I never remove the bay leaf, but if you don't share my superstition, feel free to take it out before serving.

serves 6

1^1/2 teaspoons salt

^{1}/4 teaspoon freshly ground black pepper

all-purpose flour for dusting the meat

2^1/2 pounds beef round or chuck, cut into 1^1/2-inch cubes

2^1/2 tablespoons olive oil

1 medium onion, diced

1 stalk celery, diced

1 medium carrot, diced

2 cloves garlic, chopped

1 cup peeled, seeded, and chopped tomatoes

2-inch strip fresh orange zest, white pith removed

^{1}/4 cup fresh flat-leaf parsley, chopped

1 bay leaf

1   In a medium bowl, combine 1 teaspoon of the salt, the pepper, and about ^{1}/3 cup flour. Lightly dust the meat with the seasoned flour, shaking off any excess.

2   In a stewpot over medium heat, heat 1 tablespoon of the olive oil. Working in batches, brown each piece of beef on all sides. Transfer the beef to a plate and set aside.

3   In the same pot over medium heat, heat the remaining 1^1/2 tablespoons of olive oil. Add the onion, celery, and carrot and cook for 3 minutes. Add the garlic and cook, stirring, for 1 minute. Add the tomatoes, orange zest, parsley, bay leaf, thyme, and the remaining ^{1}/2 teaspoon of salt and cook for 2 minutes longer.

4   Pour in the wine and broth. Scrape the bottom with a wooden spoon to loosen any browned bits.

5   Return the meat to the pot. Reduce the heat to medium-low. Cover and simmer until the meat is tender, about 1 1/2 to 2 hours. Garnish with Crispy Shallots, if desired.

note   *This dish can be made ahead, and it reheats well. It can be frozen for 2 to 3 months.*

3 sprigs fresh thyme leaves, about 2 teaspoons, or 3/4 teaspoon dried thyme leaves

1 1/2 cups full-bodied red wine

1/2 cup beef broth or water

Crispy Shallots, p. 272 for garnish, optional

13

serve with any of the following:

starch   Anna's Crusty French Loaf, *page 222*; or Garlic & Herb Mashed Potatoes, *page 235*; or Round Country Loaf, *page 224*   **salad**   Roasted Beet & Onion Salad on Watercress, *page 247*; or Mesclun Salad with Goat Cheese, *page 262*; or Arugula Salad, *page 265*   **dessert**   Nectarines with Tarragon & Pepper, *page 213*

Beef Rendang

THIS IS ONE OF THE WORLD'S best beef stews, and it is my favorite. Rendang, a specialty from Sumatra which was originally made with buffalo meat, now commonly features beef simmered in chili-spiced coconut milk. The aroma while it is cooking is absolutely heavenly. The flavor is rich and satisfying. In this country, rendang is not everyday fare, but we all need to treat ourselves every now and then.

I first ate this dish over twenty years ago in a restaurant in Amsterdam. The Indonesian chef graciously offered to show me his secrets for preparing rendang. The coconut sauce should not be soupy, but should be extremely thick and only glaze the meat. The rendang is ready when the beef has absorbed most of the coconut milk, a process that can't be rushed. Patience is essential.

serves 6

Red Chili Paste

4 plump cloves garlic, sliced

4 medium shallots, sliced

1/2-inch piece fresh ginger

2 stalks lemon grass, sliced, optional

**5 to 7 small red chili peppers (such as bird's eye, cayenne, or other), seeded and chopped or
2 teaspoons of *sambal ulek* (page 276) or ground chili paste**

2 teaspoons tomato paste, optional

1   *To prepare the paste:* In a food processor fitted with the metal blade or a blender, combine the garlic, shallots, ginger, and lemon grass and puree until smooth, adding 1 to 2 teaspoons of warm water if necessary to make a paste. Add the chopped chilis or sambal ulek. Puree until a smooth paste forms. Transfer to a small bowl and stir in the tomato paste.

2   *To prepare the stew:* In a stewpot over medium heat, heat the vegetable oil. Add the red chili paste from above or 3 tablespoons prepared Thai-style red chili paste; cook, stirring occasionally until the aroma is very strong, about 7 to 10 minutes. Add the brown sugar and cook, stirring constantly, for 1 minute longer. Pour in the coconut milk and cook, stirring occasionally, until the liquid comes to a gentle boil, about 3 to 5 minutes.

3 Add the beef. Reduce the heat to medium-low. Simmer, uncovered, stirring every 30 minutes or so, until the beef is tender, about 1½ to 2 hours. The liquid should be gently bubbling during the cooking process.

4 Reduce the heat to low. Continue simmering, stirring often, until the sauce is very, very thick and clings to the meat, about 30 to 45 minutes. Timing can vary slightly, but this part cannot be hurried. When the sauce begins to thicken noticeably, you will need to stir almost constantly to prevent scorching, as if you were stir-frying the meat. The meat should absorb most of the coconut milk, and the sauce should turn brown and coat the meat. Garnish with Crispy Shallots.

note *This dish can be made ahead and gently reheated in a double-boiler or over medium-low heat, stirring often. You may need to add a very small amount of coconut milk when reheating directly on the stovetop. This stew does not freeze well because of the coconut milk, but it can be refrigerated for 3 to 5 days.*

Stew

2½ tablespoons vegetable oil

2 tablespoons brown sugar

3 cups unsweetened coconut milk

2½ pounds beef bottom round or chuck, cut into ¾-inch cubes or strips

Crispy Shallots (page 272) for garnish, optional

15

serve with any of the following:

starch   white, basmati, or Texamati rice; or Spiced Rice or Yellow Spiced Rice variation, *page 244*   salad   Pickled Cucumber Salad, *page 258*; or Rujak, *page 246*; or Carrot Orange Sambal, *page 256*

Beef Goulash

I THINK OF THIS DISH as gourmet kid's fare that adults like, probably because it was one of those recipes that my mother made for company. She could make it ahead and actually sit with guests rather than be sequestered in the kitchen. As a bonus, my brother and I would eat it when we were small and not complain. As we got older, we even requested it, and I still like it today. It's no bother to make—you can make it while doing nine other things, it doesn't mess up the kitchen too much, and people actually think you've gone to some trouble. It's one of those old standbys that has stood the test of time.

16

serves 6

2 whole cloves garlic

2 sprigs fresh marjoram or
   $1/2$ teaspoon dried

$2^1/2$ pounds beef bottom round or
   chuck, cut into $1^1/2$- inch cubes

$1/2$ teaspoon salt

2 tablespoons olive oil

1 medium onion, chopped

2 tablespoons tomato paste

1 tablespoon Hungarian sweet
   paprika

1 cup beef broth

1 cup full-bodied red wine

1 tablespoon Worcestershire sauce

$1/8$ to $1/4$ teaspoon cayenne

1 Preheat oven to 325°. Wrap the garlic and marjoram in a small piece of cheesecloth; tie it to form a sack.

2 Pat the beef dry with paper towels, then season it with salt.

3 In a large ovenproof stewpot over medium heat, heat about 1 tablespoon of the olive oil. Working in batches, lightly brown each piece of beef on all sides. Add more of the oil as necessary between batches, letting it get hot before putting in more meat. Repeat until all the meat is browned. Return all the beef to the pot.

4 Add the onion and cook, stirring occasionally, until it is tender, about 10 minutes. Stir in the tomato paste and paprika and cook, stirring constantly so nothing burns, for about 2 minutes.

5 Pour in the broth and wine. Add the cheesecloth sack, Worcestershire sauce, and cayenne. Stir, scraping the bottom to loosen any browned bits.

6 Cover the pot and put it in the oven. Bake until the beef is tender, about 1¹/₂ to 2 hours. Remove the cheesecloth sack before serving.

note *This dish can be made ahead, and it reheats well. It can be frozen for 2 to 3 months. You may need to add a little liquid when reheating on a stove to keep it from burning.*

serve with any of the following:

starch   broad noodles or Great Potato Pancakes, *page 232*; or Mashed Turnips & Apples, *page 238*; or Oven-Roasted Red Potatoes with Rosemary, *page 234*

salad   Tomato & Sautéed Mushroom Salad, *page 250*; or Herbed Vegetable Slaw, *page 252*   dessert   Spiced Dried Fruit Compote, *page 207*

Kentucky Burgoo

THERE'S NOTHING QUITE LIKE a Kentucky Burgoo—a stew of meat, poultry, and vegetables spiked with bourbon. It's an outstanding Southern tradition. It is one of those dishes that improves when made ahead and reheated.

Old-time recipes call for game such as rabbit and squirrel, but I use a combination of beef, chicken, and ham with excellent results. The ingredient list may be long, but it's worth the effort. I like to use Rebel Yell or Jack Daniels in the burgoo, but you can use any good bourbon or sour-mash whiskey.

serves 6

1 1/2 pounds beef bottom round or chuck, cut into 1 1/2-inch cubes

3/4 pound boneless skinless chicken thighs

1/2 pound smoked ham, sliced 1/2-inch thick, cut into strips

2 cups beef broth or water

2 cups chopped, peeled, and seeded tomatoes

2/3 cup good bourbon or sour-mash whiskey

1 medium potato, peeled and cubed

3 tablespoons chopped fresh parsley

1 1/2 teaspoons fresh chopped thyme leaves or 3/4 teaspoon dried leaves

1   In a stewpot over medium heat, combine the beef, chicken, ham, broth, tomatoes, bourbon, potato, parsley, thyme, bay leaf, salt, black pepper, and cayenne. Bring the mixture to a boil, uncovered.

2   As soon as the liquid comes to a boil, reduce the heat to medium-low. Cover and simmer for 1 1/4 hours.

3   Stir in the lima beans, corn, and okra. Cook, covered, until the meat is tender and the vegetables have been infused with the meat and other flavors, about 45 minutes longer. While the stew is cooking, check to see if the okra has thickened it too much; add a little water, if necessary. Serve with Tabasco sauce on the side.

18

note   This dish can be made ahead, and it reheats well. It can be frozen for 2 to 3 months.

1 bay leaf

1 teaspoon salt

$1/2$ teaspoon freshly ground black pepper

$1/4$ teaspoon cayenne

$1^1/4$ cups (one 10-ounce package) frozen or fresh lima beans

$1^1/4$ cups (one 10-ounce package) frozen or fresh corn kernels

$1^1/4$ cups (one 10-ounce package) frozen or fresh sliced okra

Tabasco sauce as a garnish

serve with any of the following:

starch   Buttermilk Cornbread, *page 219*; or Biscuits Any Which Way, *page 230*; or Spiced Mashed Sweet Potatoes, *page 237*   salad   Warm Greens, *page 251*, with Hot Pepper Vinegar, *page 271*

Malmö Meatballs

MALMÖ IS A CITY on the southern coast of Sweden. While Swedish meatballs, or *panbiffan*, are not really a stew, I include the dish in this book because, like many stews, they act as the comfort food of a nation and are one of the world's best dishes. Perhaps this is just my Viking heritage talking, but I hope you agree that these are delicious.

20

serves 6

Meatballs
1 pound beef ground round or sirloin
1/2 pound beef ground chuck
1 medium onion, chopped
1/2 cup unseasoned bread crumbs
1/3 cup whole or 2% milk
1 egg
1 teaspoon salt
1/2 teaspoon white pepper
1/4 teaspoon freshly ground black pepper
1/2 teaspoon freshly grated nutmeg
1 1/2 tablespoons vegetable oil

Sauce
1 1/4 cups beef broth
3/4 cup light cream or half and half
2 tablespoons dry red wine

1   In a large bowl, using your hands, combine the ground round, ground chuck, onion, bread crumbs, milk, egg, salt, white pepper, black pepper, and nutmeg. Wet your hands, and roll the mixture into meatballs about 1 inch in diameter.

2   In a medium nonstick frying pan over medium heat, heat the vegetable oil. Working in batches, add no more than 10 meatballs at a time to the pan, and brown each on all sides. Transfer the cooked meatballs to a plate lined with paper towels and pat gently to remove excess oil.

3   *To prepare the sauce:* In a large saucepan over medium-low heat, combine the broth, cream, and wine and simmer for 5 minutes.

4   Add the meatballs to the sauce and simmer for 15 minutes.

note This dish can be made ahead and reheats well. It can
be frozen for 2 to 3 months. If frozen, add some cream to the
sauce when reheating.

serve with any of the following:

starch   boiled red potatoes; or Creamy Potato Gratin, *page 233*

salad   Pickled Cucumber Salad for savory food with dill, *page 258*; or Pickled

Beets, *page 259*; or Lemony Asparagus or Green Beans with Nuts, *page 255*

condiment   Traditionally, this dish is served with lingonberry preserves, which are

available in many supermarkets and gourmet stores. Lingonberries, native to

Scandinavia, are rather tart and the preserves are expensive in the United States.

You could substitute Cranberries in Red Wine, *page 212*, as a side dish or as a

dessert with frozen yogurt, sorbet, or ice cream.

Tangy Beef Stroganoff

RICH AND CREAMY, this classic Russian dish is undeniably superb. Many of us remember the creamed mushroom soup and hamburger meat version from 1960s American cookbooks—a far cry from the real thing. However, even ground beef tastes good in this sauce.

I once worked for someone who claimed to have the original Russian recipe for this dish—whether or not this was true, I'll never know. Apparently, the secret of the sauce is the mustard, so this version includes mustard and a few other subtle flavors. Serve the stroganoff with broad noodles as I always do.

serves 6

Sauce

1 1/2 tablespoons butter
1 1/2 tablespoons all-purpose flour
1 cup beef broth, heated
1 1/2 teaspoons Dijon mustard
1 teaspoon Hungarian sweet paprika
dash of freshly grated nutmeg (less than 1/8 of a teaspoon)
3/4 to 1 cup sour cream or nonfat sour cream

Beef

2 1/2 tablespoons butter
1 medium onion, diced
1/2 pound mushrooms, sliced
1 teaspoon salt
1 1/2 pounds beef filet, sirloin or top round, sliced into very thin strips
1/4 teaspoon white pepper
chopped fresh chives or parsley for garnish

1   *To prepare the sauce:* In a saucepan over medium heat, melt the butter. Add the flour. Cook for 1 to 2 minutes, stirring constantly with a wooden spoon or wire whisk. While stirring, gradually pour in the heated broth. Stir until the mixture is smooth. Add the mustard, paprika, nutmeg, and sour cream and stir. Set aside. You may keep the sauce warm over low heat while preparing the rest of the ingredients, but don't let it boil.

2   *To prepare the beef:* In a large, deep skillet or stewpot over medium heat, melt 1 1/2 tablespoons of the butter. Add the onion and cook until translucent, about 5 minutes. Add the mushrooms and cook until they are tender, about 5 minutes. Season with 1/2 teaspoon of the salt. Transfer to a plate and set aside.

3   Season the beef with the remaining 1/2 teaspoon salt and the white pepper. In the same large skillet or stewpot over medium heat, melt the remaining 1 tablespoon of butter. Working in batches, brown each piece of beef on all sides.

4 When the beef is browned, return it all to the skillet and add the mushrooms. Pour in the reserved sauce. Over low heat, simmer briefly until everything is heated through, less than 5 minutes. Serve immediately, garnished with chopped chives.

note *This recipe does not freeze well because the sour cream can break upon reheating. Although it can be made ahead if you reheat it gently and carefully, in my opinion it is best eaten right after it is made. The beef can get a bit overdone when reheating.*

23

serve with any of the following:

starch   broad noodles; or Herbed Dijon Beer Bread, *page 218*; or Biscuits Any Which Way, *page 230*   salad   mixed greens with Basic Vinaigrette, *page 266*; or A Good & Simple Salad, *page 264*; or Lemony Asparagus or Green Beans with Nuts, *page 255*   dessert   Pears in Ruby Port & Vanilla, *page 206*

Oxtail with Fennel & Tomatoes

I ALWAYS WONDERED what oxtail was. Where were these oxen of which only the tail was eaten? Were there tailless oxen running around? Actually, oxtail is beef—the tail from the steer we normally eat. It makes an excellent stew with a rich gravy. Fennel and tomatoes add their unique spark to this homespun dish. Forget good manners when eating this stew—the best way to get all the meat is by picking up the pieces and gnawing it off the bone.

24

serves 6

3 1/2 pounds oxtail, cut into sections between the joints

all-purpose flour for dusting the meat

2 tablespoons olive oil

2 medium onions, chopped

2 carrots, chopped

1 medium fennel bulb, cored and diced

4 plump cloves garlic, minced

5 to 6 (about 1 1/2 cups or one 14 1/2-ounce can) plum tomatoes, peeled, seeded, and chopped

1 1/2 cups beef broth

1 cup dry red wine

1 bay leaf

1 tablespoon fresh thyme leaves or 1 teaspoon dried

1 Lightly dust the oxtail pieces with flour, shaking off any excess. In a stewpot over medium heat, heat the olive oil. Working in batches, brown each oxtail piece on all sides. Return all the oxtail to the pot.

2 Add the onions, carrots, fennel, garlic, tomatoes, broth, and wine. Scrape the bottom of the pan with a wooden spoon to loosen any browned bits. Cook for approximately 2 minutes, stirring often.

3 Add the bay leaf, thyme, 2 tablespoons of the parsley, lemon zest, lemon juice, brown sugar, salt, and pepper and stir.

4 Reduce the heat to medium-low. Cover and simmer until the meat is tender, about 2 to 2 1/2 hours. With a ladle, skim off any fat that has risen to the surface. Stir in the remaining 2 tablespoons of parsley and serve garnished with fennel fronds.

note This dish can be made ahead, and it reheats well. It can be frozen for 2 to 3 months.

$1/4$ **cup chopped fresh flat-leaf parsley**

finely grated zest and juice of 1 lemon

$1 1/2$ **teaspoons brown sugar**

$3/4$ **teaspoon salt**

$1/2$ **teaspoon freshly ground black pepper**

fennel fronds reserved for garnish

25

serve with any of the following:

starch   Oven-Roasted Red Potatoes with Rosemary, *page 234*; or Basic Risotto or Risotto with Mushrooms, *page 242*; or Onion Flat Bread, *page 222*   salad   Arugula Salad, *page 265*; or Mesclun Salad with Goat Cheese, *page 262*   dessert   Figs in Red Wine, Ginger, & Thyme, *page 210*

World War II Bride's Ragu

DURING WORLD WAR II, there was food rationing, and Americans were allotted a certain number of points for the purchase of butter, fresh meat, canned meat, and other items. If you ate in a restaurant, however, you didn't waste any points. A meal out let you stretch your points for home-cooked meals and could prevent a daily diet of Spam.

26 Consequently, my dad used to take my mother to an Italian restaurant. The owner's wife knew my mother was a young bride and taught her how to make this basic spaghetti sauce with only a small amount of meat. That stretched the points even farther and fed many mouths. Although this is classified a pasta sauce, its preparation, a long-simmering fusing of flavors, is similar to that of many stews. I have included it because I love this ragu, and it's an economical meal.

serves 6 to 8

2 tablespoons olive oil
2 medium onions, chopped
1 green bell pepper, chopped
3 plump cloves garlic, chopped
1/2 pound lean ground beef
1/3 pound lean ground pork
6 tablespoons tomato paste
1/2 cup full-bodied red wine
1/3 cup water
3 1/2 cups (one 28-ounce can) canned crushed plum tomatoes
1 bay leaf
2 tablespoons chopped fresh basil or 2 1/2 teaspoons dried

1 In a stewpot or large deep skillet over medium heat, heat the olive oil. Add the onions and bell pepper and cook, stirring occasionally, until the vegetables are softened, about 5 minutes. Add the garlic and cook, stirring often, for 1 minute.

2 Add the ground beef and pork in small pieces, breaking up any lumps with the back of a spoon, and cook until the meat is browned, about 7 to 10 minutes.

3 Add the tomato paste and cook, stirring often, until the paste darkens slightly, about 2 minutes. Pour in the wine, water, and tomatoes. Add the bay leaf, basil, oregano, black pepper, and salt.

4   Reduce the heat to medium-low. Partially cover and simmer for 1¹/₂ to 2 hours. Stir in the olives if using and simmer for 20 to 25 minutes. Taste for salt and add more if you wish. Serve with Parmesan cheese on the side.

note   *This recipe can be made ahead, and it reheats well. It can be frozen for up to 3 months.*

2 teaspoons chopped fresh oregano or 1 teaspoon dried

¹/₄ teaspoon freshly ground black pepper

³/₄ to 1 teaspoon salt or to taste

¹/₂ cup coarsely chopped, pitted black Italian olives, optional

freshly grated Parmesan cheese for garnish

27

serve with any of the following:

starch   pasta such as spaghetti, tagliatelle, or linguine; Anna's Crusty French Loaf, *page 222*, turned into garlic bread; or Onion Flat Bread, *page 220*

salad   A Good & Simple Salad, *page 264*; or mixed greens tossed with Basic Vinaigrette using balsamic or red wine vinegar, *page 266*

Wine-Marinated Beef Stew

BASED ON THE MARVELOUS FRENCH classic, boeuf bourgignon, the beef in this stew is marinated overnight in red wine, spices, and herbs, imparting the robust character of the marinade to the meat.

Don't let the long list of ingredients or the two-day process keep you from at least trying the dish. Although there appear to be many steps, they are easy, and there is very little hands-on work.

28

serves 6

Marinade

1 medium onion, peeled and studded with 4 whole cloves

3³/4 pounds beef bottom round, cut into 2¹/2- to 3-inch cubes

1 bottle (about 3¹/2 cups) good-quality red wine, such as Cabernet Sauvignon, Merlot, a Cabernet-Merlot blend, or Burgundy

¹/4 cup good-quality cognac or brandy

2 tablespoons extra virgin olive oil

1 bay leaf

3 black peppercorns

2 white peppercorns

3 whole coriander

3 sprigs fresh thyme or ¹/2 teaspoon dried

2 cloves garlic, peeled and smashed slightly

1   *To prepare the marinade:* The day before serving, place the onion in the center of a large, deep glass or stainless-steel bowl. Surround the onion with the meat. Add the wine, brandy, and olive oil for the marinade. Wrap the bay leaf, peppercorns, coriander, thyme, and garlic in a small piece of cheesecloth and tie it to form a sack. Submerge the sack in the wine mixture. Make sure the meat is covered completely. Cover the bowl with plastic wrap and put it in the refrigerator for 12 to 24 hours. Once or twice, lift or stir the beef from the bottom to the top so that it marinates evenly.

2   Preheat the oven to 325°. With a slotted spoon, remove the beef from the marinade. Spread the beef on a clean baking sheet, and pat it with paper towels until it is dry. Set aside. Reserve the marinade, cheesecloth sack, and onion.

3   In a large saucepan over medium-high heat, bring the marinade, spice, and onion mixture to a boil. Reduce the heat to medium and boil for 5 to 10 minutes, making sure the liquid doesn't boil over. (It can boil over rather quickly.) The liquid should be reduced slightly, by

about 1 cup. With a slotted spoon, remove and discard the onion. Set the mixture aside.

4   To prepare the stew: In a medium skillet over medium heat, heat 1 tablespoon of the olive oil for the stew. Add the carrots, celery, and onion and cook, stirring occasionally, until the vegetables are tender, about 10 minutes. Set aside.

5   In a small bowl, combine the flour, salt, and pepper. Lightly dust the beef with the seasoned flour, shaking off any excess.

6   In an ovenproof stewpot over medium heat, heat a third of the remaining olive oil. Working in batches, lightly brown each piece of meat on all sides. Transfer the browned meat to a plate. Add more of the oil as necessary between batches, letting it get hot before putting in the meat. Repeat until all the meat is browned.

7   Return all the beef to the pot. Add the reduced marinade, cheesecloth sack, and cooked vegetables and stir. Cover and bake until the beef is almost tender, about 2 1/2 hours. If the stew is too thick, add a little water.

8   Stir the mushrooms and lardons into the stew. Cover and bake until the beef is completely tender, about 30 to 40 minutes longer. Before serving, garnish with parsley.

Stew

3 tablespoons olive oil
2 medium carrots, sliced
1 celery stalk, sliced
1 medium onion, diced
1/3 cup all-purpose flour
1 teaspoon salt
1/2 teaspoon freshly ground black pepper
1/2 pound mushrooms, sliced
Lardons (page 274)
chopped fresh flat-leaf parsley for garnish

29

note   *This dish can be made ahead, and it reheats well. It can be frozen for 3 months.*

serve with any of the following:

starch   Anna's Crusty French Loaf, *page 222*; or Mashed Potatoes with Cucumber, *page 236*; or Garlic and Herbed Mashed Potatoes, *page 236*   **salad**   A Good & Simple Salad, *page 264*; or Lemony Asparagus or Green Beans with Nuts, *page 255*; or Tomato & Sautéed Mushroom Salad, *page 250*   **dessert**   Spiced Apples in Cider & Brandy, *page 211*

All-Beef Chili

CHILI IS AN AMERICAN STANDARD that is always a hit. There are many versions of it: some with beans, some with tomatoes. The list is as varied and endless as the people making the dish. This recipe is a straightforward beef chili with beer, some tomatoes, and no beans that adapts well to individual preferences. I like beef chili sans beans, but add some if you want it to serve more people. Depending on my mood, I like to garnish it with either shredded cheese or sour cream.

serves 6 to 8

2 tablespoons olive or vegetable oil

1 1/2 teaspoons salt

3 1/2 pounds beef chuck, bottom round, or brisket, cut into 1/2-inch cubes

2 medium onions, chopped

5 cloves garlic, minced

1/3 cup chili powder, about 5 tablespoons

1 1/2 teaspoons ground cumin

1/2 teaspoon cayenne

2 1/2 cups canned crushed tomatoes

1/2 cup beer or water

1 tablespoon fresh chopped oregano or 1 teaspoon dried

1 teaspoon brown sugar

1 tablespoon *masa harina* or 1/2 tablespoon fine cornmeal combined with 1/2 tablespoon all-purpose flour, optional

grated Monterey Jack cheese, sour cream, or nonfat sour cream for garnish, optional

1 In a large stewpot over medium heat, heat the vegetable oil. Pat the meat dry with paper towels, and season with 1 teaspoon of the salt. Working in batches, brown each piece of beef on all sides. Return all the beef to the pot.

2 Add the onions and cook, stirring, until the onion is tender, about 10 minutes. Add the garlic, chili powder, cumin, and cayenne and cook, stirring often, about 2 minutes.

3 Add the crushed tomatoes, beer, oregano, and sugar. Reduce the heat to medium-low. Simmer, uncovered, until the meat is tender, about 1 1/2 to 2 hours. Stir occasionally while the chili is cooking. Stir in the masa harina and simmer for about 5 minutes.

note   This dish can be made ahead, and it reheats well. It can be frozen for 3 months.

serve with any of the following:

starch   warm tortillas; or rice; or Herbed Corn Biscuits, *page 229*; or Buttermilk Cornbread, *page 219*   salad   Avocado Salad, *page 260*; or Cucumber Tomato Salsa, *page 261*

31

Curried Ground Beef

IT'S AMAZING HOW MANY places this dish appears. Versions of curried ground beef, also known as *kheema,* are found in India, throughout the Caribbean, in South Africa, and in many metropolitan neighborhoods in the United States. It is quick and easy to prepare and can be used as a filling for a snack or rotis, the flat Caribbean Indian-style bread, available at some Caribbean or Indian markets. In a pinch, you can use a flour tortilla. This is not a fancy recipe, and it can be put together in a flash. I make it when I'm bored with burgers.

serves 6

2 tablespoons vegetable oil

2 medium onions, chopped

1-inch piece fresh ginger, minced

2 cloves garlic, minced

2 tablespoons good quality curry powder, such as Madras brand

1^1/2 pounds lean ground beef

2 medium tomatoes, peeled, seeded, and chopped, about 1 cup

1 medium potato, peeled and diced in ^{1}/2-inch cubes

^{1}/2 teaspoon salt

1^1/4 cups (one 10-ounce package) frozen peas

2 tablespoons chopped fresh cilantro, optional

1 In a large deep skillet over medium heat, heat the vegetable oil. Add the onions and cook, stirring occasionally, until they are translucent, about 5 minutes. Add the ginger, garlic, and curry powder and cook, stirring constantly, for 2 minutes.

2 Add the ground beef and cook, stirring occasionally, until it is browned. Add the tomatoes and cook, stirring occasionally, for 5 minutes.

3 Add the potatoes. Reduce the heat to medium-low. Cover and simmer until the potatoes are tender, about 30 minutes.

4 Add the salt and stir, then add the peas. Cook until the peas are heated through, about 5 minutes. Stir in the cilantro and serve.

note   This dish can be made ahead, and it reheats well. It
can be frozen for 2 to 3 months.

serve with any of the following:

    starch   white, basmati, Texamati rice; or Spiced Rice, *page 244*

salad   Pickled Cucumber Salad for spicy dishes with chilis and mint, *page 258*;

    or Raita, *page 257*

Marjory's Beef Horseradish

BEEF AND HORSERADISH ARE LIKE long-time lovers—perfectly matched. This is one of those dishes whose origin is lost in the family archives. I used to eat it on special occasions as a child, and it was a hit whenever served. Because this recipe can be made ahead and needs only a few finishing touches at the end, it is a blessing for the cook who likes to entertain.

34

serves 6

3 tablespoons vegetable oil

2 onions, thinly sliced

1-inch piece fresh ginger, minced

1 clove garlic, minced

1 teaspoon chopped fresh thyme
  leaves or $^{1}/_{2}$ teaspoon dried
  thyme leaves

$^{1}/_{8}$ teaspoon ground cloves

1 bay leaf

2 pounds round steak, cut into
  1$^{1}/_{2}$-inch cubes

all-purpose flour for dusting the
  meat

$^{3}/_{4}$ teaspoon salt

$^{1}/_{4}$ teaspoon freshly ground black
  pepper

1$^{2}/_{3}$ cups beef broth or water

1 tablespoon Worcestershire sauce

1 tablespoon molasses

$^{3}/_{4}$ cup sour cream or nonfat sour
  cream

1$^{1}/_{2}$ tablespoons prepared, grated
  white horseradish

1. Preheat the oven to 350°. In a medium skillet over medium heat, heat 1 tablespoon of the vegetable oil. Add the onions and cook, stirring occasionally, until they are translucent, about 5 minutes. Add the ginger, garlic, thyme, cloves, and bay leaf and cook, stirring often, for 1 to 2 minutes. Set the skillet aside.

2. Pat the meat dry with paper towels. In a bowl, combine about $^{1}/_{3}$ cup of the flour, salt, and pepper. Lightly dust the meat with the seasoned flour, shaking off any excess.

3. In an ovenproof stewpot over medium heat, heat the remaining 2 tablespoons of vegetable oil. Working in batches, brown each piece of beef on all sides.

4. Return all the beef to the pot. Add the onions and stir to mix evenly. Add the broth, Worcestershire sauce, and molasses. Stir and scrape the bottom with a wooden spoon to loosen any browned bits.

5. Cover and bake until the meat is tender, about 1$^{1}/_{2}$ hours. The stew can be made ahead up to this point.

6 In a small bowl, combine the sour cream and horseradish. Stir the horseradish cream into the stew. On the stovetop over medium-low heat, simmer until everything is heated through, about 5 minutes.

note *This dish can be made ahead, up to the addition of the horseradish cream. It reheats well and can be frozen for 2 to 3 months. The horseradish cream must be added right before serving.*

35

serve with any of the following:

starch   broad noodles; or Mashed Potatoes with Cucumber, *page 236*; or Buttermilk Raisin Spice Bread, *page 216*   salad   Sugar Snap Peas with Orange & Herbs, *page 249*; or Make-Ahead Herbed Garden Salad, *page 263*   dessert Rhubarb with Cardamom, *page 209*

Root Cellar Beef Stew

MY GRANDMOTHER, WHO LIVED in Pennsylvania, had a root cellar—an underground cavern in which she stored vegetables during the winter. As a child, I thought the cellar was both fascinating and eerie. She stocked it with turnips, rutabagas, carrots, parsnips, potatoes, and onions— vegetables that survive, even thrive in the frosty months. This old-fashioned beef stew, flavored with root vegetables, is perfect for a chilly day.

serves 6

1 1/2 pounds beef bottom round or chuck, cut in 1 1/4-inch cubes

1 1/4 teaspoons salt

1/4 teaspoon freshly ground black pepper

2 tablespoons vegetable oil

2 medium onions, diced

2 tablespoons tomato paste

1 3/4 cups beef broth or water

12 ounces turnip or rutagaba, coarsely diced in 1/2-inch chunks, about 2 cups

3 medium carrots, sliced

2 medium parsnips, sliced (woody core removed)

2 medium potatoes, peeled and coarsely diced in 1/2-inch chunks

1/3 cup chopped flat-leaf parsley

1   Pat the beef dry with paper towels and season it with 3/4 teaspoon of the salt and the pepper.

2   In a stewpot over medium heat, heat the vegetable oil. Working in batches, brown each piece of beef on all sides. Add onions and cook, stirring occasionally, until they are tender, about 10 minutes.

3   Stir in the tomato paste and cook, stirring constantly, for about 2 minutes. Add the broth, turnips, carrots, parsnips, and potatoes and stir to mix well.

4   Reduce the heat to medium-low. Simmer until the beef and vegetables are tender, about 1 1/2 to 2 hours. Stir in the parsley and serve.

note *This dish can be made ahead, and it reheats well. I don't recommend freezing for longer than a couple of weeks— the potatoes tend to get mealy.*

serve with any of the following:

starch broad noodles; or South African Garlic, Herb & Cheese Pot Bread, *page 226*; or Herbed Dijon Beer Bread, *page 218*; or Lemon Scallion Soda Bread, *page 217* **salad** A Good & Simple Salad, *page 264*; or Make-Ahead Herbed Garden Salad, *page 263*; or Sugar Snap Peas with Orange & Herbs, *page 249* **dessert** Spiced Dried Fruit Compote, *page 207*

Veal with Chanterelles & Asparagus

THIS IS A TRULY ELEGANT STEW. It shouldn't be reserved for guests—any excuse will do. Fresh chanterelles are not always available, so I use dried ones in this recipe as well the fresh or white cultivated mushrooms. The flavor of dried chanterelles can vary from nutty to almost spicy. Consequently, this stew reveals a different character each time I make it, but it is always superb. You can preview the flavor of the mushrooms by smelling them. I usually add cream because the mushrooms beg for it—but the choice is up to you.

serves 6

1/4 ounce (about 6) dried chanterelles
1/2 cup boiling water
3 tablespoons butter
1 medium onion, chopped
3/4 teaspoon salt
1/4 teaspoon freshly ground black pepper
all-purpose flour for dusting the meat
1 1/4 pounds trimmed boneless veal shoulder, cut into 1-inch cubes
1/2 cup dry white wine
1 tablespoon cognac or brandy
3/4 cup chicken broth
bowl of ice water
1/4 pound asparagus, trimmed and sliced on an angle into 2-inch pieces
1/2 pound fresh chanterelles or white mushrooms, sliced
1/2 cup cream or half and half, optional
chopped fresh chives for garnish

1 Put the dried chanterelles in a small bowl and pour the boiling water over them. Let them stand until they are soft, about 20 to 30 minutes. Remove the mushrooms from the liquid and chop them coarsely or cut them with scissors. Pour the soaking liquid through a strainer lined with a paper coffee filter and reserve.

2 Meanwhile, in a skillet over medium-low heat, melt 1 tablespoon of the butter. Add the onion and cook, stirring occasionally, until it is translucent, about 5 minutes. Set the onion aside.

3 In a small bowl, combine the salt and pepper with about 1/3 cup of flour. Pat the meat dry with paper towels. Lightly dust the meat with the seasoned flour, shaking off any excess.

4 In a stewpot over medium heat, melt 1 tablespoon of the butter. Working in batches, lightly brown each piece of meat on all sides. Transfer the cooked veal to a plate.

5   Pour the wine and cognac into the stewpot and stir with a wooden spoon to loosen any browned bits. Add the reserved mushroom liquid and the broth.

6   Return the veal and its juices to the pot. Reduce the heat to medium-low. Cover and simmer until the veal is tender, about 1¼ to 1½ hours.

7   Meanwhile, have a bowl of ice water ready. In a large saucepan over high heat, cook the asparagus in plenty of lightly salted boiling water until tender but crisp, about 3 minutes. Immerse the asparagus immediately into the ice water to stop the cooking, and let cool. Drain the asparagus in a colander and set aside.

8   In a skillet over medium-low heat, melt the remaining tablespoon of butter. Add the mushrooms and cook, stirring occasionally, until they are cooked through, about 10 minutes.

9   Add the mushrooms and their juices, asparagus, and cream to the veal. Simmer, uncovered, until everything is heated through, about 5 minutes. To serve, garnish with chopped chives.

note   *This dish can be made ahead, and it reheats well. It can be frozen for 2 to 3 months.*

serve with any of the following:

starch   broad noodles; or Basic Polenta or Herbed Polenta, *page 240*; or Basic Risotto, *page 242*   **salad**   Mesclun Salad with Goat Cheese, *page 262*; or mixed greens with Basic Vinaigrette using raspberry or balsamic vinegar, *page 266*   **dessert**   Nectarines with Tarragon & Pepper, *page 213*

Veal with Artichokes & Tomatoes

SOME DISHES COME UPON ME like a light bulb clicking on—why not try *x* with *y*? I had a friend who would only eat red meat—preferably beef and veal—and who had a passion for artichokes. Tired of life in the big city, she bought a ramshackle farm and moved to Pennsylvania where she could see the sky and write songs. One day, I heard a song of hers on the radio and I came up with this dish. It deserves an award for the best veal stew on this side of the Atlantic, even though it borrows its flavor from Italy.

40

serves 6

2 tablespoons olive oil

1 medium onion, chopped

2 cloves garlic, chopped

1 1/2 tablespoons chopped fresh rosemary or 2 1/4 teaspoons dried and crumbled

2 pounds trimmed boneless veal shoulder, cut into 2-inch cubes

all-purpose flour for dusting the meat

3/4 cup dry red wine

1 1/4 cups beef broth or water

2 tablespoons soy sauce

1 1/2 cups artichoke hearts or bottoms, cut in half (use either fresh; canned, packed in water, and rinsed; or frozen and thawed)

5 plum tomatoes, each one peeled, seeded, and sliced lengthwise into 6 thin strips

1   Preheat the oven to 325°. In an ovenproof stewpot over medium heat, heat half of the olive oil. Add the onion and cook, stirring occasionally, until soft, about 5 minutes. Add the garlic and rosemary and cook, stirring constantly, for 2 minutes. With a slotted spoon, transfer the seasoned onions to a plate and set aside.

2   Pat the veal dry with paper towels. Lightly dust the meat with flour, shaking off any excess. In the same stewpot over medium heat, heat half of the remaining olive oil. Working in batches, lightly brown each piece of meat on all sides. Transfer the browned meat to a plate. Add more of the oil as necessary between batches, letting it get hot before putting in the meat. Repeat until all the meat is browned.

3   Add the wine and scrape the bottom with a wooden spoon to loosen any brown bits. Cook until the wine is reduced by half.

4 Return all the veal and the onions to the pot. Add the broth, soy sauce, artichokes, and tomatoes. Cover and bake until the meat is tender, about 1¹/₂ to 2 hours.

note *This dish can be made ahead, and it freezes well. It can be frozen for 2 to 3 months.*

serve with any of the following:

starch   Oven-Roasted Red Potatoes with Rosemary, *page 234*; or Basic Risotto or Parmesan Herb Risotto or Saffron Risotto, *page 242*; or Onion Flat Bread, *page 220*   salad   Roasted Beet & Onion Salad on Watercress, *page 247*; or Sugar Snap Peas with Orange & Herbs, *page 249*   dessert   Figs in Red Wine, Ginger, & Thyme, *page 210*

Sultry Spiced Veal

OFTEN WHEN I COOK, I leave the outside door wide open. Invariably, my neighbors pop in to taste what I am making. The aroma of this stew attracts the neighbors in a big way. In this unusual dish, the veal is simmered in spices in the Malay style, creating fragrantly aromatic, succulent stew.

42

serves 6

2 1/2 pounds trimmed boneless veal shoulder, cut into 1 1/2-inch cubes

1 teaspoon salt

1/4 teaspoon white pepper

2 tablespoons vegetable oil

1/2 cup water

2 medium onions, thinly sliced

8 cardamom pods

1/4 teaspoon whole coriander

1 bay leaf

1/3 cup orange juice

2 tablespoons brown sugar

3/4 cup chopped canned tomatoes

1-inch strip fresh orange zest, white pith removed

1 clove garlic, minced

1/2-inch piece fresh ginger, minced

2 medium potatoes, peeled and diced in 1/2-inch cubes, optional

1 Pat the meat dry with paper towels. Season the veal with 1/2 teaspoon of the salt and the pepper. In a large stewpot over medium heat, heat 1 tablespoon of the vegetable oil. Working in batches, brown each piece of veal on all sides. Transfer the browned veal to a plate and set aside.

2 In the same stewpot over medium heat, combine the water, onions, cardamom pods, coriander, and bay leaf. Bring the water to a boil and cook until all the water has evaporated.

3 Add the remaining tablespoon of vegetable oil. Cook until the onions are very tender, about 10 minutes.

4 Return the veal to the pot. Add the orange juice, brown sugar, tomatoes, orange zest, garlic, and ginger. Reduce the heat to medium-low. Cover and simmer until the veal is tender, about 1 1/2 hours. Season with the remaining 1/2 teaspoon salt or to taste.

5 Add the potatoes, cover, and cook until the potatoes are tender, about 20 to 30 minutes longer.

note *This dish can be made ahead, and it reheats well. It can be frozen for 2 to 3 months if you don't use potatoes.*

serve with any of the following:

starch   white, basmati, or Texamati rice; or Spiced Rice or Yellow Spiced Rice variation, *page 244*; or Buttermilk Raisin Spice Bread, *page 216*; or, if you do not use the potatoes, Lemon Couscous, *page 239*   **salad**   Cucumber Tomato Salsa, *page 261*; or Avocado Salad, *page 260*   **dessert**   Pineapple in Coconut Milk, *page 208*

43

Lemon Saffron Veal Stew

LEMON, ALMONDS, AND SAFFRON are used together in parts of Spain, Italy, and southern France. Here they are wedded to veal to create a delicately flavored stew. The ground almonds thicken the sauce. Saffron, the stamen of crocuses harvested by hand, is quite expensive, but a little bit goes a long way. You might decide to use less or to omit it from this dish, but please, *please* don't substitute turmeric.

serves 6

$2^{1}/2$ **pounds trimmed boneless veal shoulder, cut into $1^{1}/2$-inch cubes**

$1^{1}/4$ **teaspoons salt**

$^{1}/4$ **teaspoon freshly ground black pepper**

2 tablespoons olive oil

1 medium Spanish onion, thinly sliced

3 cloves garlic, minced

$1^{1}/2$ **teaspoon chopped fresh lemon thyme or thyme leaves or $^{1}/2$ teaspoon dried leaves**

1 cup dry white wine

$1^{1}/4$ **cups chicken broth, heated**

1 cup finely ground almonds

1 tablespoon finely grated fresh lemon zest

$^{1}/2$ **to $1^{1}/2$ teaspoons loosely packed Spanish saffron threads, toasted***

$1^{1}/2$ **cups (6 ounces) sliced fresh green beans**

1 Season the veal with salt and pepper. In a stew-pot over medium heat, heat the olive oil. Working in batches, brown each piece of veal on all sides. Transfer the meat to a plate and set aside.

2 In the same pot, add the onion and cook, stirring occasionally, until it is tender and golden, about 10 to 13 minutes. Add the garlic and thyme and cook, stirring often, for 2 minutes.

3 Return the veal and its juices to the pot. Add the wine and 1 cup of the broth. Stir in the ground almonds and lemon zest. Reduce the heat to medium-low, cover partially, and simmer for $1^{1}/4$ hour or until the veal starts to become tender.

4 Put the toasted saffron in a small bowl and crush it with the back of a teaspoon. Pour the remaining $^{1}/4$ cup of the heated broth over the saffron so it dissolves. Add the saffron liquid to the stew and stir.

*To toast the saffron: Enclose the threads in a small piece of foil. Place a small skillet over medium heat and add the foil packet. Cook about 1 minute, turning the packet over once. Remove the saffron from the foil and use in the recipe as directed.

5   Add the green beans and cook, uncovered, until the veal and green beans are tender and the sauce is slightly yellow, about 20 to 30 minutes longer. Combine the remaining lemon zest and parsley for the garnish and stir into the stew right before serving.

¹/2 tablespoon extra finely grated fresh lemon zest for garnish

2 tablespoons chopped fresh flat-leaf parsley for garnish

note   *This dish can be made ahead, and it reheats well. It can be frozen for 2 to 3 months.*

45

serve with any of the following:

starch   rice; or Oven-Roasted Red Potatoes with Rosemary, *page 234*; or Mashed Potatoes with Cucumber, *page 236*   salad   Tomato & Sautéed Mushroom Salad, *page 250*; or A Good & Simple Salad, *page 264*   dessert   Pears in Ruby Port & Vanilla, *page 206*

Veal Paprika

THIS RICH, LUSCIOUS STEW with its brilliant reddish-orange color is both eye- and palate-pleasing. Paprika, its primary spice, is made from ground red peppers. Hungarian paprika has the best flavor and comes in two versions, sweet and hot. This dish calls for Hungarian sweet paprika.

Veal Paprika was standard early 1960s dinner party fare. As a child, I used to sneak some spoonfuls in the kitchen when my mother wasn't looking. But trends change. Due to the current focus on dietary fat, it has taken a back seat to lighter stews. If you must, make it with nonfat sour cream. It will still be absolutely fantastic.

serves 6 to 8

2 tablespoons butter

2 medium onions, diced

1 large red or yellow bell pepper, coarsely diced

2 cloves garlic, minced

2 3/4 pounds trimmed boneless veal shoulder, cut into 1 1/2-inch cubes

1 teaspoon salt

all-purpose flour for dusting the meat

2 tablespoons Hungarian sweet paprika

1/2 cup extra dry white vermouth

1 1/4 cups beef or chicken broth

1 cup sour cream or nonfat sour cream

chopped fresh parsley for garnish

1   In a stewpot over medium heat, melt 2 teaspoons of butter. Add the onions and bell pepper and cook, stirring occasionally, until soft, about 5 minutes. Add the garlic and cook, stirring constantly, for 2 minutes. Transfer the onions and pepper mixture to a plate and set aside.

2   Pat the meat dry with paper towels. Season the meat with salt and lightly dust it with flour, shaking off any excess. In the same stewpot over medium heat, heat half of the remaining butter. Working in batches, lightly brown each piece of veal on all sides. Transfer the browned meat to a plate. Add more of the butter as necessary between batches, letting it get hot before putting in the meat. Repeat until all the meat is browned.

3 Return the veal to the pot. Add the paprika, stir-ring constantly to coat the meat and vegetables evenly. Pour in the vermouth and scrape the bottom to loosen any brown bits; cook for 2 to 3 minutes. Add the broth and onion bell pepper mixture.

4 Reduce the heat to medium-low. Cover, and simmer until the meat is tender and the sauce is reduced, about 1^1/$_2$ to 2 hours.

5 Stir in the sour cream. Simmer until everything is heated through, about 5 minutes. Do not let the sauce boil.

note *This stew reheats well, but be careful not to let the sauce boil or it may separate. It can be made ahead, but for the best result do not add the sour cream until just before serving time. The dish does not freeze well because of the sour cream.*

47

serve with any of the following:

starch   broad noodles; or Lemon Scallion Soda Bread, *page 217*; Biscuits Any Which Way, *page 230*; or Great Potato Pancakes, *page 232*   salad   Pickled Beets, *page 259*; or Herbed Vegetable Slaw, *page 252*   dessert   Spiced Apples in Cider & Brandy, *page 211*

Sage-Scented Veal Stew with Tomatoes

IN EARLIER CENTURIES, sage was believed to create clear thinking and ensure long life, and consequently it found its place in teas, tonics, ales, soups, and stews. Whether or not this belief is true, sage and veal are perfect partners in this Italian stew. Fresh sage is recommended; it is available at greengrocers and in the produce section of many supermarkets. If you have the space, grow a bush of broad-leaf sage. It is a lovely addition to a garden, and you can use it in many dishes including your Thanksgiving stuffing.

48

serves 6

3 tablespoons olive oil

2 medium onions, chopped

2 cloves garlic, chopped

6 plum tomatoes, peeled, seeded, and chopped, about 1 1/2 cups

1 1/2 tablespoons fresh chopped sage

3/4 teaspoon salt

1/4 teaspoon freshly ground black pepper

all-purpose flour for dusting the meat

1 3/4 pounds trimmed boneless veal shoulder, cut into 1-inch cubes

2/3 cup dry white or red wine

2/3 cup beef broth

1 1/4 cups (one 10-ounce package) frozen or fresh peas

1   In a large, deep skillet over medium heat, heat 1 tablespoon of the olive oil. Add the onions and cook, stirring occasionally, until soft, about 5 minutes. Add the garlic and cook, stirring constantly, for 2 minutes. Add the tomatoes and sage and cook for 5 minutes and set aside.

2   In a small bowl, combine the salt and pepper with about 1/3 cup of flour. Lightly dust the meat with the seasoned flour, shaking off any excess.

3   In a stewpot over medium heat, heat half of the remaining olive oil. Working in batches, lightly brown each piece of veal on all sides. Transfer the cooked veal to a plate. Add more of the olive oil as necessary between batches, letting it get hot before adding more veal. Repeat until all the meat is browned.

4   Pour in the wine and stir with a wooden spoon to loosen any browned bits. Add the broth. Return the veal to the pot. Add the onion-tomato mixture.

5 Reduce the heat to medium-low. Cover and simmer until the veal is tender, about 1^1/4 to 1^1/2 hours.

6 Add the peas and stir. Continue simmering, uncovered, until the peas are cooked, about 5 minutes for frozen or 12 minutes for fresh.

note *This dish can be made ahead, but add the peas a few minutes before serving so they remain fresh-tasting and bright green. It reheats well, and can be frozen for 2 months.*

49

serve with any of the following:

starch   Basic Polenta, *page 240*; or Mashed Potatoes with Cucumber, *page 236*; or Anna's Crusty French Loaf, *page 222*; or Round Country Loaf, *page 224*

salad   mixed green salad with Basic Vinaigrette using balsamic vinegar, *page 266*; or Arugula Salad, *page 265*

venison

Venison in Orange-Spiced Wine

AN OFT-ASKED AUTUMN and winter question is, "What can I do with venison?" Farm-raised and wild venison are both available then. In this recipe, the classic combination of venison, wine, and juniper berries is accented with orange to create a spectacular stew that should turn even the most unadventurous and skeptical diner into a venison enthusiast. This recipe can also be made with beef chuck, round, or bottom round.

serves 4 to 6

2 $1/2$ tablespoons vegetable oil

2 medium onions, diced

2 plump cloves garlic, minced

2 pounds trimmed boneless venison shoulder, cut into 1 $1/2$-inch cubes

$3/4$ teaspoon salt

all-purpose flour for dusting the meat

1 $1/3$ cups dry red wine

1 $1/2$ cups beef broth

$1/2$ cup chopped or crushed tomatoes

1 medium orange, seeded and quartered

1 bay leaf

1 tablespoon juniper berries

1 teaspoon minced fresh thyme leaves or $1/2$ teaspoon dried leaves

1 teaspoon finely grated fresh lemon zest

6 ounces sliced mushrooms

Lardons (page 274)

2 tablespoons chopped fresh flat-leaf parsley

1 Preheat the oven to 350°. In a medium skillet over medium heat, heat 1 tablespoon of the vegetable oil. Add the onions and cook, stirring occasionally, until the onion is translucent, about 5 minutes. Add the garlic and cook, stirring often, for 2 minutes. Set aside.

2 Season the venison with salt. Lightly dust the meat with flour, shaking off any excess. In an ovenproof stewpot over medium heat, heat the remaining 1 $1/2$ tablespoons of vegetable oil. Working in batches, brown each piece of venison on all sides. Transfer the meat to a plate.

3 Pour in the wine and broth. Stir and scrape the bottom with a wooden spoon to loosen any browned bits. Add the onions, tomatoes, orange, bay leaf, juniper berries, thyme, and lemon zest.

4 Return the venison and its juices to the pot and stir. Cover and bake for 1 hour.

5 Add the mushrooms and Lardons and stir to mix. Cover and continue baking until the meat is very tender, about to 1 to 1 $1/2$ hours longer. Stir in the parsley before serving.

note   *If using wild venison, marinate the meat in red wine for 24 hours to remove the gamey taste. Discard the wine afterward. If using farm-raised venison, you do not need to marinate the meat. This dish can be made ahead, and it reheats well. It can be frozen for 2 to 3 months. Discard the oranges before freezing.*

51

serve with any of the following:

starch   Round Country Loaf, *page 224*; or Mashed Turnips & Apples, *page 238*; or Creamy Potato Gratin, *page 233*; or Garlic & Herb Mashed Potatoes, *page 235*

salad   mixed green salad with Basic Vinaigrette using red wine vinegar, *page 266*; or Roasted Beet & Onion Salad on Watercress, *page 247*; or Herbed Vegetable Slaw, *page 252*

Venison & Beans in Bourbon Sauce

WHEN I THINK OF THE TASTE of venison, I think "personality." Venison holds its own against the strong taste of bourbon, red wine, and spices in this sweet and pungent sauce. Bake it with beans, and it's an excellent country-style stew. If you can't find venison and want to make this dish, substitute beef chuck, round, or bottom round.

serves 6

1¹/2 pounds trimmed boneless venison shoulder, cut into 1¹/2-inch cubes*

1 teaspoon salt

1/4 teaspoon freshly ground black pepper

2 tablespoons vegetable oil

2 medium onions, thinly sliced

2 plump cloves garlic, minced

1/2 cup dry red wine

3/4 cup good-quality bourbon

2 tablespoons Worcestershire sauce

1¹/3 cups chopped or crushed tomatoes

1/3 cup brown sugar

1/3 cup maple syrup

1/2 teaspoon ground allspice

1/4 teaspoon ground cinnamon

1/4 teaspoon ground cloves

1/4 teaspoon white pepper

1 bay leaf

2 cups cooked navy, white, or pinto beans (if canned, drain and rinse well)

Crispy Shallots (page 272) for garnish, optional

1 Preheat the oven to 350°. Season the venison with salt and pepper. In an ovenproof stewpot over medium heat, heat the vegetable oil. Add the meat and cook, stirring occasionally until the meat is lightly browned.

2 Add the onions and cook, stirring occasionally, until the onions are translucent, about 5 minutes. Add the garlic and cook, stirring often, for 2 minutes.

3 Add the wine, bourbon, Worcestershire sauce, tomatoes, brown sugar, maple syrup, allspice, cinnamon, cloves, white pepper, and bay leaf. Cover and bake for 1 hour.

4 Add the beans and stir to mix. If the stew is beginning to get dry, add a little water at this time. Cover and bake until the meat is very tender, about 1 hour longer.

5 Before serving, garnish with Crispy Shallots, if desired.

note *This dish can be made ahead, and it reheats well. Although some dishes with beans can't be frozen, I have frozen leftovers of this dish for 1 to 2 months with good results. Add a little extra liquid when reheating if it has been frozen.*

serve with any of the following:
    starch   Spiced Mashed Sweet Potatoes, *page 237*; or Herbed Corn Biscuits, *page 229*; or Biscuits Any Which Way, *page 230*   salad   Colorful Crunchy Slaw, *page 253*; or Make-Ahead Herbed Garden Salad, *page 263*   dessert   Spiced Dried Fruit Compote, *page 207*

*If using wild venison, marinate the meat in red wine for 24 hours to remove the gamey taste. Discard the wine afterward. If using farm-raised venison, you do not need to marinate the meat.

two   LAMB & PORK

Lamb

High IQ Irish Stew

Lamb with Figs

Moroccan Lamb Stew

Mediterranean Lamb with Lentils

Cape Malay Sweet & Sour Lamb
   & Bean Curry

Lamb & Eggplant Tarkhari

Spanish Lamb Stew with Bell Peppers

Herbed Lamb Ragout

Pork

Chili Pork with Pinto Beans

Reading Railroad Pork with Cabbage

Pork with Ruby Port & Shiitake
   Mushrooms

Indonesian Peanut Pork

BBQ Pork Stew

Fruity Spiced Pork

Rosemary Pork in Milk

Additional Recipe (Chapter Six)

lamb

High IQ Irish Stew

TO ME, THIS IRISH MASTERPIECE is the quintessential lamb stew. It is humble in origin, yet always outstanding. Preparation is totally painless—put it on, take a bath, read a book, play with the cat, and when the allotted time has passed, serve it and eat it. There is no trick. This is a brilliant stew because it almost makes itself.

54

serves 6

1 tablespoon butter

2 medium leeks, white part only, thinly sliced

2 pounds trimmed boneless lamb from leg or shoulder, cut into 1 1/2-inch cubes

2 medium onions, coarsely chopped

3 medium carrots, coarsely sliced

1 medium turnip, about 4 ounces, coarsely chopped

2 large potatoes, about 1 1/2 pounds, peeled and cubed

2 sprigs fresh thyme or 1 teaspoon dried thyme leaves

1 teaspoon salt

1/2 teaspoon freshly ground black pepper

2 cups water

1/2 cup chopped flat-leaf parsley

1 In a stewpot over medium heat, melt the butter. Add the leeks and cook, stirring, until the leeks are softened, about 5 minutes. Transfer the leeks to a plate and set aside.

2 Add the following to the pot in layers: half of the meat, half of the onions, half of the carrots, half of the turnip, half of the potatoes, and half of the leeks. Top with all of the thyme, 1/2 teaspoon salt, and 1/4 teaspoon pepper. Do not stir.

3 Repeat the layering. Pour the water into the pot, but do not stir.

4 Cover the pot. Over medium-low heat, simmer for 1 1/2 to 2 hours, until the lamb is tender. Stir in the chopped parsley and serve.

note   This dish can be made ahead and reheats well. Like some stews with potatoes, I do not recommend freezing because the potatoes get mealy.

serve with any of the following:

starch   Herbed Dijon Beer Bread, *page 218*; or Lemon Scallion Soda Bread, *page 217*   salad   A Good & Simple Salad, *page 264*; or Colorful Crunchy Slaw, *page 253*; or Lemony Asparagus or Green Beans with Nuts, *page 255*   dessert   Spiced Apples in Cider & Brandy, *page 211*

Lamb with Figs

OUT OF ADVERSITY CAME A BLESSING—an extraordinary stew. I once had a landlord whose primary redeeming feature was that he had planted fig trees around the house where I lived. When the figs came into season, I would pluck them from the tree and eat them in abundance. In the dead of winter, when the furnace didn't work and I missed those fresh figs, I made this stew with dried ones. The lamb is marinated in wine and spices, the figs in cognac. Together they create a melodious symphony of taste.

serves 6

Marinade

1 large clove garlic, sliced in half lengthwise

1 cinnamon stick

2 sprigs of thyme or 3/4 teaspoon dried thyme leaves

1-inch piece fresh ginger, sliced

2 whole cloves

2 whole allspice berries

2 1/2 cups full-bodied red wine

Stew

2 1/2 pounds trimmed boneless lamb from shoulder or leg, cut into 1 1/2-inch cubes

1 1/2 teaspoon salt

1/2 teaspoon freshly ground black pepper

3 tablespoons olive oil

2 medium leeks, white part only, thinly sliced

1   *To prepare the marinade:* Wrap the garlic, cinnamon stick, thyme, ginger, cloves, and allspice in a piece of cheesecloth and tie it to form a sack. Put the wine and cheesecloth sack in a large glass, stainless-steel, plastic, or ceramic bowl. Add the lamb, making sure it is submerged. Cover the bowl, and refrigerate it for 2 to 4 hours. Stir the ingredients once or twice during that time.

2   Remove the lamb from the marinade, reserving 2 1/2 cups of the marinade. Discard the cheesecloth sack.

3   *To prepare the stew:* Pat the meat dry with paper towels. Season the meat with 3/4 teaspoon of the salt and the pepper. In a stewpot over medium heat, heat 2 tablespoons of the olive oil. Working in batches, lightly brown each piece of lamb on all sides. Transfer the lamb to a plate and set aside.

*This can be used to thicken almost any stew. If the sauce is too thin for your taste, ten minutes before serving, prepare the beurre manie by kneading together 1 tablespoon softened butter with 1 tablespoon flour. Add to the stew in 1/2-teaspoon pieces, stirring to fully incorporate after each addition. Cook a few minutes longer to allow the sauce to thicken slightly.

4 In the same pot, over medium heat, add the remaining tablespoon of olive oil. Add the leeks, garlic, and ginger. Cook, stirring occasionally, until the leeks are softened, about 5 minutes.

5 Return the lamb to the pot. Add the reserved 2¹/₂ cups of marinade. Reduce the heat to medium-low. Cover and simmer for 1¹/₄ hours.

6 Meanwhile, in a small saucepan over medium heat, heat the cognac and brown sugar and bring to a boil. Remove the pan from the heat and add the figs. Let the figs soften in the cognac, about 30 minutes.

7 After 1¹/₄ hours of cooking the lamb, add the figs and the cognac to the stew and stir well. Simmer 30 to 40 minutes longer, or until the lamb is very tender. Serve garnished with fresh chopped parsley.

note *This dish can be made ahead, and it reheats well. It can be frozen for 2 to 3 months.*

1 plump clove garlic, minced
1-inch piece fresh ginger, minced
¹/₂ cup cognac or brandy
1 tablespoon brown sugar
1 cup dried Calmyrna figs, stems removed and quartered
***beurre manie,* optional**
chopped fresh parsley for garnish

57

serve with any of the following:

starch   Anna's Crusty French Loaf, *page 222*; or Buttermilk Raisin Spice Bread, *page 216*; or Mashed Potatoes with Cucumber, *page 236*; or Basic Risotto, *page 242*   **salad**   Roasted Beet & Onion Salad on Watercress, *page 247*; or Mesclun Salad with Goat Cheese, *page 262*; or Tomato Sautéed Mushroom Salad, *page 250*

Moroccan Lamb Stew

I LOVE MOROCCAN FOOD; however, many of the traditional recipes for tagines and stews have ingredient lists almost as long as the phone book and require more steps than I am willing to follow. After much reading, experimentation, and tasting, I came up with this sumptuous-yet-uncomplicated Moroccan-spiced stew that always seems to please my guests. If you have a larger pot, it can easily be doubled or tripled for a crowd.

58

serves 6 to 8

1^1/2 pounds trimmed boneless lamb from leg or shoulder, cut into 1^1/2-inch cubes

1 teaspoon salt

2^1/2 tablespoons vegetable oil

2 medium onions, thinly sliced

1-inch piece fresh ginger, minced

1 cinnamon stick or 1 teaspoon ground cinnamon

^{3}/4 teaspoon turmeric

^{1}/2 teaspoon freshly grated nutmeg

^{1}/2 teaspoon crushed red pepper flakes

2 cups vegetable or beef broth or water

^{1}/3 cup honey

3 plum tomatoes, peeled, seeded, and chopped

1 medium carrot, sliced

12 ounces butternut squash cut into 1-inch cubes, about 2 cups

^{1}/2 cup dried apricots, sliced in half

1 Pat the meat dry with paper towels and season it with salt. In a stewpot over medium heat, heat 1^1/2 tablespoons of the vegetable oil. Working in batches, lightly brown each piece of meat on all sides. Transfer the meat to a plate and set aside.

2 Reduce the heat to medium-low. In the same pot, heat the remaining 1 tablespoon of the vegetable oil. Add the onions and cook, stirring occasionally, until the onions are very tender, about 15 minutes. Add the ginger, cinnamon, turmeric, nutmeg, and crushed red pepper flakes and cook, stirring constantly, for 2 minutes.

3 Pour in the broth. Scrape the bottom with a wooden spoon to loosen any browned bits. Stir in the honey.

4 Return the lamb to the pot. Add the tomatoes, carrot, butternut squash, apricots, and raisins. Partially cover the pot and simmer until the lamb is very tender, about 1^1/2 hours.

*The skins of the chickpeas can give an unpleasant texture to the stew and get caught between your teeth. To remove them, place the chickpeas in a colander and rinse. Rub the chickpeas between your fingers and the skins will slip off easily. This is a tedious task, though not overly time-consuming, and it is worth the effort.

5   Add the chickpeas and stir. Simmer for ¹/2 hour longer. Garnish with almonds and cilantro and serve with Harissa on the side.

note   *This recipe can be made ahead, but I don't recommend freezing it. Leftovers can be kept in the refrigerator for 2 to 3 days.*

¹/4 cup raisins

1 cup cooked chickpeas (if canned: drain, rinse, and remove the skins*)

¹/2 cup toasted sliced almonds for garnish

¹/4 cup chopped fresh cilantro for garnish

Harissa as accompaniment, optional**

59

serve with any of the following:

    starch   Lemon Couscous, *page* 239   salad   Carrot Orange Sambal, *page 256*

**Harissa, available in gourmet and Middle Eastern food shops, is a spicy condiment used in North African and Middle Eastern dishes. Although there are complicated recipes for it, you can make a simple version by combining in a small bowl 3 cloves of finely minced garlic, 1¹/2 teaspoons crushed red pepper flakes, and a splash of olive oil to bind the ingredients. Use it sparingly. If you can't find Harissa and don't feel like making your own, try a little Tabasco as a condiment.

Mediterranean Lamb with Lentils

WHEN I WAS A YOUNG, A LOT OF PEOPLE—especially children—didn't eat lentils. No one went around boasting to their school friends that they had lentils for dinner, or invited their friends over for lentils. The threat of the "yuk" from classmates loomed greatly. It was hamburgers yes, lentils no. However, when it got cold outside, my mother made this lamb and lentil stew. Although I didn't admit it outside the family, I liked lentils very much and am living proof that even the youngest can enjoy this hearty stew.

60

serves 4 to 6

2^1/2 tablespoons olive oil
1 medium onion, diced
2 celery stalks, diced
1 carrot, diced
2 cloves garlic, minced
1^1/2 pounds trimmed boneless lamb
   from leg or shoulder, cut into
   1-inch cubes
^{1}/2 teaspoon salt
all-purpose flour for dusting the
   meat
^{1}/2 cup dry red wine
2^1/2 cups beef broth
1 bay leaf
1 tablespoon chopped fresh thyme
   or lemon thyme leaves or
   1 teaspoon dried leaves
^{1}/2 cup brown lentils
chopped fresh parsley for garnish

1 In a large stewpot over medium heat, heat 1 tablespoon of the olive oil. Add the onion, celery, and carrot and cook, stirring occasionally, until the vegetables are tender, about 10 minutes. Add the garlic and cook, stirring constantly, for 2 minutes. Transfer the vegetables to a plate and set aside.

2 Pat the lamb dry with paper towels. Season the meat with salt and lightly dust it with flour, shaking off any excess.

3 In the same stewpot over medium heat, heat half of the remaining olive oil. Working in batches, lightly brown each piece of meat on all sides. Transfer the browned lamb to a plate. Add more of the oil as necessary between batches, letting it get hot before putting in the meat. Repeat until all the meat is browned.

4 Return all the lamb to the pot. Add the wine and scrape the bottom with a wooden spoon to loosen any browned bits. Cook, stirring occasionally, until the wine is almost evaporated, about 4 to 5 minutes.

5 Return the vegetables to the pot. Add 2 cups of the broth, the bay leaf, and the thyme. Reduce the heat to medium-low. Cover and simmer for 1 1/2 hours.

6 Add the lentils and the remaining 1/2 cup of broth and stir. Simmer, uncovered, until the lamb is tender and the lentils are cooked but still hold their shape, about 40 minutes. If the liquid boils out too quickly and the stew becomes dry while the lentils are cooking, add a little more broth or water. Garnish with parsley and serve.

note   This recipe can be made ahead, and it reheats well. It can be frozen for 2 months.

serve with any of the following:

   starch   Oven-Roasted Red Potatoes with Rosemary, *page 234*; or Onion Flat Bread, *page 220*; or Round Country Loaf, *page 224*; or Basic Polenta, *page 240*

   salad   Arugula Salad, *page 265*; or Herbed Vegetable Slaw, *page 252*; or Make-Ahead Herbed Garden Salad, *page 263*

Cape Malay Sweet & Sour Lamb & Bean Curry

THE CAPE MALAYS are descendants of Malays from Java and the Indonesian islands who were brought in the seventeenth and eighteenth centuries to the Cape Town area in South Africa on ships that traveled the spice route to Indonesia. Historians differ as to whether they were political exiles, slaves, or indentured servants. One undeniable fact is that their cuisine has survived intact for centuries.

This spectacular dish, which presents a unique balance of sweet, sour, and spicy, is based on a recipe that is over 300 years old. I learned to make it while living in the Western Cape Province of South Africa. Back in the United States, I've made it for friends, special events, and cooking demonstrations, and every last bit is always eaten. I have been asked many times for this recipe, so here it is.

serves 6 to 8

2 tablespoons vegetable oil
2 medium onions, thinly sliced
1 bay leaf
4 peppercorns
2 allspice berries
2 whole cloves
2 plump cloves garlic, minced
1-inch piece fresh ginger, minced
1 to 1 1/2 tablespoons good-quality curry powder, such as Madras brand
1 teaspoon ground cumin
1 teaspoon ground coriander

1   In a large stewpot over medium heat, heat the vegetable oil. Add the onions, bay leaf, peppercorns, allspice, and cloves; cook, stirring occasionally, until the onions are tender, about 10 minutes. Add the garlic, ginger, curry powder, cumin, and coriander; cook, stirring occasionally, for 3 minutes.

2   Reduce the heat to medium-low. Add the vinegar, water, and sugar. Add the lamb and cook, stirring as often as necessary, until the lamb changes color.

3   Cover and simmer until the lamb is tender, about 1 1/2 hours.

4   Add the cooked beans and salt and stir. Simmer, uncovered, until the beans are thoroughly heated and the liquid is reduced by one fourth, about 20 to 30 minutes.

note   *This dish can be made ahead and it reheats well. Although some dishes with beans can't be frozen, I have frozen leftovers of this dish for 1 to 2 months with good results. Add a little extra liquid when reheating if it has been frozen.*

- 3/4 cup white wine vinegar or cider vinegar
- 1/4 cup water
- 1/2 cup dark brown sugar
- 1 1/2 pounds trimmed boneless lamb from the shoulder or leg, cut into 1 1/2-inch cubes
- 2 cups cooked small white or navy beans (if canned, drain and rinse well)
- 1/2 teaspoon salt

63

serve with any of the following:

starch   white, basmati, or Texamati rice; or Spiced Rice, *page 244*; or Basic Polenta with 1/3 cup chopped scallion greens, *page 240*   **salad**   Carrot Orange Sambal, *page 256*; or Pickled Cucumber Salad for spicy food with cilantro and chilis, *page 258*

Lamb & Eggplant Tarkhari

IN THIS CURRIED LAMB DISH, the meat is first marinated in spices and then is simmered with eggplant and tomatoes to form a thick, rich-tasting sauce. I learned how to make it from an Indian woman who owned a wonderful little restaurant.

Although, many purists say that curry powder is not a "real" spice, not everyone has the time to blend their own combination of spices, as in the marinade in this dish. So if you are rushed or feeling lazy, feel free to substitute 2 to 3 tablespoons of good-quality curry powder for the spices in the marinade.

64

serves 6

Marinade

1 1/2 tablespoons vegetable oil

1 1/2 tablespoons fresh lemon juice

1 tablespoon ground coriander

2 teaspoons ground cumin

1 teaspoon turmeric

1/2 to 3/4 teaspoon cayenne, to your taste

2 plump cloves garlic, minced

1-inch piece fresh ginger, minced

1 teaspoon salt

2 pounds trimmed boneless lamb from leg or shoulder, cut into 1-inch cubes

Tarkhari

2 1/2 tablespoons vegetable oil

2 medium onions, thinly sliced

2 cinnamon sticks

5 whole cloves

5 cardamom pods

1 To prepare the marinade: In a stainless steel or glass bowl, combine the vegetable oil, lemon juice, coriander, cumin, turmeric, and cayenne. Stir in the garlic, ginger, and salt. Add the lamb and toss to coat evenly. Let the meat marinate at room temperature for at least 1/2 hour and up to 1 hour. If you are in a very hot place, refrigerate the meat while marinating.

2 To prepare the Tarkhari: In a stewpot or large, deep skillet over medium heat, heat the vegetable oil. Add the onions, cinnamon, cloves, and cardamom and cook, stirring occasionally, until the onions are very soft and begin to turn a golden color, about 15 to 20 minutes. (Don't try to rush this step. The slow cooking over low heat brings out the onions' natural sweetness.)

*3 Add the lamb, with its marinade, and eggplant. Cook, stirring occasionally, until the lamb is lightly browned on all sides, about 5 to 8 minutes. Add the tomatoes and water.

4   Reduce the heat to medium-low. Cover and simmer for 1 hour.

5   Stir in the yogurt and cook, uncovered, until the lamb is very tender and the sauce is thick, about 45 minutes. Sprinkle garam masala on top and stir. Garnish with cilantro.

note   *This dish can be made ahead, and it reheats well over low heat. Even with the small amount of yogurt in it, leftovers can be frozen for 1 to 2 months. Be sure to reheat gently.*

¹/2 pound eggplant, peeled and cut into 1-inch cubes

2 medium tomatoes, peeled, seeded, and chopped, about 1 cup

1 cup water

2 tablespoons plain yogurt

2 teaspoons *garam masala* for garnish, optional

chopped fresh cilantro for garnish

65

serve with any of the following:

starch   Basmati or Texamati rice   salad   Pickled Cucumber Salad for spicy dishes with chili and fresh mint, *page 258*; or Raita, *page 257*

condiment   Fresh Mango Chutney, *page 270*; or chopped onions or commercial chutney

Spanish Lamb Stew with Bell Peppers

SOMETIMES I WANT A DISH that is uncomplicated yet distinctive, and this stew fits the bill. It features the pure tastes of Spain—olive oil, sherry, garlic, and peppers. They team up with the lamb and bring forth a delightful and colorful stew.

serves 4 to 6

66

2 tablespoons olive oil

1 medium onion, chopped

1 red bell pepper, coarsely diced

1 yellow or green bell pepper,
   coarsely diced

2 to 3 plump cloves garlic, minced

2 1/2 pounds trimmed boneless lamb
   from leg or shoulder cut into
   1 1/2-inch cubes

1 teaspoon salt

1/4 teaspoon freshly ground black
   pepper

all-purpose flour for dusting the
   meat

1/2 cup plus 2 tablespoons good -
   quality dry sherry

1 cup beef broth

1 In a stewpot over medium heat, heat 1 table-spoon of the olive oil. Add the onion and bell peppers and cook, stirring occasionally, until the vegetables are softened, about 5 minutes. Add the garlic and cook, stirring often, for 2 minutes. Transfer the vegetables to a plate and set aside.

2 Pat the lamb dry with paper towels. Season the meat with salt and pepper. Lightly dust the meat with flour, shaking off any excess.

3 In the same stewpot over medium heat, heat half of the remaining oil. Working in batches, lightly brown each piece of meat on all sides. Transfer the browned meat to a plate. Add more oil as necessary between batches, letting it get hot before putting in the meat. Repeat until all the meat is browned.

4 Add 1/2 cup of the sherry, and scrape the bottom with a wooden spoon to loosen any browned bits. Cook until the sherry is slightly reduced, about 2 to 3 minutes. Add the broth. Return the lamb and vegetables to the pot and stir.

5   Reduce the heat to medium-low. Cover and simmer until the meat is tender, about 1¹/₂ hours. Add the remaining 2 tablespoons of sherry and simmer about 10 minutes longer.

note   *This dish can be made ahead, and it reheats well. It can be frozen for 2 to 3 months.*

67

serve with any of the following:

    starch   white, basmati, or Texamati rice; or Basic Risotto or Saffron Risotto, *page 242*; or Onion Flat Bread, *page 220*; or Lemon Scallion Soda Bread, *page 217*

    salad   Tomato & Sautéed Mushroom Salad, *page 250*; or A Good & Simple Salad, *page 264*; or Lemony Asparagus or Green Beans with Nuts, *page 255*

    dessert   Pears in Ruby Port & Vanilla, *page 206*

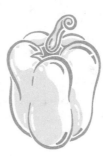

Herbed Lamb Ragout

THIS IS A SATISFYING RAGOUT with a Mediterranean flair. The rich, flavorful sauce with wine, rosemary, bay leaf, and a touch of mint enhances the lamb. It's a straightforward, no-nonsense entree that is complemented by a range of side dishes. I like to dip bread in the sauce or let the gravy seep into the potatoes. It's a wonderful cold weather treat.

68

serves 6

2^1/2 tablespoons olive oil

1 medium onion, diced

1 celery stalk, diced

1 medium carrot, diced

1 plump clove garlic, minced

2 pounds trimmed boneless lamb from leg or shoulder, cut into 1^1/2-inch cubes

1 teaspoon salt

^{1}/4 teaspoon freshly ground black pepper

all-purpose flour for dusting the meat

^{3}/4 cup dry red wine

^{3}/4 cup beef broth

1 cup crushed plum tomatoes

2 teaspoons chopped fresh rosemary or 1^1/2 teaspoons dried and crumbled

^{1}/2 teaspoon chopped fresh mint or ^{1}/4 teaspoon dried

1 bay leaf

2-inch strip fresh lemon zest

2 medium zucchini or yellow squash, diced, about 2 cups

1 In a large stewpot over medium heat, heat 1 tablespoon of the olive oil. Add the onion, celery, and carrot and cook, stirring occasionally, until the vegetables are tender, about 10 minutes. Add the garlic and cook, stirring constantly, for 2 minutes. Transfer the vegetables to a plate and set aside.

2 Pat the lamb dry with paper towels. Season the meat with salt and pepper. Lightly dust it with flour, shaking off any excess.

3 In the same stewpot over medium heat, heat half of the remaining oil. Working in batches, lightly brown each piece of meat on all sides. Transfer the browned lamb to a plate. Add the remaining oil as necessary between batches, letting it get hot before putting in the meat. Repeat until all the meat is browned.

4 Return all the lamb to the pan. Add the wine and scrape the bottom with a wooden spoon to loosen any browned bits. Cook, stirring occasionally, about 2 minutes. Add the broth, tomatoes, rosemary, mint, bay leaf, and lemon zest. Reduce the heat to medium-low. Partially cover and simmer for 1^1/2 hours.

5 Add the zucchini and stir. Simmer uncovered until the lamb and zucchini are tender, about 20 minutes longer.

note *This dish can be made ahead, and it reheats well. It can be frozen for 2 to 3 months.*

serve with any of the following:

starch Great Potato Pancakes, *page 232*; or Garlic & Herb Mashed Potatoes, *page 235*; or Anna's Crusty French Loaf, *page 222*; or Creamy Potato Gratin, *page 233*; or Lemon Couscous, *page 239* salad Mesclun Salad with Goat Cheese, *page 262*; or Roasted Beet & Onion Salad on Watercress, *page 247*; or Sugar Snap Peas with Orange & Herbs, *page 249* dessert Spiced Dried Fruit Compote, *page 207*

pork

Chili Pork with Pinto Beans

AMERICANS, AND I AM NO EXCEPTION, are chili-crazed. This medium-hot version gives a new twist to the standard chili by bringing together pork, beer, and pinto beans. The beer tenderizes the meat and boosts the sauce's flavor. If you like more heat, add a chopped, seeded jalapeño or serrano to the vegetables in step 2. Like most chilis, it is always better when made ahead and reheated.

serves 6

2 pounds trimmed boneless pork, either Boston butt, shoulder, or fresh ham from leg, cut into 1$^{1}/_{2}$-inch cubes

1$^{1}/_{4}$ teaspoons salt

2 tablespoons vegetable oil

1 medium onion, chopped

1 large green bell pepper, chopped

4 cloves garlic, chopped

4 to 6 tablespoons chili powder

1 teaspoon ground cumin

$^{1}/_{4}$ to $^{1}/_{2}$ teaspoon cayenne

1$^{1}/_{2}$ cups beer (12-ounce bottle)

2 cups tomato puree or canned crushed tomatoes

2 cups cooked pinto beans (one 16-ounce can, rinsed and drained)

1 Season the pork with $^{1}/_{2}$ teaspoon of the salt. In a stewpot over medium heat, heat 1 tablespoon of the vegetable oil. Working in batches, lightly brown each piece of meat on all sides. Transfer the pork to a plate and set aside.

2 In the same stewpot over medium heat, heat the remaining 1 tablespoon of vegetable oil. Add the onion and bell pepper and cook, stirring occasionally, until the vegetables are softened, about 5 minutes. Add the garlic and cook, stirring, for 1 minute. Add the chili powder, cumin, and cayenne and cook, stirring often, for 1 to 2 minutes.

3 Return the pork to the pot and stir to mix well. Add the beer and tomatoes. Reduce heat to medium-low. Simmer uncovered until the pork is tender, about 1$^{1}/_{2}$ to 2 hours.

4 Add the pinto beans and the remaining $^{1}/_{2}$ teaspoon salt, and simmer uncovered for 25 to 35 minutes longer.

note This dish can be made ahead, and it reheats well. Although some dishes with beans can't be frozen, I have frozen leftovers of this dish for 1 to 2 months with good results. Add a little extra liquid when reheating if it has been frozen.

serve with any of the following:

starch warm flour tortillas; or Buttermilk Cornbread, *page 219*; or Buttermilk Raisin Spice Bread, *page 216* salad Jicama Mango Salad, *page 248*; or Cucumber Tomato Salsa, *page 261*; or Avocado Salad, *page 260*

Reading Railroad Pork with Cabbage

THE READING RAILROAD, now just a property to collect when playing Monopoly®, used to be a real railroad connecting towns in Pennsylvania to the Reading Terminal in Philadelphia. Farmers from Pennsylvania Dutch country would leave their red barns bedecked with hex signs, and bring the bountiful products of their farms to the Terminal marketplace. There they would set up stalls and sell fresh meat, chicken, dairy products, produce, baked goods, and egg noodles. Their pork is still renowned as some of the best available. This hearty stew, based on a Pennsylvania Dutch recipe, pairs pork with produce available throughout the autumn and winter.

serves 4 to 6

1 1/2 pounds trimmed boneless pork shoulder, cut into 1 1/2-inch cubes

1 teaspoon salt

1/2 teaspoon freshly ground black pepper

1 1/2 tablespoons butter or vegetable oil

2 medium onions, chopped

1 medium Granny Smith apple, peeled and coarsely grated

1 pound green cabbage, shredded (about 6 cups)

1/2 teaspoon caraway seeds

1 cup hard apple cider or apple cider

1 tablespoon chopped fresh chives for garnish

1 tablespoon chopped fresh dill for garnish, optional

1   Season the pork with 3/4 teaspoon of the salt and the pepper.

2   In a stewpot over medium heat, melt the butter. Working in batches, lightly brown each piece of pork on all sides. Return all the meat to the pot.

3   Add the onions and cook, stirring as necessary to keep them from browning, until they are tender, about 10 minutes.

4   Stir in the apple, cabbage, and caraway seeds. Pour in the cider.

5   Reduce the heat to medium-low. Cover and simmer until the pork is tender, about 1 1/2 hours. Stir in the remaining 1/4 teaspoon of salt, chives, and dill, and serve.

note This dish can be made ahead, and it reheats well. It can be frozen for 2 months.

serve with any of the following:

starch egg noodles; or Creamy Potato Gratin, *page 233*; or Great Potato Pancakes, *page 232*; or Herbed Dijon Beer Bread, *page 218*

salad Pickled Beets, *page 259*; or Lemony Asparagus or Green Beans with Nuts, *page 255* **dessert** Spiced Dried Fruit Compote, *page 207*

Pork with Ruby Port & Shiitake Mushrooms

GOOD FOOD OFTEN RESULTS from improvisation. When living in a rural community in upstate New York, I had to be very flexible and accept that many ingredients were not as available as in metropolitan centers. I made this stew after driving from town to town vainly trying to find a liquor store that had Madeira. Ruby port, however, was sold everywhere. The sweetness of the port blends beautifully with the pork and is offset by the earthy undertones of the mushrooms. Perhaps you will find Madeira in your cupboard and try it that way, with equally good results.

74

serves 4 to 6

2 1/2 tablespoons butter

1 medium onion, chopped

3/4 teaspoon salt

1/4 teaspoon freshly ground black pepper

all-purpose flour for dusting the meat

1 1/2 pounds trimmed boneless pork shoulder, cut into 1 1/2-inch cubes

1 cup ruby port

2/3 cup chicken broth

1 tablespoon chopped fresh thyme leaves or 1 teaspoon dried thyme leaves

1/8 teaspoon freshly grated nutmeg

1 pound shiitake mushrooms, stems removed and sliced or 3/4 pound white mushrooms, sliced

1/4 cup chopped flat-leaf parsley

_1_   In a small skillet over medium heat, melt 2 teaspoons of the butter. Add the onion and cook, stirring occasionally, until it is translucent, about 5 minutes. Set aside.

_2_   In a bowl, combine the salt, pepper, and about 1/3 cup of flour. Pat the meat dry with paper towels. Lightly dust the meat with the seasoned flour, shaking off any excess.

_3_   In a stewpot over medium heat, melt 1 tablespoon of the butter. Working in batches, brown each piece of meat on all sides. Transfer the meat to a plate and set aside.

_4_   Pour the port into the pot and scrape the bottom with a wooden spoon to loosen any browned bits. Add the broth. Return the pork and its juices to the pot. Add the onion, thyme, and nutmeg, and stir.

5   Reduce the heat to medium-low. Cover and simmer until the pork is tender, about 1¹/₄ to 1¹/₂ hours.

6   Meanwhile, in a skillet over medium-low heat, melt the remaining 2¹/₂ teaspoons of butter. Add the mushrooms and cook, stirring occasionally, until tender, about 5 minutes.

7   Add the mushrooms and their juices to the stewpot, and simmer uncovered until the sauce is reduced slightly, about 15 minutes. Stir in the parsley and serve.

note   *This dish can be made ahead, and it reheats well. It can be frozen for 2 to 3 months.*

serve with any of the following:

starch   Oven-Roasted Red Potatoes with Rosemary, *page 234*; or Garlic & Herb Mashed Potatoes, *page 235*; or Round Country Loaf, *page 224*   **salad**   Tomato & Sautéed Mushroom Salad, *page 250*; or Lemony Asparagus or Green Beans with Nuts, *page 255*; or Sugar Snap Peas with Orange & Herbs, *page 249*

dessert   Nectarines with Tarragon & Pepper, *page 213*

Indonesian Peanut Pork

PORK SATE HAS BEEN NEAR the top of my world's-best food list ever since I tasted it at a Rijstaffel in Amsterdam. Traditionally, the meat is marinated, threaded on skewers, then grilled and served with a spicy peanut-coconut sauce on the side.

For many years, I lived in a small apartment with no grilling facilities or exhaust fan, and the broiler always set off the smoke alarm. Refusing to be denied the pleasurable flavor of sate, I came up with this stew. In this recipe, the meat is gently simmered in what would be considered the marinade. Toward the end of the cooking process, the peanut sauce is added to the pan.

serves 6

Chili Paste

3 medium onions, coarsely diced, about 8 ounces

6 plump cloves garlic, coarsely chopped

2-inch piece fresh ginger, peeled and coarsely chopped

1 to 2 jalapeño, serrano, bird's-eye, or cayenne chilis, seeded

2 stalks lemon grass, tender inside part only, coarsely sliced, optional

2 tablespoons water

Stew

2 tablespoons peanut oil

2 pounds trimmed boneless pork shoulder, cut into 1 1/2-inch cubes

1 1/2 tablespoons brown sugar

2 1/2 tablespoons rice wine vinegar

1 *To prepare the chili paste:* In a food processor fitted with the metal blade, combine the onions, garlic, ginger, chilis, lemon grass, and water; pulse until a puree forms.

2 In a large, deep skillet or stewpot over medium heat, heat the peanut oil. Add the chili paste and cook, stirring constantly, until the liquid is evaporated from the paste and the aroma is very strong, about 5 to 7 minutes.

3 Add the pork and stir to coat the meat completely with the paste. Cook, stirring constantly, until the pork begins to turn white, about 4 to 6 minutes. Add the brown sugar and stir so the meat is coated. Cook, stirring constantly, for 1 to 2 minutes. Add the vinegar, water, and Kecap Manis.

4 Reduce the heat to medium-low. Cover and simmer until the meat is tender and almost all of the liquid

*Be sure to use natural-style peanut butter—the kind you have to stir—or you will not get a good result. Smucker's and Erewohn are well-known brands.

is evaporated, about 1 to 1¼ hours. Do not boil; the liquid should be barely bubbling. If necessary, reduce the heat to low. Check occasionally to see how much liquid is in the pot. You might be amazed at the amount of liquid that is produced. (This depends on how juicy the pork is.) If there is too much liquid in the pot when the meat is almost tender (after about 50 minutes), remove the cover and continue cooking until the liquid is evaporated. If the liquid has evaporated before the meat is tender (which will occur if the heat is a little too high or the pork is dry), add a tablespoon or so of water.

5 Meanwhile, prepare the peanut sauce. In a large liquid measuring cup, use a fork to stir together the coconut milk, peanut butter, cayenne, and salt. (This can also be done in a blender.)

6 When most of the liquid in the pot has evaporated, pour in the peanut sauce and stir to coat the pork. Simmer uncovered over medium-low heat until the peanut sauce is heated through and the flavors are developed, about 15 to 20 minutes. Do not let the sauce boil. Garnish if desired.

note *This dish can be made ahead and reheated if a little extra coconut milk is added to the pan or if it is reheated in a double-boiler. It doesn't freeze well because of the coconut milk.*

2 tablespoons water

1 tablespoon Kecap Manis, or
1 tablespoon soy sauce and
1 tablespoon brown sugar

chopped red bell pepper, chopped fresh cilantro, or mint garnish, optional

Peanut Sauce

3/4 cup unsweetened coconut milk

1/3 cup natural unsalted peanut butter*

1/2 teaspoon cayenne

1/2 teaspoon salt

77

serve with any of the following;

starch   white, basmati, or Texamati rice; or Spiced Rice, *page 244*

salad   Rujak, *page 246*; or Spicy Green Bean Sambal, *page 254*; or Carrot Orange Sambal, *page 256*

BBQ Pork Stew

THIS TASTY STEW, REMINISCENT of country barbecue, features tender pork slowly cooked in a tangy tomato sauce. It is marvelous the day it is made and even better the next day. It can be served as a stew or can be put on French bread or buns for a sloppy but delicious sandwich.

serves 6

78

3^1/2 cups (one 28-ounce can) tomato puree

2/3 cup cider vinegar

1/3 cup molasses (not blackstrap)

1/3 cup strong brewed coffee

3 plump cloves garlic, finely minced

3 tablespoons Worcestershire sauce

2 tablespoons soy sauce

1^1/2 tablespoons chopped fresh oregano or 1^1/2 teaspoons dried

2^1/2 teaspoons dry English mustard such as Coleman's

3/4 teaspoon cayenne

1/2 teaspoon white pepper

1/2 teaspoon freshly ground black pepper

2^1/2 pounds trimmed boneless pork shoulder, cut into 1^1/2-inch cubes

1 teaspoon salt

1^1/2 tablespoons vegetable oil

1   In a heavy, large saucepan over low heat, combine the tomato puree, vinegar, molasses, coffee, garlic, Worcestershire sauce, soy sauce, oregano, mustard, cayenne, white pepper, and black pepper. Cover and simmer for at least 30 to 40 minutes and set aside. (You can cook the sauce up to 1 hour.)

2   Preheat the oven to 325°. Pat the pork dry with paper towels. Season the meat with salt.

3   In an ovenproof stewpot over medium heat, heat half of the vegetable oil. Working in batches, lightly brown each piece of pork on all sides. Remove the browned meat to a paper-towel-lined plate. Add more of the oil as necessary between batches, letting it get hot before putting in the meat. Repeat until all the meat is browned.

4   Return all the pork to the pot and pour in the sauce, stirring to coat the meat evenly. Cover and bake until the pork is very tender, about 1^1/2 to 2 hours.

VARIATION

To use the sauce as a barbecue sauce for grilled meat or chicken, follow step 1, but cover and simmer over low heat for 2 to 2$^1/_2$ hours.

note   *This dish can be made ahead, and it reheats well. It can be frozen for 2 to 3 months.*

79

serve with any of the following:

starch   Buttermilk Cornbread, *page 219*; or South African Garlic, Herb, & Cheese Pot Bread, *page 226*; or Biscuits, *pages 229–230*; or Spiced Mashed Sweet Potatoes, *page 237*   **salad**   Colorful Crunchy Slaw, *page 253*; or Warm Greens, *page 251*, with Hot Pepper Vinegar, *page 271*

Fruity Spiced Pork

PORK MARRIES WELL WITH DRIED FRUIT and fragrant spices. In this stew, the meat and fruit are simmered in apple cider and beer. This is a fall, winter, and spring stew. It is a wonderful dish served with apple cider or mulled cider when the air gets nippy but is equally delightful in warmer weather with a glass of cold beer.

80

serves 6

1 3/4 teaspoons dry English mustard, such as Coleman's

1 teaspoon ground coriander

1/2 teaspoon ground cardamom

1/2 teaspoon cayenne

1/8 teaspoon ground cumin

2 pounds trimmed boneless pork shoulder, cut into 1 1/2-inch cubes

1 teaspoon salt

2 tablespoons peanut oil

2 medium onions, chopped

1 medium sweet apple such as Golden Delicious or Rome, peeled, cored, and sliced very thinly

1 plump clove garlic, minced

3/4 cup apple cider or apple juice

3/4 cup beer

1 cup dried apricots

3/4 cup pitted prunes

1 In a small bowl, combine the dry mustard, coriander, cardamom, cayenne, and cumin and set aside. Pat the pork dry with paper towels. Season the meat with salt.

2 In a large stewpot over medium heat, heat the peanut oil. Add the onions and cook until they are translucent, about 5 minutes.

3 Add the pork, and cook, stirring occasionally, just until the pork has turned white. Do not brown the meat.

4 Add the spice mixture and stir well to coat the pork and onions evenly. Cook, stirring constantly so the spices don't burn, for 1 to 2 minutes. Add the apples and garlic and cook, stirring often, for 2 minutes. Pour in the cider and beer and cook until the liquids are hot and gently bubbling.

5 Reduce the heat to medium-low. Cover and simmer until the pork is almost tender, about 1 hour.

6 Stir in the apricots and prunes. Cover and simmer until the pork and fruit are tender, about 20 to 30 minutes longer. The sauce will thicken substantially after the dried fruit is added. If the stew is too thick, add a little cider or water.

note *This dish can be made ahead, and it reheats well. When reheating, add extra liquid as the fruit can thicken the stew even more after it has been refrigerated. I do not recommend freezing it.*

81

serve with any of the following:

starch rice; or Lemon or Orange Couscous, *page 239*; or Spiced Mashed Sweet Potatoes, *page 237*; or Herbed Corn Biscuits, *page 229*; or Buttermilk Raisin Spice Bread, *page 216* **salad** Make-Ahead Herbed Garden Salad, *page 263*; or Spicy Green Bean Sambal, *page 254*; or Pickled Cucumber Salad for savory dishes with chives, *page 258*

Rosemary Pork in Milk

I FIRST CAME ACROSS the custom of combining pork and milk in a recipe for roasted pork Venetian style in a book by Ada Boni, the gifted cookbook author and authority on Italian cooking. In this delicate stew, the tradition continues. Simmering the pork in milk both tenderizes the meat and imparts a subtle sweetness to it. Subtly scented with garlic and rosemary, this is a lovely, gentle stew.

82

serves 6

2 plump cloves garlic

1 sprig fresh rosemary or
　2 teaspoons fresh or dried leaves

1 bay leaf

1 teaspoon salt

1/4 teaspoon freshly ground black
　pepper

all-purpose flour for dusting the
　meat

2 1/2 pounds trimmed boneless pork
　shoulder, cut into 1 1/2-inch
　cubes

2 tablespoons olive oil

2 medium leeks, white part only,
　diced

2 medium carrots, diced

1 celery stalk, diced

1/2 cup vermouth

1/3 cup chicken broth

1 cup milk

3/4 cup frozen or fresh peas

1　Wrap the garlic, rosemary, and bay leaf in a small piece of cheesecloth and tie it to form a sack.

2　In a small bowl, combine about 1/3 cup of flour, the salt, and the pepper. Pat the meat dry with paper towels. Lightly dust the meat with the seasoned flour, shaking off any excess. Set aside.

3　In a stewpot over medium heat, heat 1 tablespoon of the olive oil. Add the leeks, carrots, and celery and cook, stirring occasionally, until the vegetables are very tender, about 15 minutes. Transfer the vegetables to a plate and set aside.

4　In the same stewpot over medium heat, heat the remaining tablespoon of olive oil. Working in batches, brown each piece of pork on all sides. Return all the meat to the pot.

5　Add the vermouth. Cook, scraping the bottom with a wooden spoon to loosen any browned bits. When the vermouth is reduced by two-thirds, add the broth, milk, and the cheesecloth sack. Stir in the cooked vegetables.

6 Reduce the heat to medium-low. Simmer uncovered until the pork is tender, about 1¹/₄ to 1¹/₂ hours.

7 Stir in the peas and simmer until they are heated through, about 5 minutes for frozen or 12 minutes for fresh.

note *This stew can be made ahead, and it reheats well. It can be frozen for 2 to 3 months.*

83

serve with any of the following:

starch   Basic Risotto or Wild Mushroom Risotto, *page 242*; or Basic Polenta or Parmesan Herb Polenta, *page 240*; or Oven Roasted Red Potatoes with Rosemary, *page 234*   salad   Tomato & Sautéed Mushroom Salad, *page 250*; or Herbed Vegetable Slaw, *page 252*; or Make-Ahead Herbed Garden Salad, *page 263*

dessert   Figs in Red Wine, Ginger, & Thyme, *page 210*

three ## CHICKEN, TURKEY, & DUCK

Chicken

African Chicken Peanut Stew

Catalan Chicken with Olives

Cape Malay Chicken Curry

Chicken with Porcini

Ginger Chicken with Jamaican Pumpkin

Chicken Paprikash

Jambalaya Chicken

Dijon Tarragon Chicken

Thai Green Chicken Curry

Old-Fashioned Creamed Chicken
    with Ham

Chipotle Chicken

Rustic Waterzooie

South African Tomato Chicken Bredie

Four-Herb Ground Chicken with
    Vegetables

Turkey

Turkey Stew with Sage

Turkey Mole

Turkey Picadillo

Leftover Turkey with Tomatillo Sauce

Duck

Cajun Duck Ragout

Malaysian Duck

Additional Recipes (Chapter Six)

chicken

African Chicken Peanut Stew

GROUND PEANUTS ARE OFTEN USED as a flavoring agent and thickener for stews and soups throughout Africa—including Nigeria, Senegal, Ghana, and areas of Zimbabwe. There are several versions of what is commonly known as groundnut stew; some with a thin broth, others with a thick sauce. It typically contains peanuts and tomatoes, but may also include other vegetables such as okra, eggplant, spinach, or cabbage.

This interpretation has a spicy sauce, made from peanuts, tomatoes, onions, and bell peppers, which permeates the chicken as it cooks. I have often served this marvelous, "May I have more, and are there leftovers?" stew. Fortunately, the recipe can be doubled.

Although it can be served immediately, I prefer to make it ahead and reheat it so the flavors have time to intensify. As with any thick sauce, you may need to add a little water when reheating to prevent scorching, or reheat it in a double boiler.

serves 4 to 6

Chicken

2 pounds boneless skinless chicken thighs or breasts, cut in 1 1/2-inch strips
juice of 1/2 lemon
1/2 teaspoon salt
1 tablespoon peanut oil

Sauce

1 tablespoon peanut oil
3 bunches scallions (about 15), white part only, sliced
1 medium onion, diced
2 medium green bell peppers, diced

1 Rub the chicken pieces with the lemon juice and season them with salt. Set aside for 10 to 15 minutes.

2 In a stewpot over medium heat, heat the peanut oil. Working in batches, if necessary, add the chicken pieces and cook until they turn white, about 5 to 7 minutes. Transfer the chicken to a plate and set aside.

3 In the same pot over medium heat, heat the peanut oil. Add the scallions, onion, and bell peppers. Cook until the vegetables are tender, about 10 minutes. Add the garlic, ginger, and chili powder and cook, stirring constantly, for 2 to 3 minutes. Add the tomatoes, thyme, and crushed red pepper flakes and cook for 5 minutes. Add the peanut butter; stir until blended evenly. Add the broth and cook for 5 minutes.

4 Reduce the heat to medium-low. Return the chicken to the pot. Simmer uncovered until the sauce is reduced and is quite thick, and the chicken is tender, about 30 to 40 minutes.

note *This dish can be made ahead, and it reheats well. It can be frozen for 2 to 3 months.*

3 plump cloves garlic, minced

$1^{1}/_{2}$-inch piece fresh ginger, minced

1 tablespoon chili powder

2 cups peeled chopped tomatoes

1 teaspoon minced fresh thyme leaves or $^{1}/_{2}$ teaspoon dried thyme leaves

$^{1}/_{4}$ to $^{1}/_{2}$ teaspoon crushed red pepper flakes, to taste

$^{1}/_{3}$ cup natural peanut butter

$1^{1}/_{4}$ cups chicken broth or water

87

serve with any of the following:

starch   white, basmati, or Texamati rice; or Basic Polenta, *page 240*

salad   sautéed spinach with garlic; or Warm Greens, *page 251*; or Avocado Salad,

page 260; or Jicama Mango Salad, replacing the mango with oranges, *page 248*;

or for a crowd serve also with South African Garlicky Eggplant with Potatoes, *page 162*

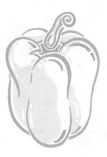

Catalan Chicken with Olives

A FRIEND USED TO MAKE this quick stew for impromptu dinner parties. An "urban pioneer," she lived in a Tribeca loft in New York before it was approved by the City for residential living. I never got a formal recipe, so here is my sense memory version. This is a terrific meal that you can make even after a hard day of work. I sometimes use pitted imported black olives instead of stuffed green olives.

88

serves 4 to 6

2 tablespoons olive oil

1 medium onion, chopped

1 medium green bell pepper, chopped

1 medium red or yellow bell pepper, chopped

3 plump cloves garlic, minced

1 3/4 pounds boneless skinless chicken breasts, cubed

1 teaspoon salt

3 1/2 cups canned crushed or chopped tomatoes in puree

1/4 teaspoon cayenne

1/4 teaspoon freshly ground black pepper

1 bay leaf

1/3 cup sliced pimento-stuffed green olives

1 In a large, deep skillet over medium heat, heat the olive oil. Add the onion and bell peppers. Cook, stirring occasionally, until the vegetables are very tender, about 10 to 15 minutes. Add the garlic and cook, stirring constantly, for 1 minute.

2 Season the chicken pieces with 1/2 teaspoon of the salt. Add them to the skillet and cook, stirring occasionally, until they turn white, about 5 minutes. Add the tomatoes, cayenne, pepper, bay leaf, and the remaining 1/2 teaspoon of the salt and stir.

3 Reduce the heat to medium-low. Simmer uncovered until the chicken is tender, about 25 to 30 minutes. Stir in the olives and simmer until the olives are heated through, about 5 minutes longer.

note *This dish can be made ahead, and it reheats well. It can be frozen for 2 to 3 months.*

serve with any of the following:

starch white, basmati, or Texamati rice; or Garlic & Herb Mashed Potatoes, *page 235*; or Anna's Crusty French Loaf, *page 222* **salad** Mesclun Salad with Goat Cheese, *page 224*; or A Good & Simple Salad, *page 262*; or Avocado Salad, *page 260* **dessert** Rhubarb with Cardamom, *page 209*

Cape Malay Chicken Curry

CURRIES ARE A NATIONAL PASSION in South Africa. They are available in most restaurants, delis, take-out shops, and street stalls; are sold frozen, canned, and bottled in supermarkets; and of course are prepared in homes. Grocery shelves stock several types of curry powder and spice mixtures called masalas, and there are shops solely devoted to the sale and blending of spices to create various curries and spice rubs.

South African Indian-style curries are eye-popping hot; however, Cape Malay-style curries, such as this one, are more fragrantly spiced and moderately hot. You may use a smaller amount of chili peppers if you wish. Although we don't have the range of curry blends in the United States, I've had good results with high-quality curry powders. This curry is one of my favorites.

serves 4 to 6

3 tablespoons vegetable oil

1 1/2 pounds boneless skinless chicken breasts, cut into thin strips

2 medium onions, chopped

4 cardamom pods

2 cinnamon sticks

4 plump cloves garlic, minced

1 1/2-inch piece fresh ginger, minced

1/2 to 1 red or green chili such as cayenne, jalapeño, or serrano, seeded and minced

1 to 1 1/2 tablespoons good-quality curry powder, such as Madras brand

1 teaspoon ground cumin

1 teaspoon ground coriander

1/4 teaspoon turmeric

1 In a stewpot or large deep skillet over medium heat, heat 1 tablespoon of the vegetable oil. Add the chicken strips and cook until they turn white, about 5 to 7 minutes. Transfer the chicken to a plate and set aside.

2 In the same pot over medium heat, heat the remaining 2 tablespoons of vegetable oil. Add the onions, cardamom, cinnamon, garlic, ginger, chili, curry powder, cumin, coriander, and turmeric. Cook, stirring often, for 2 to 3 minutes. Add the tomatoes and broth and cook for 15 minutes.

3 Reduce the heat to medium-low. Return the chicken to the pot. Simmer until the chicken is cooked through and tender, about 30 to 40 minutes. Garnish with chopped cilantro.

note This dish can be made ahead, and it reheats well. It can be frozen for 2 to 3 months.

5 plum tomatoes, peeled, seeded, and chopped, about 1 $^1/_3$ cups

$^1/_2$ cup chicken broth or water

2 tablespoons chopped fresh cilantro or mint for garnish

serve with any of the following:

starch   white, basmati, or Texamati rice; or Spiced Rice, *page 244*

salad   Carrot Orange Sambal *page 256*; or Pickled Cucumber Salad with chilis and

mint, *page 258*   condiment   Fresh Mango Chutney, *page 270*; or commercial

chutney

Chicken with Porcini

DRIED PORCINI, ALSO KNOWN AS CEPES, impart a heavenly yet earthy aroma to this stew. A native of Italy and France, as well as areas of the United States and Canada, these precious mushrooms can be bought dried in good supermarkets and specialty or Italian food shops. Although dried porcini are costly, you won't use very much in this dish. The roasted garlic puree adds a more subtle flavor than minced garlic. If you don't have the puree, use fresh garlic.

serves 4

1 ounce dried porcini mushrooms

1 cup boiling water

1 1/2 pounds boneless skinless chicken breasts, cut into thin strips

1/2 teaspoon salt

1/4 teaspoon freshly ground black pepper

all-purpose flour for dusting the chicken

2 tablespoons olive oil

4 scallions, white and green part, thinly sliced

1/2 cup dry white wine

1/2 cup chicken broth

2 tablespoons roasted garlic puree* (page 275)

2 plum tomatoes, peeled, seeded, and chopped, about 2/3 cup

2 tablespoons chopped fresh flat-leaf parsley

1 Place the porcini in a small bowl, pour the boiling water over them, and let them stand for 20 to 30 minutes. Then pour the liquid through a strainer lined with a paper coffee filter, and reserve. Rinse the porcini with a little bit of water to remove any lingering grit, and squeeze them dry. Chop or cut with scissors into small pieces. Set the porcini aside.

2 Season the chicken strips with salt and pepper. Lightly dust them with flour, shaking off any excess.

3 In a deep skillet over medium heat, heat the olive oil. Add the scallions. Cook, stirring occasionally, until they are softened, about 5 minutes. Add the chicken and cook, stirring occasionally, until the strips are lightly golden.

4 Pour in the wine and scrape the bottom with a wooden spoon to loosen any browned bits. Cook until the wine is reduced by about half, about 7 minutes.

*If you don't have any roasted garlic puree on hand, after the scallions are tender in step 3, add 1 clove of minced garlic and cook, stirring constantly, for 1 minute; add the chicken and proceed with the directions.

5 Add the reserved mushroom liquid and broth. Stir in the roasted garlic puree. Add the tomatoes and the reserved mushrooms.

6 Reduce the heat to medium-low. Simmer until the chicken is tender and the sauce is reduced, about 35 to 40 minutes longer. Garnish with parsley and serve.

note *This dish can be made ahead, and it reheats well. It can be frozen for 2 to 3 months.*

serve with any of the following:

starch Basic Risotto or Saffron Risotto, *page 242*; or Great Potato Pancakes, *page 232*; or Oven-Roasted Red Potatoes with Rosemary, *page 234*; or Lemon Scallion Soda Bread, *page 217* salad Sugar Snap Peas with Orange & Herbs, *page 249*; or Arugula Salad, *page 265*; or mixed green salad with Basic Vinaigrette using balsamic vinegar, *page 266*; or Mesclun Salad with Goat Cheese, *page 262*

Ginger Chicken with Jamaican Pumpkin

JAMAICAN GINGER, JAMAICAN PUMPKIN, Jamaican rum—you get the theme, especially when you add coconut milk and the traditional spices for Jamaican jerked chicken: allspice and cinnamon. Although this is not a traditional dish, it is a fun and tasty way to fuse the terrific tastes of Jamaica in a stew. If you can't find Jamaican pumpkin, use butternut squash.

94

serves 4 to 6

3/4 cup raisins

1/3 cup dark rum

2 tablespoons butter

2 medium onions, sliced thinly

2-inch piece fresh ginger, minced

1 to 2 jalapeño or serrano or
    1/2 Scotch bonnet pepper, seeded
    and minced

2 allspice berries or 2 whole cloves

1 cinnamon stick

1/2 teaspoon fresh thyme leaves

1 green or red bell pepper, sliced in
    thin strips

3/4 teaspoon salt

1 1/4 pounds boneless skinless
    chicken thighs, cut into strips

2 pounds Calabaza (Jamaican
    pumpkin) or butternut squash,
    cut into 1 1/2-inch cubes

1/3 cup unsweetened coconut milk

2 tablespoons brown sugar

1   In a small saucepan over high heat, combine the raisins and rum; bring the liquid to a boil and remove the pan from the heat. Let the raisins soak in the rum until they are added to the stew later.

2   In a stewpot over medium heat, melt the butter. Add the onions, ginger, chilis, allspice, cinnamon, and thyme and cook, stirring occasionally, until the onions are translucent, about 5 minutes. Add the bell pepper and cook, stirring occasionally, for 5 minutes.

3   Season the chicken strips with 1/4 teaspoon of the salt. Add the chicken to the stewpot and cook, stirring occasionally, until the strips turn white, about 5 to 7 minutes. Add the pumpkin, raisins with the rum, coconut milk, and brown sugar and stir.

4   Reduce the heat to medium-low. Cover and simmer until the pumpkin is quite soft but still holds its shape and the flavors are fully blended, about 50 to 60 minutes. Stir in the remaining ¹/₂ teaspoon salt before serving.

note   *This stew can be made ahead, and it reheats well. It can be frozen for 2 to 3 months.*

95

serve with any of the following:

starch   rice; or Spiced Rice or Yellow Spiced Rice variation, *page 244*; or Spiced Mashed Sweet Potatoes, *page 237*   salad   Sugar Snap Peas with Orange & Herbs, *page 249*; or Jicama Mango Salad, *page 248*; or leaf lettuce with cubed papaya and Basic Vinaigrette using lime juice and garnished with chopped fresh mint, *page 266*

Chicken Paprikash

THIS CHICKEN STANDARD OF HUNGARIAN origin is—what can I say?—simply scrumptious. I know it is rich, so feel free to substitute nonfat sour cream. The success of the dish lies in the quality of the paprika you use, and I recommend imported Hungarian sweet paprika.

serves 4 to 6

96

2 tablespoons butter

2 medium onions, diced

1 1/2 pounds boneless skinless chicken breasts, cut into 1 1/2-inch cubes

3/4 teaspoon salt

1/8 teaspoon white pepper

1 tablespoon all-purpose flour

2 1/2 tablespoons Hungarian sweet paprika

1 1/2 tablespoons tomato paste

1/2 cup dry white wine

1 cup chicken broth

1 teaspoon fresh thyme leaves or 1/2 teaspoon dried

6 ounces mushrooms, sliced

1/2 teaspoon Dijon mustard

2/3 cup regular or nonfat sour cream

chopped fresh parsley for garnish, optional

1   In a stewpot or large deep skillet over medium heat, melt 1 tablespoon of the butter. Add the onions and cook, stirring occasionally, until they are tender, about 10 minutes.

2   Season the chicken pieces with 1/2 teaspoon of the salt and the pepper. Add the chicken to the onions and cook, stirring occasionally, until the pieces turn white, about 5 to 7 minutes.

3   Add the flour and cook, stirring constantly, for 1 minute. Add the paprika and tomato paste and cook, stirring constantly, for 1 to 2 minutes.

4   Pour in the wine and chicken broth. Add the thyme. Reduce the heat to medium-low. Cover and simmer until the chicken is tender, about 15 to 20 minutes.

5   Meanwhile, in a large skillet over medium heat, melt the remaining tablespoon of butter. Add the mushrooms and cook until tender, about 7 to 10 minutes. Season with the remaining 1/4 teaspoon of salt. Add the mushrooms to the chicken and stir.

6 Reduce the heat to low. Stir in the mustard and sour cream. Simmer until everything is heated through and the chicken is very tender, about 10 minutes. Garnish with parsley before serving.

note *This stew can be made ahead if you reheat it gently over low heat or in a double boiler. Do not allow the mixture to boil, as the sour cream may curdle. It cannot be frozen.*

97

serve with any of the following:

starch broad noodles; or Mashed Potatoes with Cucumber, *page 236*; or Round Country Loaf, *page 224*; or Herbed Dijon Beer Bread, *page 218*

salad Herbed Vegetable Slaw, *page 252*; or Lemony Asparagus or Green Beans with Nuts, *page 255*; or mixed green salad with Basic Vinaigrette using red wine vinegar, *page 266*

Jambalaya Chicken

JAMBALAYA, THE CELEBRATED SPICY Cajun rice dish made with various combinations of meat, sausage, poultry, and seafood, takes its cue from the best of Cajun cooking and the Joloffe rice dishes of West Africa.

In Mississippi, where some of my family lives, chicken Jambalaya is very popular. The first time I tasted it, it was so delicious that I wondered if I had achieved nirvana. When I read a recipe for it, I nearly passed out when I saw the fat content, and I shied away from it. This full-flavored, sock-it-to-me rendition uses a lot less fat than most recipes, although I wouldn't call it a dieter's special. Despite the many ingredients, jambalaya is a snap to make.

serves 6 to 8

$1/2$ **pound spicy smoked sausage links, such as Andouille or chorizo, sliced**

$2^1/2$ **tablespoons butter**

1 pound boneless skinless chicken breasts, cut into thin strips

2 medium onions, chopped

2 celery stalks, chopped

1 large green bell pepper

3 plump cloves garlic, minced

1 bay leaf

1 tablespoon chopped fresh oregano or 1 teaspoon dried

1 teaspoon fresh thyme leaves or $1/2$ teaspoon dried leaves

$1/2$ **teaspoon white pepper**

$1/2$ **teaspoon cayenne**

$1/4$ **teaspoon freshly ground black pepper**

1 In a large stewpot over medium heat, lightly brown the sausage slices, then place them on a paper towel-lined plate and blot the excess fat.

2 Wipe out the stewpot with a clean paper towel. In the stewpot over medium heat, melt 1 tablespoon of the butter. Add the chicken strips and cook, stirring occasionally, until they turn white, about 5 to 7 minutes. Transfer the chicken to a plate and set aside.

3 In the same stewpot, melt the remaining $1^1/2$ tablespoons butter. Add the onions, celery, and bell pepper and cook, stirring occasionally, until the onions are translucent, about 5 minutes. Add the garlic and cook, stirring often, for 2 minutes. Add the bay leaf, oregano, thyme, white pepper, cayenne, and black pepper and cook, stirring occasionally, for 15 minutes. Add the tomatoes and cook for 10 minutes.

4   Add the chicken, sausage, and ham to the vegetable mixture. Add the rice, heated broth, and Tabasco. Bring the liquid to a boil, then reduce the heat to medium-low. Cover and simmer until the rice is tender, about 20 minutes.

5   Stir in the parsley and scallions for garnish. Taste for salt and add additional if desired. Serve with extra Tabasco on the side.

note   *This dish can be made ahead and reheated in a microwave or on the stovetop with a little extra liquid added to it. It does not freeze well, as the texture of the sausage and ham changes when frozen.*

4 medium tomatoes, peeled, seeded, and chopped, about 2 cups

4 ounces diced smoked ham, about 1 cup

1 cup long-grain white rice

2^1/4 cups chicken broth, heated

^{1}/4 teaspoon freshly ground black pepper

^{1}/2 teaspoon Tabasco

^{1}/4 cup chopped fresh parsley for garnish

4 scallions, white and green parts, thinly sliced for garnish

^{1}/2 teaspoon salt, optional (Add at the end after tasting; the ham may provide enough salt.)

99

serve with any of the following:

starch   Biscuits Any Which Way, *page 220*; or Herbed Corn Biscuits, *page 229*   salad   Colorful Crunchy Slaw, *page 253*; or Warm Greens, *page 251*, with Hot Pepper Vinegar, *page 271*   dessert   Spiced Dried Fruit Compote, *page 207*

Dijon Tarragon Chicken

ALMOST EVERY TAKE-OUT and catering shop has some version of Dijon chicken. Many adults adore this classic combination, but I wondered if this would hold true for children as well.

I have watched my niece and nephew eat mustard straight from the jar on too many occasions, and I know the amazing appeal of mustard to children's palates. However, I wasn't sure this stew would pass the mustard test with kids. I have since tried it on many children and have found that this simple one-pot meal with plenty of vegetables is a hit with them as well.

serves 4 to 6

2 tablespoons butter

1 medium onion, coarsely diced

1 stalk celery, coarsely diced

2 medium carrots, coarsely diced

1¼ pounds boneless skinless chicken breasts, cut into thin strips

1 medium potato, about 4 ounces, peeled and cubed, or 6 tiny red or new potatoes, quartered

1½ cups chicken broth, heated

1 cup cream or half and half

¼ cup dry sherry

2½ tablespoons Dijon mustard

2 tablespoons mild whole-grain mustard

1 tablespoon honey

1 tablespoon fresh chopped tarragon or 1 teaspoon dried

½ teaspoon salt

1 In a stewpot or deep skillet over medium heat, melt the butter. Add the onion, celery, and carrots. Cook, stirring occasionally, until the vegetables are very tender, about 15 to 20 minutes.

2 Add the chicken and potatoes. Pour in the heated broth. Reduce the heat to medium-low and simmer until the chicken is cooked through and the vegetables and potatoes are tender, about 15 to 20 minutes.

3 Meanwhile, in a small saucepan over medium heat, combine the cream, sherry, both mustards, honey, and tarragon. Bring the mixture to a boil, then reduce the heat to medium-low. Simmer until the sauce is thick enough to lightly coat the back of a spoon, about 5 minutes. Add the salt and set aside.

4 Strain the chicken and vegetables from the broth. Discard the broth or reserve it for another use.

5 Return the chicken, vegetables, and potatoes to the stewpot. Pour the Dijon cream sauce over the chicken and vegetables. Simmer over medium-low heat until everything is heated through, about 10 minutes.

note *This dish can be made ahead, and it reheats well. It can be frozen for 2 to 3 months.*

101

serve with any of the following:

starch   Biscuits Any Which Way, *page 230*; Round Country Loaf, *page 224*

salad   A Good & Simple Salad, *page 264*; or Herbed Vegetable Slaw, *page 252*

dessert   Spiced Apples in Cider & Brandy, *page 211*

Thai Green Chicken Curry

I ADORE THIS CURRY—it's a perfect marriage of hot and sweet. I started eating Thai food in the 1970s, and for a long time I found it difficult to consider ordering anything besides this dish when I went to a Thai restaurant.

A friend who lived in Bangkok for many years described to me the seemingly intricate, lengthy process of mashing the paste by hand. Although untraditional, using a food processor makes preparing your own curry paste easy. The paste will keep in the refrigerator for up to 2 weeks and can be frozen in an airtight container for up to 2 months. If you prefer, use 3 tablespoons commercially made Thai green or Thai red curry paste. Of course, you can adjust the amount of curry paste depending on your personal taste.

To make a really good paste, puree the ingredients in a blender or food processor, then place the puree in a mortar and pound until the paste is completely smooth. If you don't have the time, go ahead and use it straight from the food processor.

serves 4 to 6

Green Curry Paste
**2 medium shallots, sliced, or
   1/4 cup finely minced onion**
**4 to 6 green bird's-eye chilis or
   jalapeños, stems removed**
4 cloves garlic, thinly sliced
2-inch piece fresh ginger, thinly sliced
**2 stalks fresh lemon grass (the
   softer inner core), thinly sliced**
**finely grated zest of 1 Thai
   (makrud) lime, or 1 teaspoon
   finely grated fresh lemon zest,
   optional**
1/4 cup warm water

1 *To prepare the curry paste:* In a blender or food processor, combine the shallots, chilis, garlic, ginger, lemon grass, lime zest, and water. Puree until a smooth paste forms, adding up to 1 tablespoon of additional warm water if necessary.

2 In a deep skillet or stewpot over medium heat, heat the vegetable oil. Add 3 tablespoons of the green curry paste and cook, stirring constantly, until the aroma is very strong and the curry paste is almost dry, about 5 to 7 minutes.

3 Add the coconut milk, lime leaves, chicken, peas, and bamboo shoots. Simmer until the chicken is cooked through, 10 to 15 minutes.

4 Stir in the fish sauce and simmer for 3 to 5 minutes. Serve garnished with chopped mint or basil.

note *This dish does not freeze well because of the coconut milk.*

Chicken

1 tablespoon vegetable oil

$1^3/4$ cups unsweetened coconut milk

1 to 2 Thai (makrud) lime leaves, optional

$1^1/4$ pounds boneless skinless chicken breasts, cut into strips

$1^1/4$ cups frozen (one 10-ounce package) peas

$1/2$ cup canned bamboo shoots, drained, rinsed, and julienned

2 to 3 tablespoons Thai fish sauce or $1/2$ to $3/4$ teaspoon salt

2 tablespoons fresh chopped mint, Thai holy basil, or small basil leaves for garnish

103

serve with any of the following:

starch   white or jasmine rice   **salad**   Jicama Mango Salad, *page 248*; or Pickled Cucumber Salad for spicy dishes with chili and cilantro, *page 258*

Old-Fashioned Creamed Chicken with Ham

THIS TRADITIONAL, LUSCIOUS DISH with a hint of Parmesan cheese is a holdover from my childhood, when we ate something because it tasted good and didn't think about dietary effects. I still crave it when I am feeling blue, and it seems to soothe the soul the same way a peanut butter and jelly sandwich with an ice-cold glass of milk does. Perhaps it is a desire for the return to the innocence of childhood. And so I indulge myself with a helping of this rich dish because it tastes oh so good.

104

serves 4 to 6

Sauce

2 tablespoons butter
2 1/2 tablespoons all-purpose flour
3/4 cup chicken broth, heated
3/4 to 1 cup milk or light cream, heated
1/4 cup freshly grated Parmesan or romano cheese

Chicken

1 tablespoon butter
1 small onion, chopped
3-ounce slice smoked ham, 1/4-inch thick, trimmed of fat, diced
1 1/4 pounds boneless skinless chicken breasts, cut into strips
6 ounces sliced mushrooms, about 2 cups
1/3 cup dry sherry
1 cup frozen or fresh peas, optional
freshly ground black pepper to taste

1 To prepare the sauce: In a large saucepan over medium heat, melt the butter. Add the flour and cook, stirring constantly, about 2 minutes. While stirring, gradually add the heated broth and 3/4 cup of the milk. Bring to a gentle boil, stirring often. Reduce the heat to medium-low and simmer about 5 minutes. Stir in the Parmesan cheese. The sauce should be thick enough to lightly coat the back of a spoon. Set aside. (If the sauce becomes too thick while it sits, add some of the remaining milk, 1 tablespoon at a time.)

2 To prepare the chicken: In a large, deep skillet over medium heat, melt the butter. Add the onion and ham and cook, stirring occasionally, until the onion is tender, about 10 minutes. Add the chicken strips and cook, stirring occasionally until they turn white, about 5 to 7 minutes. Add the mushrooms and cook, stirring, until the mushrooms are cooked through, about 5 minutes.

3 Add the sherry to the chicken mixture and cook for 1 to 2 minutes. Pour the cream sauce into the chicken mixture.

4 Reduce the heat to medium-low. Add the peas and simmer until they are tender, about 5 minutes for frozen or 12 minutes for fresh. Before serving, add freshly ground black pepper to taste.

note *This dish can be made ahead, and it reheats well. It can be frozen for 2 to 3 months.*

serve with any of the following:

starch   broad noodles; or rice; or Buttermilk Raisin Spice Bread, *page 216*; or Biscuits Any Which Way, *page 230*; or Spiced Mashed Sweet Potatoes, *page 237*

salad   A Good & Simple Salad, *page 264*; or mixed greens with Basic Vinaigrette, *page 266*   condiment   Cranberries in Red Wine, *page 212*

Chipotle Chicken

THIS COLORFUL, SPICY STEW is a celebration of the native bounty of the American continents—tomatoes, corn, and chilis. Chipotle peppers, which add their unique flavor to this dish, are smoked jalapeños. I prefer to use the dried ones rather than the canned ones. To me this stew is better when it is made ahead, but beware! It seems to get hotter as it stands. Feel free to substitute turkey thighs for the chicken.

serves 6

2 dried chipotle peppers, reconstituted,* seeded, and stems removed, or 2 jalapeño peppers, seeded and minced

2 tablespoons vegetable oil

2 medium onions, chopped

3 cloves garlic, chopped

1 1/2 teaspoons ground cumin

1 1/2 teaspoons chopped fresh oregano or 3/4 teaspoon dried

1/4 teaspoon ground cinnamon

1 1/4 teaspoons salt

1 3/4 pounds boneless skinless chicken thighs, cut in 1 1/2-inch strips

1 3/4 cups canned crushed or chopped tomatoes (one 14 1/2-ounce can)

1 1/4 cups chicken broth

3 tablespoons orange juice

3 tablespoons fresh lemon juice

1 1/4 cups frozen (one 10-ounce package) corn kernels

1/4 cup chopped fresh cilantro

1 In a food processor fitted with the metal blade or a blender, combine the chipotles with 2 tablespoons of water. Pulse until a puree forms. (Omit step if using jalapeños.)

2 In a large stewpot over medium heat, heat the vegetable oil. Add the onions and cook, stirring occasionally, until translucent, about 5 minutes. Add the garlic and cook, stirring constantly, about 1 minute. Add the chipotle puree, cumin, oregano, and cinnamon. Cook, stirring often, for 2 minutes. Set aside.

3 Season the chicken strips with 1/2 teaspoon of the salt. Add the strips to the pot and cook, stirring occasionally, until the they turn white, about 5 to 7 minutes.

4 Add the tomatoes, broth, orange juice, and lemon juice. Reduce the heat to medium-low. Simmer until the chicken is tender, about 30 to 40 minutes.

*To reconstitute chipotle peppers: Place the chipotles in a small bowl. Pour enough boiling water over them to cover. Let stand for 20 to 30 minutes until softened. Discard the water and remove the stems and seeds. Finely chop the chipotles with a sharp knife or in a mini-food processor.

5 Add the remaining ³/₄ teaspoon of salt and the corn and stir. Simmer until the corn is tender and heated through, about 5 to 7 minutes. Stir in the cilantro and serve.

note *This dish can be made ahead, and it reheats well. It can be frozen for 2 to 3 months.*

serve with any of the following:

starch warm flour tortillas; or rice; or Buttermilk Cornbread, *page 219*; or Herbed Corn Biscuits, *page 229* **salad** Avocado Salad, *page 260*; or Jicama Mango Salad, *page 248*; or Cucumber Tomato Salsa, *page 261*

Rustic Waterzooie

WATERZOOIE IS A TRADITIONAL FLEMISH DISH. A cross between a stew and a thick soup, it is most often made with chicken but can also be prepared with fish. Unlike the better-known classic version with its heavy cream sauce thickened with egg yolks, this rustic interpretation has a lighter, herbed sauce.

I make it with freshly made broth and light cream and thicken it with pureed vegetables and fresh parsley and chervil. This dish requires a good homemade chicken broth. Serve the pale green Waterzooie in shallow soup bowls.

serves 4 to 6

2 tablespoons butter

5 medium leeks, white part only, thinly sliced

1 medium onion, thinly sliced

4 medium stalks celery, thinly sliced

1 bay leaf

1 1/2 teaspoons minced fresh thyme leaves or 3/4 teaspoon dried thyme leaves

1/8 teaspoon freshly grated nutmeg

1 3/4 pounds boneless skinless chicken breasts

4 cups homemade chicken broth, heated

1 teaspoon salt

1/4 teaspoon white pepper

2 1/2 tablespoons fresh lemon juice

1/2 cup cream or half and half

1/3 cup chopped fresh parsley

1/3 cup chopped fresh chervil (Do not use dried. If fresh is not available, use a total of 2/3 cup chopped fresh parsley.)

1 In a stewpot over medium-low heat, melt the butter. Add the leeks, onion, celery, bay leaf, thyme, and nutmeg. Cook, stirring occasionally, until the vegetables are extremely tender, about 15 to 20 minutes.

2 Place the chicken breasts on top of the softened vegetables. Add the broth and simmer over medium-low heat until the chicken is cooked through, about 10 to 15 minutes. The broth should be just bubbling gently; do not boil. With a slotted spoon, remove the chicken from the broth. When cool, slice the chicken into bite-size strips.

3 Meanwhile, strain the vegetables from the broth, reserving 2 1/2 cups of the broth (as well as the vegetables). Remove and discard the bay leaf.

4 In a food processor fitted with the metal blade, puree the vegetables until very smooth, adding a little of the reserved broth if necessary.

5 Put the pureed vegetables and reserved broth into the stewpot and simmer over medium-low heat. Add the salt, pepper, and lemon juice and stir. Add the cream and stir. When the creamy broth is gently bubbling, add the strips of cooked chicken. Simmer until the chicken is heated through, about 5 minutes.

6 Add the parsley and chervil and stir. Simmer for 2 to 3 minutes. Serve immediately in shallow soup bowls.

note *This dish can be made ahead, and it reheats well. It can be frozen for 2 months.*

109

serve with any of the following:

starch   boiled red or baby potatoes; or Anna's Crusty French Loaf, *page 222*; or Herbed Dijon Beer Bread, *page 218*   salad   Roasted Beet & Onion Salad on Watercress, *page 247*; or Tomato & Sautéed Mushroom Salad, *page 250*   dessert   Spiced Apples in Cider & Brandy, *page 211*; or Nectarines with Tarragon & Pepper, *page 213*

South African Tomato Chicken Bredie

WHAT'S A BREDIE? It is a delectable yet humble stew that has been elevated to an art form in South Africa. Bredies are always named for the primary vegetable that endows the meat and other ingredients in the dish with its flavor.

Tomatoes, green beans, cabbage, peas, and pumpkins are the usual stars of this unique one-pot meal. Although bredies are most often made with a bit of lamb, chicken is also commonplace in tomato bredies. This dish is even better if it is made ahead and reheated, allowing the aromatic spices to fully permeate the stew.

110

serves 6

2 medium onions, thinly sliced
1/2 teaspoon peppercorns
5 whole cloves
3/4 cup water
2 tablespoons vegetable oil
2 sticks cinnamon
2 cardamom pods
1-inch piece fresh ginger, minced
3 plump cloves garlic, minced
1 1/2 pounds boneless skinless chicken thighs
1/2 to 1 red or green chili such as cayenne, jalapeño, or serrano, seeded and minced
5 cups canned chopped tomatoes (three 14-ounce cans)
1 teaspoon salt

1 In a stewpot over medium heat, combine the onions, peppercorns, cloves, and water and bring to a boil. Reduce the heat to medium-low and cook until all the water has been absorbed.

2 Add the vegetable oil, cinnamon, and cardamom. Cook, stirring occasionally, until the onions are lightly golden, about 15 minutes.

3 Add the ginger, garlic, and chicken and stir thoroughly. Cover and simmer, stirring occasionally, about 10 to 15 minutes.

4 Add the chili and tomatoes and stir. Cover and simmer until the chicken is very tender, about 15 to 20 minutes.

5 Add the salt, pepper, and brown sugar and stir. Add the potatoes and stir. Cover and simmer until the potatoes are tender, about 20 to 25 minutes. Taste again for salt, and add salt if desired. Garnish with cilantro or parsely.

note *This dish can be made ahead, and it reheats well. It can be frozen for 2 to 3 months.*

1/4 teaspoon freshly ground black pepper

1 tablespoon dark brown sugar

1 pound medium potatoes, peeled and quartered

chopped fresh cilantro or parsley for garnish

111

serve with any of the following:

starch   white, basmati, or Texamati rice; or Spiced Rice or Yellow Spiced Rice, *page 244*   salad   Pickled Beets, *page 259*; or Carrot Orange Sambal, *page 256*; or Sugar Snap Peas with Orange & Herbs, *page 249*; or Pickled Cucumber Salad for spicy food with chilis and cilantro, *page 258*

Four-Herb Ground Chicken with Vegetables

THIS CASUAL, DOWN-HOME DISH accented with parsley, rosemary, thyme, and chives turns ground chicken into a refined entree. The recipe works equally well with ground turkey or veal. I also like it tossed with pasta. When spooned over French bread, it's a sophisticated Sloppy Joe.

serves 4 to 6

2 tablespoons olive oil

1 medium onion, chopped

2 cloves garlic, chopped

1 tablespoon chopped fresh rosemary or 1 1/2 teaspoons crumbled dried

1 1/2 pounds ground chicken

1/2 cup dry white wine

3 tablespoons chopped fresh flat leaf parsley

2 tablespoons chopped fresh chives

1 teaspoon chopped fresh thyme or 1/2 teaspoon dried

1/2 teaspoon salt

1/4 teaspoon freshly ground black pepper

2/3 cup chicken broth

1 medium zucchini, diced

1/2 pound mushrooms, thinly sliced

chopped fresh parsley or chives for garnish

1 In a large, deep skillet over medium heat, heat the olive oil. Add the onion and cook, stirring occasionally, until soft, about 5 minutes. Add the garlic and rosemary and cook, stirring constantly, for 2 minutes.

2 Add the chicken and cook, stirring occasionally, until it is lightly browned. Add the wine and cook until the wine is slightly reduced, about 5 minutes. Stir in the parsley, chives, thyme, salt, and pepper. Add the broth. Reduce the heat to medium-low. Simmer uncovered for 30 to 40 minutes.

3 Add the zucchini and mushrooms and stir. Simmer uncovered until the vegetables are tender and the broth is almost absorbed, about 10 to 15 minutes. Garnish with extra fresh herbs before serving.

note *This dish can be made ahead, and it reheats well. It can be frozen for 2 to 3 months.*

serve with any of the following:

starch linguine; or broad noodles; or Anna's Crusty French Loaf, *page 222*; or Round Country Loaf, *page 224*; or Onion Flat Bread, *page 220* **salad** Arugula Salad, *page 265*; or A Good & Simple Salad, *page 264*; or Mesclun Salad with Goat Cheese, *page 262*

turkey

Turkey Stew with Sage

SOMETIMES I YEARN FOR THE TASTE and perhaps the contentment associated with a traditional Thanksgiving feast. This stew fulfills that desire, and I don't have to wait for Turkey Day to come around. I like to use red wine in the sauce, but if you prefer white, go for it. You can also substitute boneless skinless chicken thighs.

It's important to use fresh sage in this recipe; don't replace it with dried sage, which does not resemble the fresh herb. If you can't find fresh sage, substitute 1 tablespoon chopped fresh rosemary and 2 tablespoons fresh chopped flat-leaf parsley. It will be different than the original, but still tasty.

serves 4

1 3/4 pounds boneless skinless turkey thighs, cut into thin strips

1/2 teaspoon salt

1/4 teaspoon freshly ground black pepper

all-purpose flour for dusting the turkey

2 tablespoons olive oil

2 medium leeks, white part only, thinly sliced

1 medium carrot, finely diced

1 celery stalk, finely diced

1 plump clove garlic, minced

6 fresh sage leaves, minced

1 teaspoon fresh chopped thyme leaves or 1/2 teaspoon dried thyme leaves

1/2 cup dry red wine

1 Season the turkey strips with salt and pepper. Lightly dust the strips with flour, shaking off any excess.

2 In a deep, medium skillet or stewpot over medium heat, heat the olive oil. Add the leeks, carrot, and celery and cook, stirring occasionally, until the vegetables are tender, about 10 minutes. Add the garlic and cook, stirring constantly, for 1 minute longer.

3 Add the turkey strips and cook, stirring occasionally, until the meat is lightly golden. Stir in the sage and thyme.

4 Pour in the wine and scrape the bottom with a wooden spoon to loosen any browned bits. Cook until the wine is reduced by about half, about 7 minutes.

5 Reduce the heat to medium-low. Simmer uncovered until the turkey is tender and the sauce is reduced, about 35 to 40 minutes longer.

note *This dish can be made ahead, and it reheats well. It can be frozen for 2 to 3 months.*

115

serve with any of the following:

starch Mashed Turnips and Apples, *page 238*; or Spiced Mashed Sweet Potatoes, *page 237*; or Mushroom Polenta, *page 198*; or Creamy Potato Gratin, *page 233* salad A Good & Simple Salad, *page 264*; or Sugar Snap Peas with Orange & Herbs, *page 249*; or Mesclun Salad with Goat Cheese, *page 262*; or Lemony Asparagus or Green Beans with Nuts, *page 255* condiment Cranberries in Red Wine, *page 212*

Turkey Mole

MOLE IS ONE OF MEXICO'S national treasures. Rich and full-bodied, this classic Mexican stew is a pleasure to make and to eat. Many recipes for this distinctive sauce can be long and complicated for the home cook. In this rendition, I've simplified the process, yet the taste remains superb. You can also use about 3^1/$_2$ to 4 cups of leftover cooked turkey instead of starting from scratch, and prepare the sauce as directed.

116

serves 6

Turkey

4 to 5 pounds turkey thighs, skinned

1^1/$_2$ quarts water, or chicken broth

Sauce

2 tablespoons sesame seeds, toasted*

^{1}/$_3$ cup sliced almonds

2 slices white bread, toasted

2 tablespoons vegetable oil

1 medium onion, chopped

3 cloves garlic, chopped

1 dried guajillo chili pepper, reconstituted, stems removed, seeded, and pureed in 2 tablespoons warm water**

1 dried pasilla or ancho chili pepper, reconstituted, stems removed, seeded, and pureed in 2 tablespoons warm water

1^1/$_2$ teaspoons ground coriander

1 teaspoon ground cinnamon

^{1}/$_2$ teaspoon ground cumin

1 *To prepare the turkey:* Place the turkey in a large stewpot or stockpot over medium-high heat. Add 1^1/$_2$ quarts of water. Simmer for 50 minutes to 1 hour until the turkey is cooked through. Remove the turkey and set aside. Strain the broth, and reserve 2^1/$_2$ cups to use in the sauce. When the turkey is cool enough to touch, remove the turkey from the bones and cut the meat into bite-size strips.

2 *To prepare the sauce:* In a food processor fitted with the metal blade, combine the sesame seeds, almonds, and bread; pulse until the seeds and nuts are ground. Set aside.

3 In a large stewpot over medium heat, heat the vegetable oil. Add the onion and cook, stirring occasionally, until it is translucent, about 5 minutes. Add the garlic and cook, stirring constantly, for 1 minute. Add the pureed guajillo and pasilla chilis, coriander, cinnamon, cumin, and cloves. Cook, stirring constantly, until the aroma is very strong, about 5 minutes.

*To toast sesame seeds: Place the seeds in a nonstick skillet over medium heat. Cook, stirring occasionally, until the seeds just begin to darken slightly, 2 to 3 minutes. Remove seeds from the pan immediately, as the residual heat will continue to darken and possibly burn them. If they burn, discard them and start over.

4 Add the reserved broth, tomatoes, and choco-late. Stir until the chocolate is completely melted. Add the ground almonds and bread mixture and stir to com-bine. Reduce the heat to medium-low. Simmer uncov-ered for 25 to 30 minutes.

5 Add the cooked turkey pieces to the sauce. Add the salt and sugar and stir. Cover and simmer for 30 to 40 minutes.

note This dish can be made ahead, and it reheats well. It can be frozen for 2 to 3 months. You can also use 3 1/2 to 4 cups of leftover cooked turkey in this recipe. Omit step 1, and use 2 1/2 cups of chicken broth in the sauce. The sauce made in steps 2 and 3 can be made up to one day ahead if you use pre-pared chicken or turkey broth; refrigerate it and reheat it to use in step 4.

1/8 teaspoon ground cloves

2 1/2 cups crushed or chopped canned tomatoes in puree

1 ounce unsweetened chocolate coarsely chopped

1 teaspoon salt

2 tablespoons sugar

117

serve with any of the following:

starch   rice; or warm flour tortillas; or Herbed Corn Biscuits, *page 229*

salad   Jicama Mango Salad, *page 248*; or Cucumber Tomato Salsa, *page 261*

**To reconstitute dried chili peppers: Place the dried chilis in a small bowl. Pour enough boiling water over them to cover. Let stand for 20 to 30 minutes until softened. Discard the water and remove the stems and seeds.

Turkey Picadillo

PICADILLO, A STEW USUALLY MADE FROM ground pork or beef, is eaten in Latin American coun-tries, particularly Brazil and the Caribbean nations. It has numerous variations: some with raisins, some with almonds, some with olives, some with combinations thereof, and all with a variety of spices. It's quick and easy, so I like to make it in the middle of the week when time always seems short.

Once made, the picadillo can be served as a traditional stew; wrapped in warm flour tortillas; or even put in a casserole, topped with pie dough, and baked at 350° until the crust is lightly gold-en, about 40 minutes. Picadillo also makes an excellent filling for empanadas (use a standard pie dough and make turnovers) and bake at 375° for 20 to 25 minutes.

serves 4 to 6

1/4 cup raisins

1/4 cup light rum

1 tablespoon olive oil

6 to 8 scallions, green and white part, thinly sliced

1 jalapeño, seeded and minced

1 clove garlic, minced

1 1/2 pounds ground turkey or chicken

1 cup chopped tomatoes

1 tablespoon cider or white wine vinegar

1/2 teaspoon chopped fresh thyme or 1/4 teaspoon dried

1 Soak the raisins in the rum and set aside.

2 In a large skillet over medium heat, heat the olive oil. Add the scallions and jalapeño and cook until softened, about 5 minutes. Add the garlic and cook, stir-ring constantly for 1 minute.

3 Add the ground turkey to the skillet and brown the meat, stirring occasionally to prevent lumps, about 5 to 7 minutes.

4 Add the tomatoes, vinegar, thyme, salt, cumin, pepper, and cloves and stir well. Strain the raisins from the rum and discard the rum. Add the raisins and the olives and stir.

5 Reduce the heat to medium-low, cover partially, and simmer for 20 to 25 minutes. Stir in the cilantro before serving.

note *This recipe can be made ahead, and it reheats well. It can be frozen for 2 to 3 months.*

$^1/_2$ **teaspoon salt**
$^1/_4$ **teaspoon ground cumin**
$^1/_4$ **teaspoon freshly ground black pepper**
$^1/_8$ **teaspoon ground cloves**
$^1/_3$ **cup chopped green olives**
1 tablespoon chopped fresh cilantro or flat-leaf parsley

119

serve with any of the following:

starch   warm flour tortillas; or rice; or Herbed Corn Biscuits, *page 229*

salad   Avocado Salad, *page 260*; or Cucumber Tomato Salsa, *page 261*; or Tomato & Sautéed Mushroom Salad, *page 250*

Leftover Turkey with Tomatillo Sauce

TOMATILLOS, THE SMALL GREEN TOMATO that is a prime player in Mexican cuisine, rejuvenates leftover turkey. Its citrus and herbal flavor is refreshing and lively. Fresh tomatillos are widely available at greengrocers and supermarkets and are preferable to canned. The piquant Mexican sauce featured in this recipe can also be served with poached boneless chicken breasts or fish.

120

serves 4 to 6

1 1/4 pounds fresh tomatillos (about 14) or two 13-ounce cans tomatillos, drained

1 medium onion, chopped

2 cloves garlic, minced

2 jalapeños or serranos, seeded and minced

1/4 cup chopped fresh cilantro

2 tablespoons vegetable oil

2 1/2 cups chicken broth

2 slices toasted bread or 2 corn tortillas, lightly fried, and made into crumbs

3 1/2 cups cooked cubed turkey

1/2 to 1 teaspoon salt, to taste

1   If using fresh tomatillos, bring 1 quart of water to a boil in a large saucepan. Add the tomatillos and cook for 10 minutes until barely tender. Drain in a colander. When cool enough to handle, peel the papery husk off the tomatillos.

2   In a food processor with the metal blade, combine the tomatillos, onion, garlic, jalapeños, and cilantro; pulse until a puree forms. Set aside.

3   In a stewpot over medium heat, heat the vegetable oil. Add the tomatillo-jalapeño puree and cook, stirring constantly, until the puree darkens slightly, about 3 to 5 minutes. Add the chicken broth and toasted crumbs; cook for 3 to 5 minutes longer.

4   Reduce the heat to medium-low. Add the turkey to the tomatillo sauce. Cook until the turkey is tender and heated through, about 20 to 25 minutes. Season with salt to taste before serving.

note This dish can be made ahead, and it reheats well. I do not recommend freezing it.

serve with any of the following:

starch   warm flour tortillas; or rice; or Buttermilk Cornbread, *page 219*

salad   Avocado Salad, *page 260*; or Cucumber Tomato Salsa, *page 261*   side dish

For a crowd, Black Bean Chili, *page 172*

121

duck

Cajun Duck Ragout

THIS TANGY STEW OF LOUISIANA origin features duck, spicy Andouille or chorizo sausage, and vegetables. It has the best flavor when it has been made up to a day before serving.

If you are short of time, use four cups cooked shredded duck, chicken, or turkey for this ragout. You can also substitute duck parts for the whole duck called for in the recipe.

122

serves 6

Duck

2 ducklings, about 7 pounds total weight, cut into pieces or halved, giblets removed

2 to 2^1/2 quarts water

1 medium onion, quartered

1 celery stalk, coarsely chopped

1 carrot, coarsely chopped

1 bay leaf

Ragout

^{1}/2 pound spicy sausage, such as andouille or chorizo, sliced

3 tablespoons vegetable oil

1 medium onion, sliced

2 bunches scallions, white and green part, thinly sliced

1 celery stalk, diced

1 green bell pepper, diced

^{1}/4 pound mushrooms, sliced

3 cloves garlic, minced

1 tablespoon paprika

1 teaspoon chopped fresh thyme leaves or ^{1}/2 teaspoon dried

1   To prepare the duck: In a large stewpot or stockpot over medium heat, combine the ducks, water, onion, celery, carrot, and bay leaf. Bring the water to a boil, reduce the heat to medium-low, and simmer until the ducks are cooked through, about 50 to 60 minutes. Remove the ducks from the broth. Strain the broth and reserve 1^3/4 cups to use in the ragout. Freeze any leftover broth or use it for soup.

This step is best done up to 1 day ahead. The broth can be put in an ice bath or cooled at room temperature, then refrigerated. Remove the excess fat that solidifies on the top of the broth and discard. When the duck is cool enough to touch, remove and discard the skin. Remove the meat from the bones and coarsely shred it. You should have approximately 4 cups of duck meat.

2   In a medium skillet over medium heat, lightly brown the sausage. Transfer the sausage to a paper towel-lined plate and pat dry to remove excess fat. Set aside.

3 In a stewpot over medium heat, heat 1 tablespoon of the vegetable oil. Add the onion, scallions, celery, and bell pepper and cook, stirring occasionally, until the vegetables are tender, about 10 minutes. Add the mushrooms, garlic, paprika, thyme, sage, salt, cayenne, and white pepper. Cook, stirring, for 2 minutes longer. Remove the vegetables from the pot and set aside.

4 Reduce the heat to medium-low. In the same stewpot, heat the remaining 2 tablespoons of vegetable oil. Add the flour and cook, stirring constantly, until the roux is a light golden color, about 7 to 10 minutes. Gradually add the heated broth and cook, stirring constantly, so no lumps form.

5 Add the vegetables, duck, and sausage to the pot and simmer for 45 to 55 minutes.

note *This dish can be made ahead, and it reheats well. It can be frozen for 2 to 3 months.*

**6 chopped fresh sage leaves
(1 teaspoon) or $^1/_2$ teaspoon
dried**

$^1/_2$ teaspoon salt

$^1/_4$ to $^1/_2$ teaspoon cayenne, to taste

$^1/_4$ teaspoon white pepper

3 tablespoons flour

123

serve with any of the following:

starch   rice; or warm flour tortillas; or Lemon Scallion Soda Bread, *page 217*; or South African Garlic, Herb, & Cheese Pot Bread, *page 226*; or Buttermilk Cornbread, *page 219*; or Biscuits Any Which Way, *page 230*   salad   Warm Greens, *page 251*, with Hot Pepper Vinegar, *page 271*; or Colorful Crunchy Slaw, *page 253*

Malaysian Duck

MALAYSIAN DUCK, LIKE ITS COUSIN, Beef Rendang, is fragrantly spiced and rich. When I make it, the delightful aroma fills me with anticipation. The coconut sauce must be simmered for about one hour before adding the duck. Unlike the fairly thin coconut sauce in Thai Green Chicken Curry, this sauce should be very thick and lightly coat the duck when it is done. This dish is equally good, and less expensive, if you substitute boneless skinless chicken breasts or thighs for the duck.

124

serves 4 to 6

3 cups unsweetened coconut milk

1 stalk lemon grass, cut into 4 pieces*

10 to 12 scallions (white part only), sliced

2-inch piece ginger, minced

3 plump cloves garlic minced

1 tablespoon dark brown sugar

1 bay leaf

1³/4 pounds boneless skinless duck breast or 4 cups raw boneless duck meat, cut into thin strips

1 tablespoon fresh lime juice

2 to 3 teaspoons *sambal ulek* or ground chili paste, or 2 teaspoons crushed red chili flakes, or 1 teaspoon cayenne

1/4 teaspoon salt, to taste

Crispy Shallots (page 272) for garnish, optional

1 In a stewpot over medium heat, combine the coconut milk, lemon grass, scallions, ginger, garlic, brown sugar, and bay leaf. Bring the liquid to a boil. Reduce the heat to low and simmer, stirring occasionally, until the liquid is somewhat thick and reduced, about 1 hour.

2 Add the duck, lime juice, and sambal ulek to the coconut milk mixture. Raise the heat to medium-low and simmer, stirring occasionally, for 40 to 45 minutes. The liquid should become quite thick.

3 Raise the heat to medium and continue cooking, stirring often, until any oil that has formed in the coconut milk is completely absorbed by the duck and the sauce is very thick and lightly coats the duck, about 1/2 hour longer. Season with salt and serve. Garnish with Crispy Shallots.

note This dish can be made ahead and gently reheated over low to medium-low heat, stirring often. This stew does not freeze well because of the coconut milk.

serve with any of the following:

starch basmati or Texamati rice; or Spiced Rice, *page 244* **salad** Spicy Green Bean Sambal, *page 254*; or Jicama Mango Salad, *page 248*; or Rujak, *page 246*; or Pickled Cucumber Salad for spicy dishes, *page 258*

*Lightly bruise the lemon grass by giving the pieces a whack with the flat of a chef's knife or a meat pounder so that the aroma will be released during cooking. Do not completely crush the stalks.

four SEAFOOD

Trout with Rice Wine & Vegetable
    Julienne

Shellfish Mariscada

Moroccan-Spiced Fish Stew

Cacciucco

Fish or Scallops in Port & Cream

Chunky Gaspacho with Shellfish

Lobster or Shrimp Fra Diavolo

South African Fish Stew

Fiery Shrimp Curry

Oyster Stew

Mussels Provençal

Off the Dock Stew

Shrimp Creole

Indonesian Fish & Corn Stew

Trout with Rice Wine & Vegetable Julienne

I HAVE BEEN FORTUNATE to have crossed paths with many friendly and hospitable people from around the globe. A Japanese neighbor who was living briefly in the United States shared some of her culinary secrets and introduced me to cooking with sake and mirin—ingredients common to dishes such as teriyaki sauce, sukiyaki, and several mild white fish dishes.

This lovely, light stew is not a traditional Japanese dish, but the fish is simmered in a broth delicately scented with rice wine and accented with toasted sesame seeds.

serves 4

1 tablespoon peanut oil

1 bunch scallions, white part, and 1 stalk greens part, thinly sliced and reserved

1 red bell pepper, sliced into thin strips

1 medium carrot, sliced into very thin strips

1-inch piece ginger, minced

1 plump clove garlic, minced

1 medium yellow squash, sliced into very thin strips

2 cups vegetable, fish, or chicken broth, or 1 cup clam juice and 1 cup water

1/4 cup *sake* (rice wine) or dry white wine

1/4 cup Japanese *mirin**, or additional sake

1 In a large, deep skillet over medium-high heat, heat the peanut oil. Add the white part of the scallions, bell pepper, and carrot and stir fry for 2 to 3 minutes. Add the ginger and garlic and stir fry for 1 minute. Add the yellow squash and stir fry for 1 minute.

2 Add the broth, sake, mirin, and soy sauce. Let the liquid come to a boil, then reduce the heat to medium.

3 Add the trout to the broth. Cover and simmer until the fish is cooked through, about 3 to 4 minutes. Stir in the reserved sliced scallion greens.

4 Serve the fish and vegetables in soup plates with some of the broth and garnish with toasted sesame seeds.

*Mirin, a sweet Japanese rice wine with a unique flavor, is used only in cooking. It is available in Asian markets, specialty food stores, or the Asian section of some supermarkets. If you have trouble finding mirin, use more sake or broth, but do not substitute rice wine vinegar.

note   *This dish cannot be made ahead and should be served immediately. It cannot be frozen.*

3 tablespoons soy sauce

1 pounds trout fillets, cut into 8 equal pieces

1 tablespoon toasted sesame seeds**

serve with any of the following:

starch   white, basmati, or Texamati rice   **salad**   Pickled Cucumber Salad using rice wine vinegar and no herbs or chilis, *page 258*; or Jicama Mango Salad, *page 248*

**To toast sesame seeds: Place the seeds in a nonstick skillet over medium heat. Cook, stirring occasionally, until the seeds just begin to darken slightly, about 2 to 3 minutes. Remove them from the pan immediately, as the residual heat will darken them and possibly burn them. If they burn, discard them and start over.

Shellfish Mariscada

I HAVE ALWAYS BELIEVED that shellfish is the most delectable and sweetest gift from ocean waters. Mariscada is South America's mixed shellfish stew. Like many other seafood stews, it is open to any combination of fresh shellfish. If scallops aren't available where you live, use more shrimp, clams, mussels, or crayfish or lobster tails cut into four pieces. The success of the dish lies in using the best-quality, freshest ingredients.

128

serves 6

2 tablespoons olive oil

1 medium onion, chopped

1 celery stalk, chopped

1 plump clove garlic, minced

1/2-inch piece fresh ginger, minced

1 jalapeño, seeded and minced

1/2 cup dry white wine

1 1/2 cups fish broth or 3/4 cup clam juice and 3/4 cup water

3 medium tomatoes, peeled, seeded, and chopped (about 1 1/2 cups)

1 bay leaf

3/4 teaspoon salt, to taste

18 littleneck clams, cleaned in cold water to remove sand

1 pound medium shrimp, peeled, deveined, tails left on

1 pound bay scallops (feet removed), left whole or sea scallops (feet removed), cut in half

2 tablespoons fresh flat-leaf parsley or cilantro

1 tablespoon finely grated fresh lemon zest

1 In a stewpot over medium heat, heat the olive oil. Add the onion and celery and cook, stirring occasionally, until the vegetables are softened, about 5 minutes. Add the garlic, ginger, and jalapeño, and cook, stirring constantly, for 1 minute.

2 Add the wine and cook until the wine is reduced by half, about 5 minutes. Add the broth, tomatoes, and bay leaf. Cover and bring the liquid to a boil. Add the salt.

3 Reduce the heat to medium-low. Arrange the clams, shrimp, and scallops in the pot. Cover and cook until the clams open, the shrimp are pink and cooked through, and the scallops are cooked thoroughly, about 3 to 5 minutes. Do not overcook.

4   Meanwhile, in a small bowl, combine the parsley and lemon zest. Stir into the stew before serving. Serve the fish with some of the broth in shallow soup plates.

note   *This dish cannot be made ahead, reheated, or frozen.*

serve with any of the following:

starch   rice; or Herbed Corn Biscuits, *page 229*; or Buttermilk Raisin Spice Bread, *page 216*; or Lemon Scallion Soda Bread, *page 217*   **salad**   Jicama Mango Salad, *page 248*; or Avocado Salad, *page 260*; or Cucumber Tomato Salsa, *page 261*

Moroccan-Spiced Fish Stew

MOROCCANS DON'T EAT their fish this way, but Moroccan spices with fish are terrific. The flavor from the spice rub permeates the fish and creates an unusual, wonderfully aromatic, exceptional stew. If you have extra time, marinate the fish for an hour in the spice rub before cooking.

serves 6

130

Spice Rub

1 tablespoon fresh lemon juice

1 tablespoon olive oil

2 teaspoons paprika

1 teaspoon salt

$^{1}/_{4}$ teaspoon ground cumin

$^{1}/_{4}$ teaspoon ground cinnamon

$^{1}/_{4}$ teaspoon cayenne

$^{1}/_{8}$ teaspoon ground cloves

2 pounds monkfish, haddock, hake, grouper, or catfish filets cut into 2- to 3-inch chunks

Stew

2 tablespoons olive oil

2 medium onions, thinly sliced

1 cinnamon stick

6 whole coriander

$^{1}/_{4}$ teaspoon crushed red chili flakes

2 cloves garlic, minced

1 large red or green bell pepper, thinly sliced

5 plum tomatoes, peeled, seeded, and diced, about 1$^{1}/_{3}$ cups

1 *To prepare the spice rub:* In a medium bowl, combine the lemon juice, olive oil, paprika, salt, cumin, cinnamon, cayenne, and cloves.

2 Add the fish to the bowl, and toss to coat evenly. Set aside while preparing the other ingredients.

3 *To prepare the stew:* In a stewpot over medium heat, heat 1 tablespoon of the olive oil. Add the onions, cinnamon stick, coriander, and chili flakes and cook, stirring occasionally, until the onions are translucent, about 5 minutes. Add the garlic, bell pepper, and tomatoes and cook, stirring occasionally, for 5 minutes.

4 Add the broth, lemon zest, and saffron. Cover the pot and cook for 5 minutes.

5 In a large skillet over medium heat, heat the remaining tablespoon of olive oil. Working in batches if necessary, cook the pieces of fish just long enough to sear them, about 2 to 3 minutes. Turn the fish once or twice while cooking, being careful not to make it crumble. You might want to use tongs to turn the fish. Do not cook the fish thoroughly; it should still be raw in the center.

6 Add the partially cooked fish to the broth. Reduce the heat to medium-low. Simmer uncovered until the fish is cooked through, about 5 to 7 minutes. Add the salt to the broth. Remove the cinnamon stick and serve immediately in soup plates.

1 1/2 cups fish broth or water or 3/4 cup clam juice and 3/4 cup water
2-inch strip fresh lemon zest
generous pinch of Spanish saffron threads, crumbled, optional
1/2 teaspoon salt

note *This dish cannot be made ahead, reheated, or frozen. The fish would be overcooked.*

131

serve with any of the following:

starch Lemon or Orange Couscous, *page 239*, topped with Spiced Nuts using slivered almonds, *page 273*; or Spiced Rice, *page 244* **salad** Carrot Orange Sambal, *page 256*; or Pickled Cucumber Salad for spicy dishes, *page 258* **dessert** Rhubarb with Cardamom, *page 209*

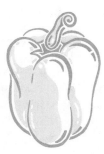

Cacciucco

CACCIUCCO, THE ITALIAN MIXED SEAFOOD stew, is served over toasted garlic-rubbed bread, which serves to thicken the broth. You can use other combinations of fish and shellfish—mussels instead of clams, scallops instead of calamari. The point is to have a varied selection. I make mine with red wine, but it's also fine to use white wine. This famous dish, of which there are many versions, is a great one-dish meal for seafood lovers.

132

serves 6

3 tablespoons extra virgin olive oil

1 medium onion, finely chopped

2 stalks celery, finely chopped

1 medium carrot, finely chopped

2 cloves garlic, minced

2/3 cup dry red wine

1/2 cup fish broth or water

2 cups chopped or crushed tomatoes

1 bay leaf

1/2 teaspoon salt

1/2 teaspoon crushed red chili flakes

1 pound firm white fish such as hake, monkfish, or haddock, cut into 2- to 3-inch chunks

1/2 pound shrimp, peeled and deveined, with tails left on

12 littleneck clams, scrubbed

3/4 pound cleaned calamari tubes

1/4 cup chopped fresh flat-leaf parsley

6 thick slices of Italian bread, toasted and rubbed with a clove of raw garlic

1 In a stewpot over medium heat, heat the olive oil. Add the onion, celery, and carrot. Cook, stirring occasionally, until the vegetables are tender, about 10 minutes. Add the garlic and cook, stirring often, for 1 minute.

2 Pour in the wine and cook until it is reduced by half, about 5 to 7 minutes. Add the broth, tomatoes, bay leaf, salt, and chili flakes. Bring the liquid to a boil, then reduce the heat to medium-low. Cover and simmer for 10 minutes.

3 Add the fish chunks to the pot and stir gently. Cover and simmer until the fish is almost cooked through, about 8 to 10 minutes. Add the shrimp, clams, and calamari and cook until the shrimp turns pink and the clams are open, about 3 to 5 minutes. Do not overcook.

4   Stir in the parsley. Divide the bread among soup plates. Ladle the stew on top.

note   *This dish cannot be made ahead, reheated or frozen. The fish may overcook when reheated.*

133

serve with any of the following:

starch   Anna's Crusty French Loaf, *page 222*; or Round Country Loaf, *page 224*   salad   Herbed Vegetable Slaw, *page 252*; or mixed green salad with Basic Vinaigrette using balsamic vinegar, *page 266*, and topped with Lardons, *page 274*

Fish or Scallops in Port & Cream

I ADORE THE SWEET TASTE of port. In Portugal, seafood and chicken are often served with a sauce of port and cream. In this magnificent stew, fish or scallops, potatoes, and vegetables are simmered in such a sauce. Richer and more luxurious than chowder, this is a filling and satisfying meal.

134

serves 4

1/2 pound potatoes, cut into 1/2-inch cubes

2 tablespoons butter

3 medium leeks, white part only, thinly sliced

1/4 pound mushrooms, sliced

1/3 cup port

1/2 cup fish or vegetable broth

3/4 cup cream or half and half

1/4 teaspoon freshly grated nutmeg

1 pound mild white fish fillets such as cod, scrod, or halibut, cut into 2-inch chunks; or 1 1/4 pounds bay scallops (feet removed), left whole or sea scallops (feet removed), cut in half

1/2 teaspoon salt

1/4 teaspoon freshly ground black pepper

2 tablespoons chopped fresh parsley

1 Put the potatoes in a medium saucepan and cover with lightly salted cold water. Over medium-high heat, boil the potatoes until they are cooked but still hold their shape, about 5 to 7 minutes. Drain in a strainer and set aside.

2 In a deep, medium skillet over medium heat, melt the butter. Add the leeks and cook, stirring occasionally, until they are very tender, about 15 minutes. Add the mushrooms and cook, stirring occasionally, until the mushrooms are cooked through, about 4 minutes.

3 Add the port, broth, cream, and nutmeg and stir. Add the cooked potatoes. Bring the liquid to a boil. Reduce the heat to medium-low, and cook for 3 minutes.

4 Season the fish or scallops with salt and pepper and add it to the creamy broth. Cook until the fish or scallops become opaque, about 3 to 5 minutes. Stir in the parsley and serve in soup plates.

note   This dish can be made ahead up to the point that the
fish is added. It should be served immediately after the fish is
cooked. It cannot be reheated or frozen.

serve with any of the following:

starch   Biscuits Any Which Way, *page* 230   salad   mixed green salad with

Basic Vinaigrette using red or white wine vinegar, *page* 266, and topped with Crispy

Shallots, *page* 272; or Lemony Asparagus or Green Beans with Nuts, *page* 255

Chunky Gaspacho with Shellfish

GASPACHO, THE CLASSIC SPANISH DISH, is often a pureed tomato-and-cucumber-based soup. This version, full of chunky vegetables, is a cold stew that is perfect for the dog days of August or anytime the weather is hot and humid. It can be put together in a flash or made ahead of time. I've used shrimp and smoked mussels, but you can use any cooked shellfish that you like.

136

serves 4 to 6

1 green or red bell pepper, diced

1 medium European cucumber, peeled, seeded, and diced

5 very ripe medium tomatoes, seeded and diced (about 2 1/2 cups)

5 to 6 scallions, white and green part, sliced

2 plump cloves garlic, minced

1 jalapeño, seeded and minced, optional

1 1/2 tablespoons fresh minced cilantro or flat-leaf parsley

1 tablespoon chopped fresh mint

1 tablespoon chopped fresh basil

3 tablespoons red wine vinegar

1 teaspoon salt

1/4 teaspoon freshly ground black pepper

5 tablespoons extra virgin olive oil

1/2 pound chilled, cooked, peeled, and deveined small shrimp

4-ounce package canned smoked mussels, drained

1 In a large bowl, combine the bell pepper, cucumber, tomatoes, scallions, garlic, jalapeño, cilantro, mint, and basil.

2 In a small bowl, combine the vinegar, salt, and pepper. Slowly whisk in the olive oil. Pour the dressing over the vegetable mixture.

3 Add the shrimp and mussels and stir to mix well. Cover and refrigerate for at least 1 hour before serving.

note *This can be made up to 1 day ahead. It cannot be frozen.*

serve with any of the following:

starch Anna's Crusty French Loaf, *page 222*; or South African Garlic, Herb, & Cheese Pot Bread, *page 226*; or Round Country Loaf, *page 224*; or Onion Flat Bread, *page 222* **dessert** Nectarines with Tarragon & Pepper, *page 213*

137

Lobster or Shrimp Fra Diavolo

New Haven, Connecticut, is known for Yale, terrific pizza, and an abundance of Italian restaurants. There used to be a fabulous restaurant hidden away on a back street near the hospital that served fra diavolo, either lobster or shrimp, with a spicy tomato sauce that was sensational. It was accompanied by plenty of napkins and a bib, a good idea because digging the lobster tail out of its shell and sopping up the sauce with crusty bread can get messy. This is how I remember the dish.

138

serves 4 to 6

1/3 cup extra virgin olive oil

8 fresh or thawed frozen lobster tails, about 4 ounces each, or 2 pounds medium or large shrimp, peeled and deveined

2 medium shallots, minced

4 plump cloves garlic, minced

1/2 cup dry white wine

2 tablespoons tomato paste

3 1/2 cups (one 28-ounce can) crushed tomatoes

1/4 cup chopped roasted red bell pepper*

1 bay leaf

1/2 teaspoon crushed red pepper flakes

3/4 teaspoon salt

1 tablespoon chopped fresh basil or 1 teaspoon dried

1 tablespoon chopped fresh flat-leaf parsley

1 In a large, deep skillet over medium heat, heat the olive oil. If using the lobster tails, put them in flesh side down and cook for 5 minutes, or until the shell is bright red. If using shrimp, add the shrimp and cook for about 2 to 4 minutes until the shrimp just turns pink. Remove the cooked shellfish from the pan and set aside.

2 Add the shallots and garlic to the skillet and cook, stirring often, for 2 to 3 minutes. Add the wine and tomato paste, stirring until the tomato paste is dissolved. Bring the wine to a boil, and boil until slightly reduced, about 1 minute. Add the crushed tomatoes, roasted red pepper, bay leaf, crushed red pepper flakes, and salt. Simmer for 15 to 20 minutes.

*To roast a bell pepper: Preheat the oven to 375°. Put the pepper on a baking sheet and bake, turning every 5 minutes until the skin turns black, about 25 to 30 minutes. (This can also be done more quickly under a broiler.) Remove the pepper from the oven and immediately put it into a paper or plastic bag. Close the bag tightly. When the pepper is cool enough to handle, take it out and peel off the skin with a paring knife. Discard the stem and seed.

3 Reduce the heat to medium-low. If using lobster, return the lobster to the pan, flesh side down, and cook 10 to 15 minutes longer. If using shrimp, return the shrimp to the pan and cook 2 to 5 minutes, until the shrimp is heated through. Stir in the basil and parsley.

note *The sauce can be prepared ahead up to the second addition of the shellfish in step 3. It cannot be reheated or frozen because the shellfish will become overcooked and toughen.*

139

serve with any of the following:

starch   linguine; or Anna's Crusty French Loaf, *page 222*, made into garlic bread if you like; or Round Country Loaf, *page 224*   salad   Arugula Salad, *page 265*; or A Good & Simple Salad, *page 264*

South African Fish Stew

FISHING IS THE LIVELIHOOD and passion of many residents along the coast of the Western Cape Province of South Africa. Adjacent to the quay on the beach in the center of the small town where I lived, there is always a spirited crowd purchasing the catch of the day from local fishermen. Choose your fish, and in the blink of an eye it is cleaned and wrapped to go.

This mildly spicy stew, infused with some of the flavors prevalent in South African food—garlic, tangerine (or naartjie, its local name), cumin, coriander, and bay leaf—is a fabulous one-pot meal of vegetables, potatoes, and fish. Don't forget to spike it with crushed red chili flakes to taste when serving.

serves 4 to 6

2 tablespoons vegetable oil
1 medium onion, thinly sliced
1 medium green or yellow bell pepper, seeded and cut into thin strips
1 medium carrot, cut into thin strips
3 plump cloves garlic, minced
1 teaspoon paprika
1 teaspoon ground cumin
1/2 teaspoon ground coriander
1/4 teaspoon turmeric
5 to 6 plum tomatoes, peeled, seeded, and chopped (about 1 1/2 cups)

_1_ In a stewpot over medium heat, heat the vegetable oil. Add the onion, bell pepper, and carrot and cook until the vegetables are softened, about 5 minutes. Add the garlic, paprika, cumin, coriander, and turmeric and cook, stirring constantly, for 2 minutes.

_2_ Add the tomatoes, broth, wine, tangerine zest, and bay leaf. Cover and bring the liquid to a boil. Add the potatoes and cook for 10 minutes.

_3_ Season the fish with salt and pepper, and then add the fish to the liquid.

4　Reduce the heat to medium-low. Cover and simmer until the potatoes are tender and the fish is cooked, about 7 to 10 minutes depending on the thickness of the fish. Stir in the cilantro. Serve in soup plates and garnish with crushed red chili flakes, to taste.

note　This dish cannot be made ahead, reheated, or frozen because the fish will become overcooked and toughen.

1 1/2 cups fish broth or water or 1 1/2 cups water and 1 cup clam juice

1/2 cup dry white wine

2-inch strip fresh tangerine zest

1 bay leaf

2 medium potatoes, peeled and cut into 1/2-inch cubes

1 3/4 pounds firm white fish fillets such as monkfish, hake, cod, catfish, or sea bass, cut into serving pieces

1 teaspoon salt

1/4 teaspoon white pepper

3 tablespoons chopped fresh cilantro or flat-leaf parsley

crushed red chili flakes for garnish

141

serve with any of the following:

starch　South African Garlic, Herb, & Cheese Pot Bread, *page 226*; or Herbed Corn Biscuits, *page 229*　**salad**　Avocado Salad, *page 260*, and Cucumber Tomato Salsa, *page 261*; or Pickled Beets, *page 259*

Fiery Shrimp Curry

SHRIMP CURRY IS ONE OF THE WORLD'S great dishes, and is found from India to England to Asia to South Africa to the Caribbean to South America. Some shrimp curries are prepared with coconut milk, some with tomatoes, some with cream. I prefer mine hot and spicy with tomatoes. If you can't take the heat, omit the Scotch bonnet pepper or jalapeño.

142

serves 6

2 1/2 tablespoons peanut or vegetable oil

1 medium onion, chopped

2 scallions, white part only, thinly sliced

3 plump cloves garlic, minced

1-inch piece fresh ginger, minced

1/4 to 1/2 Scotch bonnet pepper or 1 jalapeño or serrano, seeded and minced

2 to 3 tablespoons good-quality imported curry powder, such as Madras brand or the Caribbean brands Turban or Chief

3/4 cup shrimp or fish broth or water

2 teaspoons fresh lime or lemon juice

3 medium tomatoes, peeled, seeded, and chopped, about 1 1/2 cups

2 1/4 pounds medium shrimp, shells removed and deveined

1 In a large, deep skillet over medium heat, heat the peanut oil. Add the onion and scallions and cook, stirring occasionally, until the onions are tender, about 10 minutes. Add the garlic, ginger, and Scotch bonnet pepper, and cook, stirring constantly for 1 minute. Add the curry powder and cook, stirring often, for 2 to 3 minutes.

2 Add the broth, lime juice, and tomatoes. Reduce the heat to medium-low. Cover and simmer for 10 to 15 minutes.

3 Add the shrimp to the sauce and cook, uncovered, until the shrimp is pink and curled, about 3 to 5 minutes. Do not overcook the shrimp.

note   *The sauce can be made ahead and reheated, but do not add the shrimp. Before serving, follow step 3.*

serve with any of the following:

starch   basmati or Texamati rice   salad   Raita, *page 257*   condiment
Fresh Mango Chutney, *page 270*; or commercial chutney; and chopped onions

Oyster Stew

OYSTER STEW WAS MADE FAMOUS and fresh to order at Grand Central's Oyster Bar in New York City. Nothing could be finer, richer, or smoother than this version of the creamy oyster stew. Its taste speaks for itself—it is heavenly. So forget the calories and enjoy it.

serves 4

1 In a heavy medium saucepan over medium heat, melt the butter. Add the oysters and their liquor, the milk, cream, sherry, and Worcestershire sauce. Cook, stirring occasionally, until the cream mixture is hot and the oysters rise to the surface, about 3 to 5 minutes. Do not overcook or the oysters will become tough.

2 Season with the salt, pepper, and Tabasco. Serve immediately.

note *This dish cannot be made ahead, reheated, or frozen. It must be made and served immediately.*

2 tablespoons butter

2 cups shucked oysters, oyster liquor reserved

1^1/2 cups milk

1 cup cream

^{1}/3 cup dry sherry

1 teaspoon Worcestershire sauce

^{1}/4 teaspoon salt or to taste

^{1}/4 teaspoon freshly ground black pepper or to taste

Tabasco to taste

serve with any of the following:

starch   oyster crackers; or Biscuits Any Which Way, *page 230*   salad Colorful Crunchy Slaw, *page 253*; or Herbed Vegetable Slaw, *page 252*; or Make Ahead Herbed Garden Salad, *page 263*

Mussels Provençal

MUSSELS ARE AN OBSESSION in Belgium. There is a restaurant near the Grand Place in Brussels that serves mussels in every way imaginable. In this marvelous mussel dish, the tastes of Southern France, of Provence—garlic, tomato, olive oil, thyme, basil, and parsley—are the supporting cast. It is important to complete all of the prep prior to cooking and to keep your wits about you during the unbelievably quick cooking process. Everything is ready to serve almost at once.

144

serves 4 to 6

4 pounds fresh mussels
Pinch flour
2 cups dry white wine
4 shallots, minced
5 plump cloves garlic, minced
1 bay leaf
2 sprigs fresh thyme or 1/2 teaspoon dried
1 1/2 tablespoons extra virgin olive oil
5 to 7 plum tomatoes, peeled, seeded, and chopped (about 1 1/3 to 1 1/2 cups)
1/3 cup chopped fresh flat-leaf parsley
2 tablespoons chopped fresh basil

1 Scrub the mussels well under cold running water. Discard any mussels with broken shells or open mussels that don't close when tapped lightly; they are not safe to eat. Scrub away any barnacles with a stiff wire brush. (If you are using farm-raised mussels, which are readily available in many markets, you will not need to remove barnacles.) Let the mussels sit in a bowl of lightly salted cold water with a generous pinch of flour for about 30 minutes so the mussels spit out any sand. Pull off the beards and discard.

2 In a large, deep skillet or stewpot over medium-high heat, combine the wine, shallots, garlic, bay leaf, and thyme. Cover the pot and cook for 2 to 3 minutes.

3 Add the mussels to the skillet in a single layer. Cover the skillet and cook, shaking the pan occasionally, until the mussels are open, about 3 to 5 minutes. Discard any mussels that have not opened. With tongs or a slotted spoon, remove the mussels and divide them among soup plates. Leave the cooking liquid in the pot.

4   Meanwhile, in a medium skillet over medium heat, heat the olive oil. Add the tomatoes. Cook until the tomatoes soften slightly, about 1 to 2 minutes.

5   Add the tomatoes, parsley, and basil to the cooking liquid and stir to make the sauce. Spoon the sauce over the mussels. Serve immediately.

note   *This dish cannot be made ahead and must be served immediately.*

serve with any of the following:

starch   French fries; Anna's Crusty French Loaf, *page 222*; or Round Country Loaf, *page 224*   **salad**   Mesclun Salad with Goat Cheese, *page 262*; or Herbed Vegetable Slaw, *page 252*; or Sugar Snap Peas with Orange & Herbs, *page 249*   **dessert**   Nectarines with Tarragon & Pepper, *page 213*; or Figs in Red Wine, Ginger, & Thyme, *page 210*

Off the Dock Stew

ALONG THE SHORELINE OF LONG ISLAND SOUND, there are quaint fish markets near the docks. Boats navigating the coast avoid the submerged rocks and arrive safely to unload and sell their fresh fish and shellfish. This New England stew is delicately scented with spices and herbs that enhance the flavor of fresh seafood. Use whatever combination of fresh fish and seafood is available.

serves 4 to 6

Broth

2 tablespoons olive oil

2 onions, finely sliced

2 leeks, white part only, thinly
    sliced

1 bulb fennel, finely sliced

2 $1/3$ cups fish broth or water or
    1 $1/3$ cups water and 1 cup clam
    juice

1 cup dry white wine

3 to 4 plum tomatoes, peeled,
    seeded, and diced, about 1 cup

5 threads saffron or $1/2$ teaspoon
    turmeric

2 cloves garlic, chopped

2-inch strip fresh lemon zest

Stew

$1/2$ pound firm white fish—scrod,
    cod, halibut, monkfish, or
    snapper—cut into 4 pieces

1 medium lobster tail, cut into 4
    pieces

12 mussels, cleaned and debearded

12 littleneck clams

1 *To prepare the broth:* In a stewpot over medium heat, heat the olive oil. Add the onions, leeks, fennel, and cook for 5 minutes. Add the broth, wine, tomatoes, saffron, garlic, and lemon zest. Cover and cook for 20 minutes.

2 *To prepare the stew:* Reduce the heat to medium-low. Add the fish and lobster tail to the broth. Cover and cook for 5 minutes. Add the mussels, clams, and shrimp. Simmer until the fish, lobster, and shrimp are cooked and the mussels and clams have opened, about 3 to 5 minutes longer. Discard any mussels or clams that have not opened.

3 Stir in the cream and brandy and cook for 1 to 2 minutes longer. Serve the stew in soup plates and garnish with chopped chives.

note This stew cannot be made ahead, reheated, or frozen because the fish and shellfish will become overcooked.

¹/2 pound shrimp, peeled and deveined
¹/4 cup heavy cream
2 tablespoons brandy
fresh chopped chives for garnish

serve with any of the following:

147

starch   Biscuits Any Which Way, *page 220*; or Round Country Loaf, *page 224*

salad   Herbed Vegetable Slaw, *page 252*; or Lemony Asparagus or Green Beans with Nuts, *page 255*   dessert   Cranberries in Red Wine, *page 212*, over ice cream, frozen yogurt, or sorbet

Shrimp Creole

SHRIMP CREOLE, FOUND THROUGHOUT the South and the Caribbean, is a simple but festive dish. My mother used to make it on Christmas eve because it was always met with praise and it didn't require too much time in the kitchen on the evening she had to turn into Mrs. Claus. Make the sauce ahead and add the shrimp a few minutes before serving. I don't reserve this stew for Christmas eve only, but make it anytime, especially when I want to revive pleasant memories.

serves 4 to 6

2 tablespoons butter

1 medium onion, finely diced

5 to 6 scallions, white part only, thinly sliced

1 celery stalk, finely diced

1 large green bell pepper, finely diced

1-inch piece fresh ginger, minced

2 cloves garlic, minced

4 medium tomatoes, peeled, seeded, and chopped (about 2 cups)

1 tablespoon sugar

1 teaspoon chopped fresh thyme leaves or $1/2$ teaspoon dried thyme leaves

$3/4$ teaspoon salt

$1/4$ teaspoon white pepper

$2^1/4$ pounds medium shrimp, peeled and deveined

2 tablespoons chopped fresh parsley

1 tablespoon chopped fresh chives

1   In a large skillet over medium heat, melt the butter. Add the onion, scallions, celery, and bell pepper. Cook, stirring occasionally, until the vegetables are tender, about 10 minutes. Add the ginger and garlic and cook, stirring often, for 2 minutes.

2   Add the tomatoes, sugar, thyme, salt, and pepper. Reduce the heat to medium-low. Cover and simmer for 15 minutes.

3   Add the shrimp to the sauce and simmer, uncovered, until they are pink and curled, about 3 to 5 minutes. Do not overcook the shrimp. Stir in the parsley and chives before serving.

note   *The sauce can be made ahead and reheated, but do not add the shrimp. Before serving, follow step 3.*

serve with any of the following:

starch   basmati or Texamati rice; or Biscuits Any Which Way, *page 220*; or Herbed Corn Biscuits, *page 229*   **salad**   Avocado Salad, *page 260*; or Make-Ahead Herbed Garden Salad, *page 263*; or mixed salad with Basic Vinaigrette, *page 263*; or Jicama Mango Salad, *page 248*

Indonesian Fish & Corn Stew

IT'S AMAZING TO RECOGNIZE the scope of cultural exchange, especially when it comes to the sharing of the wealth of ingredients for food preparation. Indonesia sent spices to the West, and the best vegetables from the American continents—corn and tomatoes—found their way to the Spice Islands. Here these vegetables are matched with fresh fish and Indonesian flavors to create a refreshing but spicy warm-weather stew.

150

serves 4 to 6

1 tablespoon peanut oil

10 to 12 scallions, (white and green part) thinly sliced

1^1/2-inch piece fresh ginger, finely minced

1 plump clove garlic, minced

^{3}/4 teaspoon *sambal ulek* (page 276) or ^{1}/2 teaspoon crushed red chili flakes

^{1}/4 teaspoon turmeric

2 cups frozen corn kernels

2^1/2 cups fish broth or 1^1/4 cups clam juice and 1^1/4 cups water

1^1/2 pounds tuna, mahi-mahi, or swordfish, cut into 1^1/2-inch chunks

1 teaspoon salt

^{1}/4 teaspoon white pepper

5 ripe medium tomatoes, peeled, seeded, and coarsely chopped, about 2^1/2 cups

3 tablespoons chopped fresh mint

3 tablespoons chopped fresh basil

1 In a stewpot over medium heat, heat the peanut oil. Add the scallions and ginger and cook, stirring often, for 1 minute. Add the garlic, sambal ulek, and turmeric and cook, stirring constantly, for 1 minute. Add the corn and cook, stirring often, for 2 to 3 minutes.

2 Pour in the broth. Cover and cook for 5 minutes.

3 Season the tuna with ^{1}/2 teaspoon of the salt and the white pepper. Add the fish and the tomatoes to the broth.

4 Reduce the heat to medium-low and simmer, uncovered, until the fish is cooked through, about 5 to 7 minutes.

5 Stir in the mint, basil, and the remaining ^{1}/2 teaspoon salt and serve.

note *This dish cannot be made ahead, reheated, or frozen as the fish will overcook.*

serve with any of the following:

starch basmati rice; or Spiced Rice or Yellow Spiced Rice, coconut variation, *page 244*; or boiled potatoes salad Spicy Green Bean Sambal, *page 254*; or Carrot Orange Sambal *page 256* dessert Pineapple in Coconut Milk, *page 208*; or Rujak, *page 246*

five   VEGETABLES & LEGUMES

Farmhouse Ratatouille

Wild Mushroom Ragout

Moroccan Vegetable Stew

Mom's Vegetable Barley Stew

Indonesian Butternut in Coconut Sauce

South African Garlicky Eggplant
    with Potatoes

Lentil & Vegetable Chili

Mediterranean Swiss Chard,
    Chickpea, & Barley Stew

Red Lentil & Spinach Stew

San Francisco Pink Beans

Black Bean Chili

Yellow Dhal with Vagaar

Spicy Red Beans

Baked Maple-Rum Navy Beans

Additional Recipes (Chapter Six)

Farmhouse Ratatouille

MY GOOD FRIEND KATIE grew up in Westchester County, New York, in an antique Dutch farmhouse built in the late 1600s. The house was a magical place and sparked in the imagination the lives of previous occupants and their ghosts, who might still be lurking there. It had a hidden staircase and two brick Dutch ovens next to a large fireplace in what was known as the living room. Her mother, Emily, was an excellent cook, and her kitchen was a long, narrow galley with old copper pots adorning the walls. It was here I had my first experience cooking in copper pots and my first bites of a sensational garlicky ratatouille, the classic vegetable stew from Provence. Its flavors still haunt me, urging me to make it.

If you don't have a copper pot, make the stew anyway. Ratatouille, however it is made, is sure to please any vegetable-loving palate. It is good hot; at room temperature; or served cold the next day for a quick lunch or warmed up as a side dish for grilled steak, or as a filling for an omelet or tortilla.

serves 6

4 tablespoons olive oil
2 medium onions, chopped
5 plump cloves garlic, minced
1 1/2 pounds (about 2 medium) eggplant, unpeeled and cut into 1 1/2-inch chunks
1 1/2 pounds (about 3 medium) zucchini, sliced
1 medium green bell pepper, coarsely chopped
1 medium red bell pepper, coarsely chopped

1 Preheat the oven to 350°. In an ovenproof stewpot, heat 1 tablespoon of the olive oil. Add the onions and cook, stirring occasionally, until they are translucent, about 5 minutes. Add the garlic and cook, stirring occasionally, for 2 minutes.

2 Meanwhile, in a large bowl, combine the eggplant, zucchini, bell pepper, and tomatoes. Add the remaining 3 tablespoons of olive oil, and toss gently to coat.

3 Add the vegetables to the onion mixture in the stewpot. Add the basil, parsley, thyme, orange zest, salt, and pepper, stirring gently to mix evenly.

4 Cover and bake for 50 minutes to 1 hour until the vegetables are tender. Garnish with extra basil and parsley and serve.

note *This dish can be made ahead and reheated. It will keep for 3 to 4 days in the refrigerator. It tastes best if it has not been frozen.*

3/4 pound (about 6 to 8) plum tomatoes, peeled, seeded, and chopped, about 2 cups

3 tablespoons chopped fresh basil leaves

3 tablespoons chopped fresh flat-leaf parsley

1 large sprig thyme or 1/2 teaspoon dried

2-inch strip fresh orange zest, white pith removed

1 1/2 teaspoons salt

1/2 teaspoon freshly ground black pepper

extra chopped fresh basil and parsley for garnish

153

serve with any of the following:

starch   Garlic & Herb Mashed Potatoes, *page 235*; or Basic or Herbed Polenta, *page 240*; or Great Potato Pancakes, *page 232*; or Anna's Crusty French Loaf, *page 222*   salad   Mesclun Salad with Goat Cheese, *page 262*

dessert   Nectarines with Tarragon & Pepper, *page 213*

Wild Mushroom Ragout

WILD MUSHROOMS ARE ONE of the most pleasurable culinary jewels. Each variety possesses its own distinctive aroma and flavor. In this recipe any assortment will do.

Porcini or cepes are a wonderful addition to this stew, but are costly. Some folks, like me on occasion, are fortunate enough to be able to pick their own from among the pine needles of a forest floor. However, unless you are accompanied by a verifiable mushroom expert, I do not recommend plucking mushrooms in the woods. Play it safe by purchasing your mushrooms at the market.

serves 4 to 6

1 ounce dried porcini

1 cup boiling water

3 tablespoons olive oil

1 medium onion, diced

1 medium leek, white part only, diced

4 plump cloves garlic, minced

2 pounds assorted wild and cultivated mushrooms, such as shiitake, portabello, porcini, cremini, or white, sliced

1 teaspoon salt

1/2 teaspoon freshly ground black pepper

1/2 cup dry white wine

3 to 4 plum tomatoes, peeled, seeded, and chopped, or 1 cup canned chopped tomatoes

1 tablespoon chopped fresh sage or 2 tablespoons chopped fresh basil

1/4 cup chopped fresh flat-leaf parsley

1   Place the porcini in a small bowl and pour the boiling water over them. Let them stand in the water for 20 to 30 minutes. Pour the liquid through a strainer lined with a paper coffee filter and reserve the liquid. Rinse the porcini with a little bit of water to remove any lingering grit, and gently squeeze them dry. Chop them or cut them with scissors into small pieces. Set both the porcini and the liquid aside.

2   In a large, deep skillet or stewpot over medium heat, heat the olive oil. Add the onion and leek and cook, stirring occasionally, until both are very tender, about 15 minutes. Add the garlic and cook, stirring constantly, for 2 minutes.

3   Add the mushrooms and cook, stirring occasionally, until they are soft, about 10 minutes. Add the salt and pepper. Pour in the wine and reserved porcini liquid, and add the tomatoes and sage.

4 Reduce the heat to medium-low. Simmer, uncovered, until most of the liquid is evaporated, about 30 minutes. Stir in the parsley before serving.

note *This dish can be made a few hours ahead and reheated. Leftovers can be kept for 2 to 3 days in the refrigerator. It tastes best if it has not been frozen.*

serve with any of the following:

starch   Basic Polenta, *page 240*; or Creamy Potato Gratin, *page 233*; or Basic Risotto, *page 242*; or Onion Flat Bread, *page 220*; or South African Garlic, Herb, & Cheese Pot Bread, *page 226*   salad   A Good & Simple Salad, *page 264*; or Roasted Beet & Onion Salad on Watercress, *page 247*; or Arugula Salad, *page 265*   dessert   Pears in Ruby Port & Vanilla, *page 206*

Moroccan Vegetable Stew

MOROCCAN SPICES AND HONEY turn otherwise ordinary vegetables into a delicious, brothy stew. It is a perfect vegetarian meal any time of the year. You can substitute other seasonal vegetables with textures similar to the ones I call for here, such as butternut squash or rutabaga for the turnip or parsnip for the carrot.

156

serves 6

Spice Mix

1 teaspoon ground cumin

1/2 teaspoon fresh thyme leaves or 1/4 teaspoon dried thyme leaves

1/4 teaspoon ground cinnamon

1/4 teaspoon saffron threads, crushed; or 1/4 teaspoon turmeric

1/4 teaspoon cayenne

1/8 teaspoon ground cloves

1/8 teaspoon white pepper

Stew

2 tablespoons olive oil

3 medium onions, thinly sliced

1/2-inch piece fresh ginger, minced

13/4 cups (one 141/2-ounce can) canned whole tomatoes, crushed with the back of a spoon, and their juices

21/2 to 3 cups vegetable or chicken broth

1 *To prepare the spice mix:* In a small bowl, combine the cumin, thyme, cinnamon, saffron or turmeric, cayenne, cloves, and white pepper.

2 *To prepare the stew:* In a stewpot over medium heat, heat the olive oil. Add the onions and cook, stirring occasionally, until they are tender, about 10 minutes. Add the spice mix and ginger. Cook, stirring occasionally, for 5 minutes.

3 Add the tomatoes and their juices, the broth, honey, bay leaf, and lemon zest. Bring the liquid to a boil.

4 Add the carrots, turnips, and red bell pepper. Reduce the heat to medium-low. Cover and simmer until the turnips and carrots are tender, about 20 minutes.

5 Add the zucchini and simmer, covered, for 15 to 20 minutes. Serve in soup plates and garnish with fresh herbs.

note *This stew can be made several hours ahead, and it reheats well. It tastes best if it has not been frozen.*

3 tablespoons honey

1 bay leaf

2-inch strip fresh lemon zest

3 medium carrots, sliced
(about 1 1/2 cups)

2 medium turnips, cut into 1/2-inch
cubes (about 2 cups)

1 medium red bell pepper, coarsely
diced (about 1 cup)

2 medium zucchini or yellow
squash, sliced (about 2 cups)

chopped fresh mint, cilantro, or
parsley for garnish

157

serve with any of the following:

starch   Lemon or Orange Couscous, *page 239*; or Buttermilk Raisin Spice Bread, *page 216*   salad   mixed greens with Basic Vinaigrette using lemon juice, *page 266*   dessert   Figs in Red Wine, Ginger, & Thyme, *page 210*; or Rhubarb with Cardamom, *page 209*

Mom's Vegetable Barley Stew

I ALWAYS KNEW WINTER was approaching because my mother would make this vegetable barley stew, which is like a very thick soup. It was the dinner that announced the end of fall, usually sometime around late November, about the time the pond would freeze enough to go ice skating. Sometimes there would be beef in it, sometimes not—it's your option to make it a vegetarian dish or not. It requires little effort and always hits the spot on frosty days.

158

serves 6 to 8

3 1/2 cups (one 28-ounce can) canned whole tomatoes and their liquid

4 to 6 cups vegetable broth, beef broth, or water

1 pound short ribs of beef, cut between the ribs (optional)

2 medium onions, sliced

3 medium carrots, sliced

2 celery stalks, sliced, and the leaves chopped

1 1/4 cups (one 10-ounce package) frozen corn kernels

1 1/4 cups (one 10-ounce package) frozen lima beans

1/2 cup barley

1 bay leaf

3 sprigs fresh thyme or 1 teaspoon dried thyme leaves

1   In a small bowl, crush the tomatoes with the back of a spoon.

2   In a stewpot over medium heat, combine the tomatoes and their liquid, 4 cups of water, short ribs, onions, carrots, celery, corn, lima beans, barley, bay leaf, and thyme. Cover and bring the liquid to a boil. Using a ladle or skimmer, remove any foam that forms.

3   Reduce the heat to medium-low. Simmer, uncovered, until the meat (if included), barley, and vegetables are tender, about 1 1/4 hours.

4   Stir in the string beans and peas. Add more liquid, 1/2 cup at a time if the stew is becoming too thick. Simmer for another 20 to 30 minutes. Stir in the parsley. Season with salt and pepper to taste.

note This stew can be made several hours ahead, and it reheats well. It can be frozen for 3 months.

1¹/4 cups (one 10-ounce package) frozen or fresh sliced string beans or flat Italian broad beans

1¹/4 cups (one 10-ounce package) frozen peas

3 tablespoons chopped fresh flat-leaf parsley

salt to taste

freshly ground black pepper to taste

159

serve with any of the following:

starch   Biscuits Any Which Way, *page 230*; or Herbed Dijon Beer Bread, *page 218*; or Round Country Loaf, *page 224*; or Lemon Scallion Soda Bread, *page 217*

dessert   Spiced Dried Fruit Compote, *page 207*

Indonesian Butternut in Coconut Sauce

I CAME UP WITH THIS DISH one evening when I wanted an unusual vegetarian meal. On my shelf was a rather large quantity of butternut squashes that I had bought at a farmer's market. Throughout Indonesia, food is often simmered in spices and coconut milk. I had eaten eggplant prepared in this way, so I tried it with butternut. The spice-scented sauce permeates the squash. When served alongside rice, it can also be an unusual side dish for grilled fish or chicken.

160

serves 4 to 6

2 tablespoons peanut or vegetable oil

2 shallots or 1 small onion, thinly sliced

2 cinnamon sticks

4 allspice berries

4 cardamom pods

1/2 teaspoon whole cumin seeds

2 plump cloves garlic, minced

1-inch piece fresh ginger, minced

1/2 to 1 teaspoon crushed red chili flakes or *sambal ulek* (page 276)

1 2/3 cups coconut milk

1 tablespoon soy sauce

1 tablespoon fresh lime juice

1 1/2 tablespoons dark brown sugar

1 In a stewpot over medium heat, heat the peanut oil. Add the onions, cinnamon, allspice, cardamom, and cumin. Cook, stirring occasionally, until the onions are tender, about 10 minutes. Add the garlic, ginger, and chili flakes. Cook, stirring occasionally, for 2 to 3 minutes. The aroma of the spices should be quite strong.

2 Add the coconut milk, soy sauce, lime juice, brown sugar, and peanut butter and stir. Bring the liquid to a boil. Add the butternut and bell peppers.

3 Reduce the heat to medium-low. Cover and simmer until the vegetables are tender, about 30 minutes. Serve garnished with the macadamia nuts and mint.

note   This dish is best served immediately. It can be reheated gently, but take caution that the butternut doesn't get too soft. It cannot be frozen because of the coconut milk.

1 tablespoon natural unsalted peanut butter

2 1/2 pounds butternut squash, pared and cut into 1-inch cubes (about 6 1/2 cups)

1 small red bell pepper, thinly sliced

1 small green bell pepper, thinly sliced

1/3 cup chopped macadamia nuts or peanuts

3 tablespoons chopped fresh mint

161

serve with any of the following:

starch   basmati or Texamati rice; or Spiced Rice or Yellow Spiced Rice

page 244   salad   mixed greens with Basic Vinaigrette using lime juice, *page 266*; or Spicy Green Bean Sambal, *page 254*; or Rujak, *page 246*

South African Garlicky Eggplant with Potatoes

THIS TRADITIONAL SOUTH AFRICAN Cape Malay-style preparation pays tribute to the common eggplant in a spectacular stew accented with fresh garlic and coriander. Turmeric gently casts its appealing golden hue. Note that no liquid is added in this recipe.

I've served this dish on its own and as one of many at large gatherings. It is also a splendid accompaniment to grilled meat, poultry, or fish.

serves 4 (main course), 8 (side dish)

1 3/4 to 2 pounds eggplant, skin left on, cut into 1-inch cubes

kosher salt

2 medium potatoes (about 12 ounces), peeled and cut into 1-inch cubes

3 tablespoons vegetable oil

2 medium onions, cut in half and very thinly sliced

6 cloves garlic, minced (about 1 tablespoon)

2 teaspoons ground coriander, preferably fresh

1/2 teaspoon turmeric

1/4 teaspoon white pepper or cayenne

3 tablespoons chopped fresh cilantro for garnish

1   Lightly sprinkle the eggplant with kosher salt and let it stand in a colander over a bowl or in the sink for 20 minutes. Rinse the eggplant under cold running water and use a clean kitchen towel to pat it almost dry.

2   Meanwhile, put the potatoes in a large saucepan and cover with lightly salted cold water. Bring the water to a boil and cook the potatoes until almost tender, about 5 to 7 minutes. Drain the potatoes in a colander, spread them in a single layer on a plate, and set aside.

3   In a large, deep skillet over medium heat, heat the vegetable oil. Add the onions, garlic, and eggplant. Cook, stirring occasionally, about 5 minutes. Stir carefully so the eggplant cubes don't break up.

4   Add the potatoes, coriander, turmeric, and white pepper and stir gently.

5   Reduce the heat to medium-low. Cover and simmer until the potatoes are tender and the eggplant is soft, about 15 to 20 minutes. Garnish with cilantro.

note   *If the stew sticks, add up to $^1/_2$ cup water in step 5. This dish can be made ahead, and it reheats well. I do not recommend freezing it.*

serve with any of the following:
   starch   Spiced Rice or Yellow Spiced Rice variation, *page 244*; Tomato & Sautéed Mushroom Salad, *page 250*   **salad**   Carrot Orange Sambal, *page 256*; or Pickled Beets, *page 259*; or Avocado Salad, *page 260*; or mixed greens with Basic Vinaigrette using white wine vinegar or orange juice, *page 266*   **dessert** Pineapple in Coconut Milk, *page 208*

Lentil & Vegetable Chili

THIS PLEASING AND UNUSUAL CHILI is a colorful, piquant alliance of lentils, butternut squash, and vegetables. I've often prepared it as a casual meal for vegetarian guests. Spiced Nuts (*page* 273) as a garnish provide a delightfully crunchy and tasty contrast.

serves 6

2 tablespoons vegetable oil

1 medium onion, chopped

1 green bell pepper, diced

1 plump clove garlic, minced

2 to 3 tablespoons chili powder to taste

1 teaspoon ground cumin

2 cups vegetable broth or water

2 cups chopped canned tomatoes

2/3 cup brown lentils

1/2 pound butternut squash, cubed (about 1 1/2 cups)

1 1/4 cups (one 10-ounce package) frozen corn kernels

1 tablespoon fresh chopped oregano or 1 teaspoon dried

3/4 teaspoon salt

2 scallions, white and green part, thinly sliced for garnish

2 tablespoons Spiced Nuts (walnuts or almonds), page 273, for garnish, optional

1 In a stewpot over medium heat, heat the vegetable oil. Add the onion and bell pepper and cook, stirring occasionally, until the vegetables are softened, about 5 minutes.

2 Add the garlic, chili powder, and cumin and cook, stirring constantly, for 1 to 2 minutes.

3 Add the broth, tomatoes, lentils, butternut squash, corn, oregano, and salt. Bring the liquid to a boil, and then reduce heat to medium-low.

4 Cover and simmer until the lentils and vegetables are tender, about 40 to 45 minutes. If the stew is too thick, add a little broth; if too thin, uncover the pot and raise the heat so some of the liquid will evaporate. Garnish with scallions and Spiced Nuts.

note This dish can be made ahead, and it reheats well. It can be frozen for 1 to 2 months.

serve with any of the following:

starch rice; or Buttermilk Cornbread, *page 219*; or Lemon Scallion Soda Bread, *page 217*; or Buttermilk Raisin Spice Bread, *page 216* **salad** Avocado Salad, *page 260*

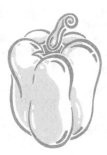

Mediterranean Swiss Chard, Chickpea, & Barley Stew

ROSINE, A LOVELY WOMAN of Armenian descent, is a talented artist and the creator of this stew. One day we were chatting about the merits of Swiss chard—especially the ruby variety—with its vibrant, magnificent, red stalks. She shared with me her way of preparing this simple and satisfying dish, and I went home and tried it that evening. Because Swiss chard is high in sodium, no salt is added in the recipe.

serves 6

2 tablespoons olive oil
1 carrot, coarsely diced
1 medium onion, diced
1 yellow bell pepper, coarsely diced
1 red bell pepper, coarsely diced
2 plump cloves garlic, chopped
2 1/3 cups vegetable broth, chicken broth, or water
1/2 cup medium pearl barley
1 tablespoon chopped fresh oregano or 1 teaspoon dried
1/4 teaspoon freshly ground black pepper
1 pound Swiss chard, washed *very* well and tough stems removed
1 medium zucchini, sliced
1 1/2 cups cooked chickpeas (one 16-ounce can, drained and rinsed)
lemon wedges for garnish

1 In a stewpot over medium heat, heat the olive oil. Add the carrot and onion and cook, stirring occasionally, until the onions are translucent, about 5 minutes. Add the bell peppers and cook, stirring occasionally, until the vegetables soften, about 5 minutes. Add the garlic and cook, stirring often, for 2 minutes. Add the broth, barley, oregano, and pepper. Cover and simmer for 35 minutes.

2 Meanwhile, prepare the Swiss chard. Wash the chard well several times; it tends to be *very* sandy. Trim off the tough ends. With scissors, separate the leaves from the stem. Cut the stems into 1/2-inch pieces, then cut the leaves into 2-inch-wide strips. Set aside.

3 After the barley and vegetables have cooked for 35 to 40 minutes, add the Swiss chard stems and zucchini to the stewpot. Cover and cook until the barley is tender, about 10 to 15 minutes longer. If the mixture is becoming too dry, add a little extra broth or water.

4 Put the Swiss chard leaves on top of the barley-vegetable mixture. Cover and cook until the leaves wilt, about 5 to 7 minutes longer. Stir the leaves and the barley-vegetable mixture together. Serve in bowls, garnished with lemon wedges.

note *This mixture can be reheated, but is best eaten on the day it is made. Add broth to leftovers to create a lovely soup. It does not freeze well.*

167

serve with any of the following:

starch Onion Flat Bread, *page 230*; or Buttermilk Raisin Spice Bread, *page 216* dessert Figs in Red Wine, Ginger, & Thyme, *page 210*

Red Lentil & Spinach Stew

DON'T LET THE NAME RED confound you—these lentils turn yellow when cooked and are nothing like the lovely salmon color they started out with. Regardless, these legumes are delicious in this delicate and savory stew scented with ginger, herbs, and orange zest.

This is one of the quickest vegetarian stews to prepare. Take care not to overcook the lentils, which can happen rather rapidly. They should be tender, but not mushy, and should still hold their shape.

serves 6

2 tablespoons olive oil

1 medium onion, chopped

1-inch piece fresh ginger, minced

1 1/2 teaspoons Hungarian sweet paprika

3 to 3 1/2 cups water

2 cups red lentils, picked for any debris, rinsed, and drained

3 plum tomatoes, peeled, seeded, and chopped, about 1/2 cup

2-inch strip fresh orange zest

1 tablespoon fresh thyme leaves or 1 teaspoon dried thyme leaves

1 tablespoon chopped fresh basil

1 bay leaf

3/4 teaspoon salt

1/2 teaspoon freshly ground black pepper

3/4 pound fresh spinach, tough stems removed, leaves coarsely chopped

Crispy Shallots (page 272) for garnish, optional

1   In a stewpot over medium heat, heat the olive oil. Add the onion and ginger and cook, stirring occasionally, until the onion is translucent, about 5 minutes. Stir in the paprika and cook, stirring constantly, about 1 minute.

2   Add the water. Cover the pot and bring the water to a boil. Add the lentils, tomatoes, orange zest, thyme, basil, bay leaf, salt, and pepper.

3   Reduce the heat to medium-low and cook, covered, until the lentils are beginning to become tender, about 10 minutes.

4   Add the spinach and cook until it is wilted and the lentils are tender, about 3 to 5 minutes. Garnish with Crispy Shallots.

note   This dish should not be made ahead. It does not reheat well, but any leftovers can be added to vegetable or chicken broth and pureed for a delicious soup. It does not freeze well unless the leftovers are frozen as a pureed soup.

serve with any of the following:

starch   barley; or Basic Risotto or Mushroom Risotto, *page 242*; or Buttermilk Raisin Spice Bread, *page 216*; or Onion Flat Bread, *page 230*   salad   Lemony Asparagus or Green Beans with Nuts, *page 255*; or Mesclun Salad with Goat Cheese, *page 262*   dessert   Nectarines with Tarragon & Pepper, *page 213*

San Francisco Pink Beans

MY FAMILY HAD A FRIEND NAMED Eleanore who grew up in San Francisco in the early 1900s. She used to serve these pink beans, scented with rosemary and garlic, which we all thought were sensational. Sometimes she would let the beans cook for 3 to 4 hours so they were so soft they could be mashed. Other times she would cook them this way. In some parts of the United States, it is hard to find pink beans, but this recipe is equally good with pinto beans.

170

serves 6

1 pound dried pink beans

6 cups water

3 1/2 cups (one 28-ounce can) canned plum tomatoes with their juice

2 medium onions, thinly sliced

2 medium green bell peppers, sliced in 1- to 2-inch strips

3 large cloves garlic, minced

1 bay leaf

2 teaspoons coarsely chopped fresh rosemary or 1 teaspoon dried and crumbled

1 1/2 teaspoons salt

1/4 cup chopped fresh flat-leaf parsley or chives

1 Place the beans in a colander and rinse under cold water; drain well. Discard any discolored or softened beans. Soak the beans overnight in water or use the quick-soak method: Place the beans in a stewpot and cover with about 3 inches of water. Over high heat, bring the water to a boil and boil for 2 minutes. Remove the pan from the heat and let the beans soak for 1 hour. Discard all the water in which the beans have soaked before proceeding with the recipe.

2 In a stewpot over medium heat, combine the soaked pink beans, water, tomatoes, onions, bell peppers, garlic, bay leaf, and rosemary. Bring the water to a boil and boil for 5 minutes. Skim off any foam that appears as the beans are cooking.

8 Reduce the heat to medium-low. Simmer, uncovered, until the beans are tender, about 2¹/₂ to 3 hours, adding more liquid if the beans become dry before they are cooked.

4 Before serving, stir in the salt and chopped parsley.

note *This dish can be made ahead, and it reheats well. You may need to add extra liquid when reheating to keep the beans from scorching. I do not recommend freezing it.*

serve with any of the following:

starch   Anna's Crusty French Loaf, *page 220*; or Herbed Dijon Beer Bread, *page 218*; or Round Country Loaf, *page 222*; or South African Garlic, Herb, & Cheese Pot Bread, *page 226*   salad   Herbed Vegetable Slaw, *page 252*; or Arugula Salad, *page 265*; or Mesclun Salad with Goat Cheese, *page 262*

dessert   Spiced Apples in Cider & Brandy, *page 211*

Black Bean Chili

BLACK BEAN CHILI HAS BECOME standard American fare that most folks seem to enjoy. Like most chilis, it's better when its made ahead. This one has no meat and is quite versatile. I like the smoky flavor of dried chipotles (smoked jalapeños), but if you can't find them, use fresh jalapeños. Add a cup of cooked corn kernels or sliced sautéed chorizo, if you feel like it. Top with a dollop of regular or nonfat sour cream. Leftovers make a fantastic filling for tortillas or omelets.

172

serves 6 to 8

1 pound dried black beans or 6 to 7 cups cooked black beans*

2 quarts water

2 tablespoons vegetable oil

2 medium onions, chopped

2 celery stalks, sliced

4 large cloves garlic, minced

2 dried chipotle peppers, reconstituted** seeded, stems removed, and pureed in 2 tablespoons warm water, or 2 to 3 jalapeño peppers, seeded and finely chopped

2 teaspoons paprika

1 1/2 teaspoons ground cumin

3 1/2 cups crushed or chopped plum tomatoes (one 28-ounce can)

1 1/2 tablespoons chopped fresh oregano or 1 1/4 teaspoons dried

1 teaspoon chopped fresh thyme leaves or 1/2 teaspoon dried thyme leaves

1 teaspoon salt

1/3 cup chopped fresh cilantro

1   Put the beans in a colander and rinse under cold water; drain well. Discard any discolored or softened beans. Soak the beans overnight in water or use the quick soak method: Place the beans in a stewpot and cover with about 3 inches of water. Over high heat, bring the water to a boil and boil for 2 minutes. Remove the pot from the heat and let the beans soak for 1 hour. Discard all the soaking water before proceeding with the recipe.

2   Put the soaked beans in a stewpot. Add the 2 quarts of water to the pot. Over medium-high heat, bring the water to a boil. When the water boils, reduce the heat to medium-low and simmer until the beans are tender, about 1 1/2 to 2 hours, adding more water if necessary. Skim off any foam that appears as the beans cook. Strain the cooked beans, reserving 2 1/2 cups of the cooking liquid. (See note if using canned, rinsed beans.)

3 In a stewpot over medium heat, heat the vegetable oil. Add the onions and celery and cook, stirring occasionally, until the vegetables are softened, about 5 minutes. Add the garlic, chipotles, paprika, and cumin. Cook, stirring, occasionally, until the vegetables are tender, about 5 minutes. Add the tomatoes, oregano, and thyme and cook for 10 to 15 minutes.

4 Add the cooked beans, the reserved $2\frac{1}{2}$ cups of cooking liquid or water, and salt. Stir to mix evenly. Cook until the beans are very tender, 40 minutes, adding more water if the beans become dry. Stir in the cilantro and serve.

173

note *This dish can be made ahead, and it reheats well. Although some dishes with beans can't be frozen, I have frozen leftovers of this dish for 1 to 2 months with good results. Add a little extra liquid when reheating if it has been frozen.*

serve with any of the following:

starch   warm tortillas; or rice; or Buttermilk Cornbread, *page 219*; or Lemon Scallion Soda Bread, *page 217*; or South African Garlic, Herb, & Cheese Pot Bread, *page 226*   salad   Avocado Salad, *page 260*; or Jicama Mango Salad, *page 248*; or Cucumber Tomato Salsa, *page 261*

*If you don't have the time to cook the black beans yourself, you can use 6 to 7 cups of canned black beans that have been rinsed and drained. Omit steps 1 and 2. Use $2^1/2$ cups water instead of the reserved cooking liquid in step 4.

**To reconstitute chipotle peppers: place the chipotles in a small bowl. Pour enough boiling water over them to cover. Let stand for 20 to 30 minutes until softened. Discard the water and remove stems and seeds.

Yellow Dhal with Vagaar

DHAL IS THE INDIAN WORD for legumes, which form a significant source of protein in a vegetarian diet. An Indian friend taught me how to make this dhal, which is cooked with spices, before the vagaar, a spiced onion mixture, is stirred into it. If you can't find yellow split peas, you can also make this with the green ones or with brown lentils.

174

I make the dhal so it is not completely dry—moist but not soupy, which is my personal preference. Feel free to adjust the amount of liquid to your own taste. Leftovers can be turned into a lovely soup with the addition of broth or water.

serves 6

Dhal

1 1/2 cups yellow split peas
3 to 3 1/2 cups water
1 teaspoon turmeric
1 1/2 teaspoons garam masala
3/4 teaspoon ground cumin
3/4 teaspoon ground coriander
1/2 teaspoon fennel seeds
1-inch piece fresh ginger, minced
2 cloves garlic, minced
1 bay leaf
1 medium tomato, peeled, seeded, and chopped
1 teaspoon sugar
3/4 to 1 teaspoon salt
chopped fresh cilantro for garnish

1 *To prepare the dhal:* Put the yellow split peas in a strainer or colander and pick them over for any debris. Wash them well under cold running water. In a stewpot over medium heat, combine the split peas and water.

2 Bring the water to a boil. Add the turmeric, garam masala, cumin, coriander, fennel seeds, ginger, garlic, bay leaf, and tomato. Cook for 30 minutes. If the dhal gets too dry, add a little water, 1/4 cup at a time.

3 Add the sugar and salt to taste. Cook until most of the liquid is absorbed and the peas are tender, about 15 to 20 minutes longer.

4 *To prepare the vagaar:* In a large skillet over medium-low heat, heat the vegetable oil. Add the onions, cinnamon, cloves, and cardamom. Cook, stirring often, until the onions are lightly browned, about 30 minutes. Remove the whole spices with a slotted spoon. Stir in the crushed red chili flakes and set aside.

5 Stir the vagaar into the dhal. Garnish with cilantro.

note *This can be made ahead and reheated in a double boiler. It cannot be frozen.*

Vagaar

2 tablespoons vegetable oil

3 medium onions, thinly sliced

2 cinnamon sticks

4 whole cloves

4 cardamom pods

2 Anaheim red chilis or 1 to 2 jalapeños, seeded and chopped, or $^1/_2$ to $^3/_4$ teaspoon crushed red chili flakes to taste

175

serve with any of the following:

starch   basmati or Texamati rice; or Spiced Rice, *page 244*

salad   Raita, *page 257*; or Cucumber Tomato Salsa, *page 261*

Spicy Red Beans

IN LOUISIANA THERE'S RED BEANS, sausage, and rice; in Jamaica, rice and peas; in Puerto Rico, red beans and rice; in India, curried beans and rice. These beans are certainly culinary travelers. I usually make my beans without meat, although sometimes I garnish them with crispy bacon lardons. Naturally, I serve them with rice.

176

serves 6

1 pound dried kidney beans or 6 to 7 cups cooked kidney beans*

2 quarts water

2^1/$_2$ tablespoons olive oil

2 medium onions, diced

5 to 6 scallions, white and green part, thinly sliced

2 celery stalks, diced

2 green bell peppers, diced

3 plump cloves garlic, minced

2 teaspoons cumin

1^1/$_2$ cups crushed tomatoes

^{1}/$_2$ teaspoon red chili flakes

2 bay leaves

1 teaspoon chopped fresh thyme leaves or ^{1}/$_2$ teaspoon dried

^{1}/$_4$ cup chopped fresh basil leaves

^{1}/$_4$ cup chopped parsley

1 teaspoon salt

2 to 3 teaspoons Tabasco, or serve on the side

Lardons (page 274) for garnish, optional

1 Put the beans in a colander and rinse under cold water; drain well. Discard any discolored or softened beans. Soak the beans overnight in water or use the quick-soak method: Place the beans in a stewpot and cover with about 3 inches of water. Over high heat, bring the water to a boil and boil for 2 minutes. Remove the pan from the heat and let the beans soak for 1 hour. Discard all the soaking water before proceeding with the recipe.

2 Put the soaked beans in a stewpot. Add 2 quarts of water to the pot. Over medium-high heat, bring the water to a boil. When the water boils, reduce the heat to medium-low. Cook until the beans are tender, adding more water if necessary, about 2^1/$_2$ hours. Skim off any foam that appears as the beans cook. Strain the cooked beans, reserving 2^1/$_2$ cups of the cooking liquid. (See note if using canned, rinsed beans.)

3 In a stewpot over medium heat, heat the olive oil. Add the onions, scallions, celery, and bell peppers. Cook, stirring occasionally, until the vegetables are very tender, about 15 minutes. Add the garlic and cumin. Cook, stirring constantly, for 2 minutes.

4   Add the beans, reserved cooking liquid or water, tomatoes, crushed red chili flakes, bay leaves, and thyme. Cook until the beans are very soft, about 1 hour, adding more liquid if necessary. Stir in the basil, parsley, salt, and Tabasco. Garnish with Lardons and serve.

note   *This dish can be made ahead, and it reheats well. I do not recommend freezing it.*

177

serve with any of the following:

starch   rice; or Herbed Corn Biscuits, *page 229*; or Biscuits Any Which Way, *page 224*; or Anna's Crusty French Loaf, *page 220*   salad   Warm Greens, *page 251*, with Hot Pepper Vinegar, *page 271*; or Cucumber Tomato Salsa, *page 261*; or Avocado Salad, *page 260*

*If you don't have the time to cook the kidney beans yourself, you can use 6 to 7 cups of canned red kidney beans that have been rinsed and drained. Omit steps 1 and 2. Use 2$1/2$ cups water instead of the reserved cooking liquid in step 4.

Baked Maple-Rum Navy Beans

IN THE BACK OF THE CUPBOARD in my mother's kitchen was a brown and white ceramic bean-pot. It was used only for making baked beans, never for anything else. I always wondered why it wasn't used as a soup tureen, but it seems beanpots are only that—beanpots. The beans in this recipe are definitely three-star—they deserve their own pot.

178 Preparing baked beans is a lengthy process requiring only patience. There is very little hands-on work, and the aroma that wafts through the house tells you it is worth the wait. If you have never had real baked beans, try these. The canned variety just doesn't cut it once you've had the real McCoy.

serves 6 as main course

1 pound dried white navy beans
2 quarts water
3/4 cup maple syrup
1/3 cup dark rum, such as Myer's
2-inch piece fresh ginger, minced
1 tablespoon English dry mustard, such as Coleman's
1 1/2 teaspoons minced fresh thyme leaves or 1/2 teaspoon dried thyme leaves
1 teaspoon salt
1/4 to 1/2 teaspoon cayenne
1/4 teaspoon white pepper
1 small onion, studded with 6 cloves
1/2 pound slab bacon, cut into several strips crosswise (optional)
Tabasco to taste, optional

1 Place the beans in a colander and rinse under cold water; drain well. Discard any discolored or softened beans. Soak the beans overnight in water or use the quick-soak method: Place the beans in a stewpot and cover with about 3 inches of water. Over high heat, bring the water to a boil and boil for 2 minutes. Remove the pan from the heat and let the beans soak for 1 hour. Discard all the soaking water before proceeding with the recipe.

2 Place the beans in a stewpot. Add 2 quarts of water to the pot. Over medium-high heat, bring the water to a boil. When the water boils, reduce the heat to medium-low. Simmer for 20 to 35 minutes or until the beans are just barely tender, adding more water if necessary. Skim off any foam that appears as the beans cook. Strain the cooked beans, reserving 3 1/2 cups of the cooking liquid.

3 Preheat the oven to 250°. In a 2-cup liquid measuring cup, combine the maple syrup, rum, ginger, dry mustard, thyme, salt, cayenne, and white pepper. Set aside.

4 Place the onion in the center of a 2¹/2 quart covered casserole dish. Arrange half of the beans and half of the bacon on top; repeat the layering, ending with bacon. Pour 2 cups of the reserved water and the maple syrup mixture over the beans and bacon.

5 Cover and bake for 5 to 6 hours until the beans are tender. Check the pot occasionally during baking, adding more water, about ¹/2 cup at a time if the beans are drying out. Uncover during the last half hour to hour of baking.

6 Let the beans cool about 5 to 10 minutes before serving. Serve with Tabasco sauce on the side, if desired.

note *This dish can be made ahead, and it reheats well. Add extra liquid when reheating so the beans don't scorch. Leftovers can be kept in the refrigerator for 4 to 5 days. I do not recommend freezing it.*

179

serve with any of the following:

starch Mashed Turnips & Apples, *page 238*; or Spiced Mashed Sweet Potatoes, *page 237*; or Buttermilk Cornbread, *page 219*; or Round Country Loaf, *page 222* **salad** Colorful Crunchy Slaw, *page 253*; or mixed green salad with Basic Vinaigrette, *page 266* **dessert** Spiced Dried Fruit Compote, *page 207*

six ## STEWS UNDER COVER

Garlic & Herb Cottage Pie

Pastel de Choclos

Quebec Tourtière

Poultry Pot Pie with Savory Cornmeal
Crust

Turkey Sausage & Roasted Peppers
Under Mushroom Polenta

Fish Bobotie

Creole Fish in Potato Crust

Mississippi Crab Gratin

Vegetable Biryani

Stewed Mushrooms Under Herbed
Polenta

Stewed Tomato & Cheddar Pie

Garlic & Herb Cottage Pie

COTTAGE PIE IS MADE WITH GROUND BEEF; shepherd's pie is made with ground lamb; both sport a topping of mashed potatoes. I've revitalized the traditional cottage pie with a topping of Garlic & Herb Mashed Potatoes (*page* 235). Although it's not a fancy meal, it is very satisfying, and it is friendly to both the cook and the budget. Make it ahead so the potatoes develop a more robust flavor.

182

serves 6

Filling
1 tablespoon butter
1 medium onion, chopped
1 leek, white part only, chopped
1/2 pound cremini or white mushrooms, sliced
1 pound lean ground beef
1/3 cup minced fresh flat-leaf parsley
1 tablespoon Worcestershire sauce
1/2 teaspoon salt
1/4 teaspoon freshly ground black pepper
3 to 4 tablespoons beef broth

Crust
1 recipe Garlic & Herb Mashed Potatoes (page 235)
1/2 cup grated sharp cheddar or Swiss cheese

1 Preheat the oven to 375°. In a large skillet over medium heat, melt the butter. Add the onion and leek and cook, stirring occasionally, until the vegetables are quite soft, about 10 minutes. Add the mushrooms and cook, stirring occasionally, until the mushrooms are tender, about 5 minutes. Transfer the vegetables to a plate and set aside.

2 In the same skillet over medium heat, brown the beef, stirring occasionally to prevent lumps. If necessary, drain the beef in a strainer to remove excess fat.

3 In a medium bowl, combine the vegetables, beef, parsley, Worcestershire sauce, salt, and pepper. Add the broth 1 tablespoon at a time to moisten the mixture. The mixture should be moist but not watery. Spread the filling evenly in a 2-quart baking dish.

4 Prepare the Garlic & Herb Mashed Potatoes.

5 While the mashed potatoes are still warm, spread them evenly on top of the filling. Sprinkle the cheese onto the potatoes. Bake until the filling is hot and the top is lightly browned, about 35 to 40 minutes.

note *This dish can be made several hours ahead and baked before serving. If it has been refrigerated, bake approximately 10 to 15 minutes longer. Leftovers can be frozen and reheated.*

183

serve with any of the following:

salad   Lemony Asparagus or Green Beans with Nuts, *page 255*; or Make-Ahead Herbed Garden Salad, *page 263*; or Herbed Vegetable Slaw, *page 252*

dessert   Spiced Apples in Cider & Brandy, *page 211*

Pastel de Choclos

WHEN I FIRST RAN ACROSS a recipe for Pastel de Choclos, I wondered who on earth could come up with this combination of ingredients—beef, chicken, olives, and hard-boiled eggs all under a pureed corn crust? Speculating, I figured someone had to throw dinner together one night with a little of this and a little of that from the pantry. Yet I was intrigued to find out how it tasted, and found it to be excellent. This is a great one-dish meal from Chile.

184

serves 6

1 pound beef round, cut into
   1/4-inch cubes

1/2 teaspoon salt

1/4 teaspoon freshly ground black
   pepper

2 tablespoons olive or vegetable oil

1 1/2 teaspoons paprika

2 medium onions, sliced

3/4 teaspoon ground cumin

1 teaspoon chopped fresh oregano
   or 1/2 teaspoon dried

2 hard-boiled eggs, sliced

12 imported black olives, pitted and
   sliced

3/4 pound skinless boneless chicken
   breasts, cut into thin strips

2 cups corn kernels

2 tablespoons cream or half and
   half or milk

1 egg, lightly beaten

2 teaspoons water

1 tablespoon sugar

1   Preheat the oven to 400°. Lightly butter a 2-quart casserole.

2   Pat the beef dry with a paper towel. Season the meat with the salt and pepper. In a deep, medium skillet over medium heat, heat 1 tablespoon of the olive oil. Add the beef and brown each piece on all sides. Add the paprika and cook, stirring constantly, for 1 minute. Remove the beef from the skillet and evenly spread it in the bottom of the prepared casserole.

3   In the same skillet, heat the remaining 1 tablespoon of the olive oil. Add the onions and cook, stirring occasionally, until they are translucent, about 5 minutes. Add the oregano and cumin, and cook, stirring occasionally, for 1 minute. Spoon half of the onions on top of the beef in the casserole. Arrange the hard-boiled eggs and the olives on top of the onions.

4   In the same skillet over medium heat, add the chicken to the remaining half of the onions. Stir fry until the chicken turns white, about 5 to 7 minutes. Spread the chicken-onion mixture evenly on top of the hard-boiled eggs and olives.

5 In a food processor fitted with the metal blade, combine the corn and the cream. Pulse until a thick puree forms. Spread the pureed corn kernels in an even layer on top of the chicken-onion mixture.

6 In a small bowl, lightly beat the egg with the water and brush the mixture onto the corn. Sprinkle the top with sugar. Bake for 35 to 40 minutes. The top should be lightly golden.

185

note *This dish can be assembled up to 2 to 3 hours ahead and then baked. When reheating in the oven, cover the top loosely with aluminum foil. It does not freeze well.*

serve with any of the following:

starch   Spiced Mashed Sweet Potatoes, *page 237*; or Herbed Corn Biscuits, *page 239*; or Biscuits Any Which Way, *page 224*   salad   Cucumber Tomato

Salsa, *page 261*; or Tomato & Sautéed Mushroom Salad, *page 250*; or Avocado Salad, *page 260*

Quebec Tourtière

TOURTIÈRE IS THE FAMED meat pie of ground pork and beef from the province of Quebec. It is a filling and hearty entree that will bolster anyone on cold weather days. Like many rural recipes, there are hundreds of versions. Everyone claims that his or her way is the best and only true way to make it. This one gets my vote.

serves 6 to 8

1/2 pound lean ground beef

1 pound lean ground pork

1 medium onion, coarsely chopped

3/4 teaspoon salt

1 teaspoon chopped fresh rosemary or 1/2 teaspoon dried and crumbled

1/4 teaspoon freshly ground black pepper

1/4 teaspoon ground cinnamon

1/8 teaspoon ground allspice

1 bay leaf

2/3 cup water

1 medium potato, peeled and very thinly sliced

2 prepared crusts for a 9-inch deep dish pie*

1   In a large nonstick skillet over medium heat, combine the beef and pork. Brown the meat, stirring occasionally to prevent lumps. Drain the meat in a strainer to remove excess fat.

2   Return the meat to the skillet and add the onion, salt, rosemary, pepper, cinnamon, allspice, bay leaf, and water. Reduce the heat to medium-low. Cover and simmer for 40 to 50 minutes, stirring occasionally. Let the mixture cool briefly so it is not too hot to put into the crust. Remove the bay leaf. The mixture should be moist but not watery.

3   Meanwhile, preheat the oven to 425°. Line a 9-inch deep dish pie plate with the bottom crust, leaving a 1/2-inch overhang. Refrigerate the crust for at least 30 minutes while the meat mixture is cooking and cooling.

4   Spoon half of the cooled meat mixture into the prepared pie crust. Arrange the potatoes in a layer, overlapping slightly, on top of the meat. Spoon the remaining meat mixture on top of the potatoes.

*The pie crust for Stewed Tomato & Cheddar Pie (*page 202*) works well with moist fillings such as this one.

5 Place the top crust onto the pie. Trim the edges so they are even and have a ³/4-inch overhang. Roll the edges of the top and bottom crusts together to form an edge that is slightly higher than the rim of the pie plate. Flute the edge or seal it with the tines of a fork. With a sharp paring knife, make 3 small slits in the center of the top crust.

6 Bake for 10 minutes, then reduce the oven temperature to 350°. Bake for an additional 30 to 35 minutes until the filling is hot and the crust is lightly golden. Let the pie stand on a cooling rack for 5 to 10 minutes before slicing.

note *This pie can be made several hours ahead, refrigerated, and then baked later. Increase the baking time at 350° by about 10 minutes if it has been refrigerated.*

serve with any of the following:

starch   Buttermilk Raisin Spice Bread, *page 216*; or Mashed Turnips & Apples, *page 238*   salad   Pickled Beets, *page 259*; or Colorful Crunchy Slaw, *page 253*   dessert   Spiced Dried Fruit Compote, *page 207*

Poultry Pot Pie with Savory Cornmeal Crust

THERE USED TO BE A FAMILY-RUN poultry farm near my house, situated at the end of a winding, hilly road off the main highway. There was a small store on the farm which sold fresh-killed chickens and turkeys as well as delicious pot pies of all sizes made daily on the premises. Although the farm is now gone and the land is covered with condos instead of chickens, it is hard to forget the taste of homemade chicken pot pie. The frozen variety is just not the same. I like broccoli in my pot pie, but feel free to substitute peas, string beans, or corn.

188

serves 6

Crust
1 cup all-purpose flour
$^1/_2$ cup cornmeal
$^3/_4$ teaspoon salt
$^1/_4$ teaspoon baking powder
2 tablespoons chopped fresh herbs of your choice, such as parsley, thyme, or chives (optional)
5 tablespoons butter or margarine, cut into small pieces
1 large egg, lightly beaten

Filling
3 tablespoons butter
1 medium onion, diced
1 celery stalk, diced
1 medium carrot, diced
$^1/_4$ pound mushrooms, sliced
1 cup chopped cooked broccoli, drained of any excess liquid
2$^1/_2$ tablespoons all-purpose flour
$^3/_4$ cup chicken broth, heated
$^1/_2$ cup cream, half and half, or milk, heated

1   *To prepare the crust:* In a small bowl, combine the flour, cornmeal, salt, and baking powder. Stir in the herbs. With your fingers or two knives, cut the butter into the dry ingredients until coarse crumbs form. Add the egg and stir with a fork until a dough forms. With your fingertips, lightly knead the dough until it just holds together, about 1 minute. Wrap the dough in plastic wrap and refrigerate it for at least 45 minutes before rolling.

2   *To prepare the filling:* In a medium skillet over medium heat, melt 1 tablespoon of the butter. Add the onion, celery, and carrot. Cook, stirring occasionally, until the vegetables are soft, about 10 minutes. Add the mushrooms and cook, stirring occasionally, until the mushrooms are cooked through, about 5 minutes. Stir in the broccoli and set aside.

3   Preheat the oven to 400°. In a medium saucepan over medium heat, melt the remaining 2 tablespoons of butter. Add the flour and cook, stirring constantly for 1 to 2 minutes. Gradually pour in the heated broth and cook, whisking or stirring constantly to make sure there are no lumps. Gradually pour in the cream, stirring constantly. Add the vegetables and the cooked chicken, parsley, thyme, salt, and pepper; stir to mix evenly. Remove the mixture from the heat and let cool. Spread the chicken mixture evenly in a 9-inch deep dish pie plate or a round 1-quart casserole dish.

4 Let the dough sit at room temperature to soften slightly before rolling, about 10 minutes. Roll out the dough between two sheets of waxed paper or plastic wrap to a 10-inch circle.

5 Cover the filling with the dough. Trim the edges of the dough so there is a $1/4$- to $1/2$-inch overhang. Lightly press the overhang around the outside edge of the pie plate to seal. Mark the edges of the crust with the tines of a fork. With a sharp paring knife, cut 3 slits in the center of the crust so steam can escape.

6 Brush the crust with the milk. Place the pie plate on a baking sheet in case the filling bubbles over slightly while baking. Bake the pot pie until the crust is golden and the filling is hot, about 30 to 35 minutes. Let the pie stand on a cooling rack for 5 to 10 minutes before serving.

VARIATION
Substitute peas, sliced string beans, or corn for the broccoli.

2 $3/4$ cups shredded or cubed cooked chicken or turkey
$1/4$ cup chopped fresh parsley
1 $1/2$ teaspoons chopped fresh thyme leaves or $3/4$ teaspoon dried thyme leaves
$1/2$ teaspoon salt
$1/4$ teaspoon freshly ground black pepper
1 tablespoon milk for brushing the crust

189

note The filling can be made up to 1 day ahead. The pie can be assembled and baked later. Do not brush the crust with milk until right before baking. Allow 10 minutes more baking time if the pie has been refrigerated. It can be wrapped and frozen for up to 2 months in a freezer-proof pie plate. Thaw in the refrigerator overnight before baking and bake as directed. Alternatively, bake the frozen pie on a baking sheet until the filling is piping hot and the crust is golden, about 1 to 1 $1/2$ hours.

serve with any of the following:

starch Biscuits Any Which Way, *page 224*; or Herbed Dijon Beer Bread, *page 218* salad A Good & Simple Salad, *page 264*; or Make-Ahead Herbed Garden Salad, *page 263* dessert Rhubarb with Cardamom, *page 209*

Turkey Sausage & Roasted Peppers Under Mushroom Polenta

THERE IS A NORTHERN ITALIAN DISH called Migliaccio Napoletano. It is a layered casserole or pasticcio of sausage, mozzarella, and polenta, upon which I have based this dish. Although excellent, I find it a little too rich and heavy. In this recipe, I've substituted turkey sausage, added some roasted red peppers, and cut out some of the cheese. The result is a marvelous and still quite filling casserole. Smaller portions can be an unusual starter.

serves 6 to 8

Polenta
1 Recipe Mushroom Polenta variation: polenta squares (page 240)

Filling
3/4 pound Italian turkey sausage, either hot or sweet or a combination

1/2 tablespoon olive oil

1 small onion, chopped

1 cup coarsely diced roasted red bell pepper*

5 ounces mozzarella cheese, grated

1/3 cup freshly grated Parmesan cheese

1 Prepare the polenta using the Mushroom Polenta variation: polenta squares, forming 2-inch squares.

2 *To prepare the filling:* Preheat the oven to 350°. With olive oil, lightly oil a 10 × 8 × 2-inch or comparable 2- to 2¹/₂-quart shallow baking dish. Arrange half of the polenta squares in the bottom of the prepared dish. Set aside.

3 Slit the sausage casing and remove the sausage meat. In a large skillet over medium heat, brown the sausage meat, stirring occasionally to prevent lumps. Drain the meat in a strainer to remove excess fat.

4 In the same skillet over medium heat, heat the olive oil. Add the onion and cook, stirring occasionally, until the onion is tender, about 10 minutes.

*To roast bell peppers: Preheat the oven to 375°. Put the pepper on a baking sheet and bake, turning every 5 minutes until the skin turns black, about 25 to 30 minutes. (This can also be done more quickly under a broiler.) Remove the pepper from the oven, immediately put it into a paper or plastic bag, and close the bag tightly. When the pepper is cool enough to handle, take it out and with a paring knife peel off the skin. Discard the stem and seeds.

5 In a small bowl, combine the onion, roasted red bell pepper, and sausage. Set aside.

6 Spread the sausage mixture evenly on top of the polenta squares in the casserole. Sprinkle with the mozzarella cheese and half of the Parmesan cheese. Top with the remaining polenta squares. Sprinkle with the remaining Parmesan cheese. Bake for 20 to 25 minutes until heated through. Let stand on a cooling rack 10 minutes before cutting.

191

note *This dish can be made several hours ahead, then baked. To reheat, cover with foil and bake for 20 to 30 minutes or until heated through.*

serve with any of the following:

salad   Arugula Salad, *page 265*; or Herbed Vegetable Slaw, *page 252*; or Sugar Snap Peas with Orange & Herbs, *page 249*

Fish Bobotie

BOBOTIE (PRONOUNCED "BABOOTY"), a traditional South African casserole with a custard topping, is made with either lamb, beef, vegetables, or, as in this rendering, fresh fish. It features a unique, exotic combination of spices that complement almost any firm white fish. This is a splendid and distinctive dish, and a delightful way to prepare seafood.

In South Africa, lemon leaves are often used in bobotie, but you can use bay leaves or lime leaves; the latter is available at Thai and Asian grocery stores. Lime leaves can be frozen in a plastic bag for several months, although their flavor will diminish the longer they are frozen.

serves 6

Bobotie

2 pounds skinless firm white fish fillets such as monkfish, hake, scrod, haddock, or orange roughy, or catfish

3 slices white bread with crusts

1/2 cup milk

2 tablespoons vegetable oil

1 medium onion, finely chopped

2 plump cloves garlic, minced

1/2 to 1 red or green chili such as cayenne, jalapeño, or serrano, seeded and minced

1 1/2 tablespoons good quality curry powder, such as Madras brand

1/2 teaspoon turmeric

1 large egg, lightly beaten

juice and finely grated zest of 1 lemon

1 Preheat the oven to 350°. Lightly butter a shallow 2-quart casserole or baking dish. Roughly cut the fish into 1 1/2-inch chunks. Put the fish into a large mixing bowl and set aside.

2 In a medium bowl, soak the bread in the milk and set aside.

3 Meanwhile, in a medium skillet over medium heat, heat the vegetable oil. Add the onion, garlic, and chili and cook until the onion is translucent, about 5 minutes. Add the curry powder and turmeric; cook, stirring constantly, for 2 minutes longer. Remove from the heat and cool slightly.

4 Gently squeeze the bread to remove excess milk. Add the, bread, onion mixture, egg, lemon juice, lemon zest, salt, and cilantro to the fish and mix well.

192

5 Spoon the mixture into the prepared baking dish and smooth the top with a dampened icing spatula. Insert the lime, lemon, or bay leaves an equal distance from each other in the fish mixture. Spread the almonds evenly on top.

6 *To prepare the custard topping:* In a glass measuring cup, lightly beat together the eggs, milk, and nutmeg. Pour the topping over the fish mixture.

7 Bake until the custard topping is set, about 35 to 45 minutes.

8 Preheat the broiler. Place the baking dish under the broiler for 2 to 3 minutes, until the top is lightly browned.

note *This dish can be made and refrigerated several hours ahead up to the point that the topping is poured on. Once the topping is added, it must be baked and served immediately. It does not freeze well, but leftovers can be kept in the refrigerator for 1 to 2 days and reheated in the microwave.*

3/4 teaspoon salt

1/3 cup chopped cilantro or parsley

4 to 6 Thai (or makrud) lime leaves or lemon leaves or 3 bay leaves, broken in half

1/2 cup sliced almonds

Custard Topping

2 large eggs

1/2 cup milk

pinch of freshly grated or ground nutmeg

193

serve with any of the following:

starch white, basmati, or Texamati rice; or Spiced Rice, *page 244*

salad Cucumber Tomato Salsa, *page 261*; or Avocado Salad, *page 260*; or Carrot Orange Sambal, *page 256* **dessert** Pineapple in Coconut Milk, *page 208*

Creole Fish in Potato Crust

THIS SAVORY PIE UNITES FRESH FISH with the Creole vegetable medley of celery, bell peppers, onions, scallions, and tomatoes under a topping of mashed potatoes and cucumber. It is a super main course for a casual supper with family or friends. Best of all, it can be assembled in advance and heated before serving.

194

serves 4 to 6

Filling

1 1/4 pounds white fish fillets such as scrod, haddock, or sea bass, or catfish

1 tablespoon olive oil

1 medium onion, chopped

5 to 6 scallions, white and green part, thinly sliced

1 small green bell pepper, finely diced

1 celery stalk, finely diced

2 cloves garlic, minced

2/3 cup tomato puree

1 tablespoon paprika

1 teaspoon thyme leaves

1/2 teaspoon salt

1/4 teaspoon dry English mustard, such as Coleman's

1/8 teaspoon white pepper

dash of Tabasco to taste, optional

Crust

1 recipe Mashed Potatoes with Cucumber (page 236)

1 Preheat the oven to 350°. Put the fish fillets on a baking sheet and bake until the fish is thoroughly cooked, about 10 minutes. Let the fish cool, and then cut it into 1 1/2- to 2-inch cubes.

2 In a medium skillet over medium heat, heat the olive oil. Add the onion, scallions, bell pepper, and celery. Cook, stirring occasionally, until the vegetables are tender, about 10 minutes. Add the garlic and cook, stirring often, for 1 minute. Add the tomatoes, paprika, thyme, salt, mustard, white pepper, and Tabasco and stir.

3 Reduce the heat to medium-low and simmer for 5 minutes. Let the sauce cool. Add the fish to the sauce and stir. Spread the fish in an even layer in a shallow 2-quart baking dish.

4 Prepare the Mashed Potatoes with Cucumber.

5 While the potatoes are still warm, spread them in an even layer on top of the fish. Bake until the fish is heated through and the top is lightly browned, about 25 minutes.

note   This dish can be made and refrigerated several hours ahead and baked just before serving. If it has been refrigerated, allow 10 minutes longer for baking. It should not be frozen.

serve with any of the following:

starch   Biscuits Any Which Way, *page 224*   **salad**   Colorful Crunchy Slaw, *page 253*; or A Good & Simple Salad, *page 264*; or mixed greens with Basic

Vinaigrette using white wine vinegar, *page 266*, and topped with Spiced Nuts, using pecans, *page 273*

Mississippi Crab Gratin

CRAB GRATIN, A LUSCIOUS AND CREAMY crab ragout under a layer of cheese, is honored by its continuing presence on many restaurant menus throughout the South. It is an exquisite entree. This tempting dish is sinfully rich, so a small portion is definitely the way to go.

serves 4

196

2 tablespoons butter

4 scallions, white part only, thinly sliced

2 tablespoons flour

1 to 1 1/4 cups cream or milk, heated

2 cups lump crabmeat (either fresh or canned), picked over for bits of shell

2 tablespoons dry sherry

1 teaspoon chopped fresh tarragon or 1/2 teaspoon dried

3/4 teaspoon salt

1/4 teaspoon white pepper

1/8 teaspoon cayenne

1/4 cup bread crumbs

1/4 cup finely grated Swiss cheese

1 Preheat the oven to 350°. Butter individual ramekins or gratin dishes.

2 In a medium saucepan over medium heat, melt the butter. Add the scallions and cook, stirring occasionally for 2 to 3 minutes. Add the flour and cook, stirring constantly for 1 to 2 minutes more. Gradually pour in 1 cup of heated cream and cook, whisking or stirring constantly, making sure there are no lumps.

3 Add the crabmeat, sherry, tarragon, salt, white pepper, and cayenne and stir. If the sauce seems too thick, add the remaining 1/4 cup of cream. Divide the mixture evenly among the prepared ramekins.

4 In a small bowl, combine the bread crumbs and Swiss cheese and sprinkle the mixture evenly on top of the crab. Bake until the crab is heated through, the crumbs are lightly browned, and the cheese is melted, about 30 to 35 minutes.

note   This dish can be made and refrigerated 2 to 3 hours
ahead and baked right before serving. It can be frozen for up to
2 months if put into a freezer- and ovenproof container. It
should be thawed in before baking. Add approximately 10 to
15 minutes to the baking time if it has been refrigerated.

serve with any of the following:

salad   Tomato & Sautéed Mushroom Salad, *page 250*; or Lemony Asparagus
or Green Beans with Nuts, *page 255*; or Sugar Snap Peas with Orange & Herbs,
   page 249; or mixed greens with Basic Vinaigrette using tarragon or raspberry
vinegar, *page 266*, and Crispy Shallots, *page 272*

Vegetable Biryani

Biryani is an elaborate, highly seasoned, Indian one-pot rice dish served at special occasions. The first time I had a biryani, an Indian friend made it with chicken. She described her method of preparing the dish: marinating and carefully cooking the chicken in yogurt and layering it between aromatic rice and baking. I prefer a vegetarian biryani.

198 | Although I like to prepare the biryani using a mixture of all the spices, feel free to substitute two to three tablespoons of good quality curry powder, such as Madras brand, for the ground spices used in the yogurt marinade in step 1.

serves 6

2^1/2 teaspoons garam masala
1^1/2 teaspoons turmeric
1^1/2 teaspoons ground cumin
1^1/4 teaspoons ground coriander
^{1}/4 to ^{1}/2 teaspoon cayenne
2 teaspoons sugar
2 cloves garlic, minced
1-inch piece ginger, minced
1^1/2 teaspoons salt
1 cup plain yogurt
1^1/2 cups peeled butternut squash
    or peeled sweet potatoes, cut
    into 1-inch cubes
2 cups bite-size cauliflower or broc-
    coli florets
1^1/4 cups sliced green beans
^{3}/4 cup fresh or frozen peas
1 recipe Spiced Rice variation:
    Yellow Spiced Rice with raisins
    (page 244)

1 In a bowl large enough to hold all the vegetables for the biryani, combine the garam masala, turmeric, cumin, coriander, and cayenne (or curry powder if you are using that instead), sugar, garlic, ginger, salt, and yogurt.

2 Add the butternut squash, cauliflower, green beans, and peas to the spiced yogurt, and let it stand for 30 to 60 minutes.

3 Lightly grease a 2^1/2- to 3-quart baking dish and set aside. Prepare 1 recipe Yellow Spiced Rice with raisins.

4 Meanwhile, preheat the oven to 350°. In a large saucepan or skillet over medium-low heat, cook the vegetable mixture, stirring often, about 5 minutes. Be careful that the yogurt doesn't burn.

5 Evenly spread half of the rice in the bottom of the prepared baking dish and top with the lentils, chickpeas, or kidney beans. Put all of the vegetables on top of the lentils or chickpeas. Put a final layer of the remaining rice on top of the vegetables. Insert the broken bay leaves into the rice.

6 Pour the water into the baking dish. Cover the dish with aluminum foil and bake until the vegetables are tender, about 50 to 60 minutes. Garnish with toasted almonds and Crispy Shallots, if desired.

1 cup cooked brown lentils or cooked chickpeas or cooked kidney beans (if canned, drain and rinse)

2 bay leaves, broken in half

1/2 cup water

3 tablespoons toasted almonds for garnish

Crispy Shallots (page 272) for garnish, optional

199

VARIATION

Use other combinations of vegetables, such as 1 1/2 cups diced potatoes or eggplant, 2 cups broccoli florets, 1 diced red or yellow bell pepper, and 1 cup peas.

note *This can be made several hours ahead through step 5. Add the water and bake as directed in step 6. It cannot be frozen.*

serve with any of the following:

salad   Raita, *page* 257; or Pickled Cucumber Salad for spicy food with mint, *page 258*

Stewed Mushrooms Under Herbed Polenta

THE FIRST TIME I HAD A PASTICCIO—a layered polenta casserole—was at a friend's home. It looked like an unusual lasagne, with cheese and mushrooms sandwiched between layers of polenta. It was absolutely delicious, and I was amazed at how filling it was. I came up with this recipe using leeks, bell peppers, and mushrooms and only a small amount of cream and cheese. It is not as rich, but is still quite filling. It is also a terrific complement to grilled or roasted meat.

200

serves 6 to 8

Polenta

1 recipe Herbed Polenta variation: polenta squares (page 240)

Stewed Mushrooms

2¹/2 tablespoons olive oil

2 medium leeks, white part only, thinly sliced

1 large red bell pepper, sliced thinly in 2-inch strips

2 pounds assorted mushrooms, such as shiitake, chanterelle, portabello, and white, sliced

¹/2 cup chicken broth

1 teaspoon salt

¹/2 teaspoon freshly ground black pepper

¹/4 cup chopped fresh flat-leaf parsley

3 tablespoons cream

²/3 cup freshly grated Romano cheese

1 Prepare the polenta using the Herbed Polenta variation. Make as directed for polenta squares, forming 2-inch squares.

2 *To prepare the stewed mushrooms:* In a very large, deep skillet or stewpot over medium heat, heat the olive oil. Add the leeks and bell pepper and cook, stirring occasionally, until the vegetables are softened, about 10 minutes. Add the mushrooms and cook, stirring occasionally, until the mushrooms are soft, about 10 minutes. Add the broth, salt, and pepper. Reduce the heat to medium-low. Simmer, uncovered, until most of the liquid is evaporated, about 30 minutes. Stir in the parsley and cream.

3 Preheat the oven to 350°. With olive oil, lightly oil a 10 × 8 × 2-inch or comparable 2- to 2¹/2-quart shallow baking dish.

4 Arrange half of the polenta squares in the prepared baking dish. Evenly spread half of the mushroom
stew on top of the squares. Sprinkle with half of the
cheese. Top with the remaining polenta squares. Add a
final layer of the remaining mushrooms and top with the
remaining cheese. Bake for 20 to 30 minutes until heated through.

note *This dish can be made up to 2 days ahead, then baked.
To reheat, cover with aluminum foil, and bake for 20 to 30
minutes until heated through. It can be frozen for 1 to 2
months, but must be thawed before baking.*

201

serve with any of the following:

salad   Roasted Beet & Onion Salad on Watercress, *page 247*; or Arugula

Salad, *page 265*; or mixed greens with Basic Vinaigrette using balsamic vinegar,

page 266   dessert   Figs in Red Wine, Ginger, & Thyme, *page 210*

Stewed Tomato & Cheddar Pie

BEING A CHEDDAR CHEESE FAN all my life, I have sought ways to use it other than in "mac and cheese" or on a cheese board. This rich and hearty pie is variation of an old English recipe.

The crust in this recipe needs time to rest before rolling. The dough can be made up to two days ahead and refrigerated. Allow it to sit a few minutes at room temperature before rolling. You can substitute any savory pie crust for this one.

serves 6 to 8

Crust
2 cups all-purpose flour
3/4 teaspoon salt
1/2 teaspoon baking powder
8 tablespoons butter, margarine, vegetable shortening, or a combination, cut into small pieces
2 large eggs, lightly beaten

Stewed Tomatoes
1 tablespoon butter
2 onions, thinly sliced
1/2 teaspoon salt
1/4 teaspoon freshly ground black pepper
1 tablespoon chopped fresh flat-leaf parsley
1 1/4 teaspoons fresh thyme leaves or 1/2 teaspoon dried leaves
1 1/2 tablespoons all-purpose flour
1 pound plum tomatoes, peeled, seeded, and cut into 1/2-inch strips

1   To prepare the crust: In a medium bowl, combine the flour, salt, and baking powder. With 2 knives or a pastry blender, cut in the butter until the mixture resembles coarse crumbs. With a fork, stir in the eggs until a dough forms. With your fingertips, lightly knead the dough until it just holds together, about 1 minute. Divide the dough in half and wrap each half separately in plastic wrap and refrigerate for at least 30 minutes or until ready to roll out. (Refrigerating will make the dough easier to roll.)

2   To prepare the stewed tomatoes: In a large skillet over medium-low heat, melt the butter. Add the onions and cook, stirring occasionally, until they are golden, about 25 minutes. Add the salt, pepper, parsley, and thyme. Cook for 10 minutes longer. Add the flour and cook, stirring constantly, for 2 to 3 minutes. Add the tomatoes. Cover and simmer until the tomatoes are softened but hold their shape, about 10 minutes. Set aside. Let the mixture cool to room temperature before using.

3 Meanwhile, remove half of the dough. Place the dough between two sheets of plastic wrap or waxed paper. Roll out the bottom crust to a 10-inch circle to fit into a 9-inch deep dish pie plate. Trim the excess dough, leaving a 1/2-inch overhang. Refrigerate while the tomatoes are cooling or until ready to use.

4 Preheat the oven to 350°. Remove the dough for the top crust from the refrigerator and let it stand at room temperature before rolling. Roll out the dough for the top crust in the same way as for the bottom crust. (If you wish, the crust can be rolled out ahead of time. The top crust can be slid onto a baking sheet and refrigerated until ready to use.)

5 Place half of the cooled stewed tomatoes into the crust-lined pie plate. Sprinkle half of the cheese on top of the tomatoes. Repeat the layering.

6 Place the top crust onto the pie. Trim the edges so they are even but have a 3/4-inch overhang. Roll the edges of the top and bottom crusts together to form an edge that is slightly higher than the pie plate. Flute the edge or seal it with the tines of a fork. With a sharp paring knife, make 3 small slits in the center of the top crust. Brush the top with milk.

7 Bake for 40 to 45 minutes until the crust is golden. Let the pie stand on a cooling rack for 5 to 10 minutes before slicing.

To Finish

1 1/2 cups grated extra sharp cheddar cheese

1 tablespoon milk

note *This dish cannot be made ahead, reheated, or frozen.*

203

serve with any of the following:

salad   Herbed Vegetable Slaw, *page 252*; or Make-Ahead Herbed Garden Salad, *page 263*; or Sugar Snap Peas with Orange & Herbs, *page 249*   dessert

Spiced Apples in Cider & Brandy, *page 211*

seven FRUIT STEWS

Pears in Ruby Port & Vanilla

Spiced Dried Fruit Compote

Pineapple in Coconut Milk

Rhubarb with Cardamom

Figs in Red Wine, Ginger, & Thyme

Spiced Apples in Cider & Brandy

Cranberries in Red Wine

Nectarines with Tarragon & Pepper

Pears in Ruby Port & Vanilla

PEARS IN RED WINE ARE GOOD, but these pears in ruby port are divine. They're terrific on their own, with ice cream, or with whipped cream. Even somewhat hard, underripe fruit works well, although they will take a little longer to become tender.

serves 6

206

²/₃ cup water

²/₃ cup ruby port

²/₃ cup sugar

**¹/₂ vanilla bean, split or 1 teaspoon
   pure vanilla extract**

2-inch strip fresh lemon zest

**1¹/₂ pounds pears (about 4
   medium), peeled and cored, each
one cut into 6 slices lengthwise**

1 In a medium saucepan over medium heat, combine the water, port, sugar, vanilla bean, and lemon zest. Bring the liquid to a boil, then reduce the heat to medium-low.

2 Add the pears to the liquid and cook, turning them occasionally, until tender, about 30 to 50 minutes depending on the ripeness of the fruit. With a slotted spoon, transfer the fruit to a medium bowl.

3 Raise the heat to medium-high and cook the liquid until it is reduced to about ²/₃ cup, about 15 minutes.

4 Let the reduced liquid cool slightly and pour it over the pears. Cool briefly. Serve the pears with some of the port wine syrup warm, at room temperature, or chilled.

note *This recipe can be made up to 3 days ahead and stored in the refrigerator.*

Spiced Dried Fruit Compote

THIS FLAVORFUL COMPOTE is a scrumptious dessert served on its own or with a dollop of whipped cream, ice cream, sorbet, or over a sweet biscuit. I also like it for brunch with a heaping spoonful of plain or vanilla yogurt.

serves 8

207

1 In a medium saucepan over medium heat, combine the wine, water, honey, sugar, nutmeg, cinnamon, and cloves. Bring the liquid to a boil.

2 Add the orange and dried fruit and reduce the heat to medium-low. Cook for 30 to 40 minutes until the fruit is tender.

3 Transfer the mixture to another container and let the fruit cool in its juices at room temperature. With a slotted spoon, remove and discard the orange slices. Serve the compote with some of its juices warm, at room temperature, or chilled.

note Strain any leftover liquid after you've finished eating the fruit. Refrigerate it and substitute it for the water the next time you make the compote. This can be made ahead. The fruit, still in its juices, will last for 1 month in a well-covered container in the refrigerator.

1 1/2 cups dry red wine

2 cups water or white grape juice

1/2 cup honey

1/2 cup sugar

1/2 teaspoon freshly grated nutmeg

1/2 teaspoon ground cinnamon

1/4 teaspoon ground cloves

1 thin-skinned orange (not navel), skin on, thinly sliced

4 cups (about 1 pound) mixed dried fruit, any combination of apples, prunes, cherries, cranberries, apricots, peaches, and pears

Pineapple in Coconut Milk

ALMOST A PINA COLADA, but—oops, no rum! This delicate and unique dish has its origins in Indonesia. It can be served warm, but I prefer it at room temperature. It is versatile enough to stand on its own or be served with vanilla ice cream or sorbet. It also can be served as a condiment to savory dishes such as grilled fish, pork, or chicken. If you have a sweet tooth, add extra sugar to taste.

208

serves 6

1 thin stalk fresh lemon grass,
  coarsely chopped
$1/2$-inch piece fresh ginger, minced
$1/4$ teaspoon whole coriander
1 cinnamon stick
2 cloves
$1^2/3$ cups unsweetened coconut
  milk
$1^1/2$ tablespoons sugar or more to
  taste
$1/4$ teaspoon turmeric
1 large pineapple, not too ripe,
  peeled, cored, and diced
fresh chopped mint for garnish

1 Wrap the lemon grass, ginger, coriander, cinnamon, and cloves in a piece of cheesecloth and tie to form a sack.

2 In a medium saucepan over medium heat, combine the coconut milk, sugar, turmeric, and cheesecloth sack. Bring the liquid to a boil and cook for 5 minutes.

3 Add the pineapple and cook, stirring occasionally, until tender, about 5 to 8 minutes. Transfer the mixture to a bowl and let the pineapple cool in the coconut milk. When the liquid is cool, remove the cheesecloth sack. Garnish with mint before serving.

VARIATION
Serve with Spiced Nuts using slivered almonds, *page 273*.

note *This recipe can be made up to three hours ahead and cooled at room temperature. Leftovers can be refrigerated for three days, but bring it to room temperature before serving.*

Rhubarb with Cardamom

WHEN I WAS VERY SMALL, we had a rhubarb patch in the backyard. My mother used to stew the plants. The trick to rhubarb is making sure you have enough sugar: sometimes it is quite sour, so taste it when it is nearly finished and add more sugar if necessary. This is terrific over vanilla ice cream or lemon or strawberry sorbet.

serves 6

209

1 Place the cardamom pods, coriander, and orange peel in a small piece of cheesecloth and tie it to form a sack.

2 In a medium saucepan over medium heat, combine the water, sugar, and cheesecloth sack. Cook until the sugar is completely dissolved, about 7 minutes.

3 Add the rhubarb and cook until it is tender, about 25 to 35 minutes depending on the thickness of the stalks.

4 With a slotted spoon, remove the cheesecloth sack. Place the rhubarb and cardamom-orange-flavored syrup in a serving bowl and cool slightly. Serve with some of its juices warm, at room temperature, or cold.

note *This recipe can be made up to 3 days ahead and stored in the refrigerator.*

3 cardamom pods, lightly crushed by tapping with the flat of a knife

4 whole coriander seeds

2-inch strip fresh orange peel

3/4 cup water

1 to 1 1/2 cups sugar, depending on the ripeness of the fruit

2 pounds rhubarb stalks, washed and sliced into 1-inch pieces (If the stalks are large and have a tough exterior, peel them with a vegetable peeler.)

Figs in Red Wine, Ginger & Thyme

I LOVE DRIED FIGS, and this combination of wine, spice, and herbs turns them into a splendid yet simple dessert. Serve with almond biscotti, top with a dollop of crème fraiche or marscapone, or serve it over ice cream. It is easy to prepare and can be made weeks ahead of time.

serves 8

3 sprigs fresh thyme or 3/4 teaspoon dried

1-inch piece fresh ginger, thinly sliced

2 cups full-bodied red wine

1/2 cup good quality honey such as orange blossom or herbal

1 pound dried figs

1 Wrap the thyme and ginger in a small piece of cheesecloth and tie to form a sack.

2 In a medium saucepan over medium heat, combine the wine, honey, and cheesecloth sack. When the liquid is gently bubbling and hot, add the figs.

3 Partially cover the pan and reduce the heat to medium-low. Simmer until the figs are tender, about 50 to 60 minutes. From time to time, turn the figs in the liquid. Do not let the liquid boil.

4 With a slotted spoon, transfer the figs to a medium bowl.

5 In the same saucepan over medium heat, cook the wine with the cheesecloth sack until the liquid is reduced by half to a thin syrup, about 10 minutes. With a slotted spoon, remove the cheesecloth sack.

6 Pour the reduced wine syrup through a fine-mesh strainer over the figs. Let the figs cool slightly. Serve with some of the syrup warm, at room temperature, or cold.

note *The figs in their liquid will keep in the refrigerator for 1 month in a well-covered container.*

Spiced Apples in Cider & Brandy

DEEP BLUE SKIES, crisp autumn air, and vibrantly colored leaves beckon me to take a trip along the back roads of New England to orchards in search of the new crop of apples and freshly pressed cider. I make these spiced apples as dessert or as an accompaniment to pork or chicken. If you tend to like things tart, use Granny Smith apples. Omit the brandy if kids are eating it; add 1/2 teaspoon vanilla extract instead.

211

serves 6

1 In a medium saucepan over medium heat, combine the cider, sugar, brandy, allspice, cloves, and orange zest. Bring the liquid to a boil, then reduce the heat to medium-low.

2 Add the apples to the liquid and cook, turning them occasionally, until tender, 15 to 25 minutes depending on the ripeness of the fruit. With a slotted spoon, transfer the fruit to a medium bowl.

3 Raise the heat to medium-high and cook the liquid until it is reduced by half, about 15 minutes.

4 Let the liquid cool slightly and pour it over the apples. Serve the apples warm, at room temperature, or chilled.

note This recipe can be made 2 to 3 days ahead and stored in the refrigerator.

1 cup fresh apple cider or water

1 cup sugar

1 1/2 tablespoons brandy or cognac

4 allspice berries

3 whole cloves

2-inch strip fresh orange zest

1 1/2 pounds apples such as Cortland, Rome, or MacIntosh (about 3 to 4 medium), peeled and cored, each one cut into 8 slices lengthwise

Cranberries in Red Wine

THIS IS A TWIST ON TRADITIONAL CRANBERRIES. It is a perfect accompaniment to many poultry and pork dishes. These sweet yet tart cranberries are also delightful spooned over ice cream or sweet biscuits or with a dollop of whipped cream.

serves 6

212

1 3/4 cups full-bodied red wine
1 1/2 cups sugar
1 bay leaf
1/8 teaspoon ground cloves or
    freshly grated nutmeg
1 pound cranberries, washed and
    picked over

1   In a medium saucepan over medium-high heat, combine the wine, sugar, bay leaf, and cloves. Bring the liquid to a boil and add the cranberries.

2   Reduce the heat to medium and cook for 10 to 15 minutes until the cranberries begin to pop. Watch carefully and lower the heat if the liquid begins to boil over.

3   Transfer the mixture to a bowl and let the berries cool at room temperature. With a slotted spoon, remove the bay leaf. Serve warm, at room temperature, or chilled.

note   *This recipe can be made up to 4 days ahead and stored in the refrigerator.*

Nectarines with Tarragon & Pepper

THESE ARE LUSCIOUS—exquisite taste and magnificent color. They are superb with lemon or raspberry sorbet or vanilla ice cream. They can also be used on top of angel food cake or sweet biscuits. If nectarines are not available, try this recipe with peaches.

serves 4 to 8

1 With a skewer, pierce the skin side of the nectarines in several places.

2 In a medium saucepan over medium heat, combine the water, sugar, lemon juice, peppercorns, and tarragon. After the sugar is completely dissolved, reduce the heat to medium-low and simmer for 5 minutes.

3 Add the nectarines, skin side up, and cook until tender, about 6 to 10 minutes depending on the ripeness of the fruit. Turn the fruit over after 4 minutes of cooking so the skin side is down.

4 With a slotted spoon, transfer the nectarines to a cutting board, skin side up. When they are cool enough to handle, use the tip of a paring knife to gently peel back the skin and remove it completely. It will slip off quite easily.

5 Meanwhile, continue cooking the tarragon-sugar liquid until it is reduced to a thin syrup, about 15 minutes longer. Let the syrup cool slightly.

6 Place the nectarines in a bowl and pour the cooled syrup over them. Let them cool to room temperature. Serve warm, at room temperature, or chilled.

4 nectarines, halved and pitted
2 cups water
1/2 cup sugar
1 tablespoon fresh lemon juice
8 black peppercorns
4 sprigs fresh tarragon, each about 3 inches long

note This recipe can be made up to 3 days ahead and stored in the refrigerator.

eight

ON THE SIDE

Bread

Buttermilk Raisin Spice Bread

Lemon Scallion Soda Bread

Herbed Dijon Beer Bread

Buttermilk Cornbread & Variations

Onion Flat Bread

Anna's Crusty French Loaf & Variations

Round Country Loaf & Variations

South African Garlic, Herb, & Cheese
    Pot Bread

Herbed Corn Biscuits

Biscuits Any Which Way

Root Vegetables & Grains

Great Potato Pancakes

Creamy Potato Gratin

Oven-Roasted Red Potatoes with Rosemary

Garlic & Herb Mashed Potatoes

Mashed Potatoes with Cucumber

Spiced Mashed Sweet Potatoes

Mashed Turnips & Apples

Lemon or Orange Couscous

Basic Polenta & Variations

Basic Risotto & Variations

Spiced Rice & Variations

Salads

Rujak

Roasted Beet & Onion Salad on
Watercress

Jicama Mango Salad

Sugar Snap Peas with Orange & Herbs

Tomato & Sautéed Mushroom Salad

Warm Greens

Herbed Vegetable Slaw

Colorful Crunchy Slaw

Spicy Green Bean Sambal

Lemony Asparagus or Green Beans
with Nuts

Carrot Orange Sambal

Raita

Pickled Cucumber Salad

Pickled Beets

Avocado Salad

Cucumber Tomato Salsa

Mesclun Salad with Goat Cheese

Make-Ahead Herbed Garden Salad

A Good & Simple Salad

Arugula Salad

Basic Vinaigrette

bread

Buttermilk Raisin Spice Bread

IN A SMALL COUNTRY INN in eastern Pennsylvania, I was served a bread basket that included a scrumptious quick bread. After a few tries, I duplicated it in my kitchen. This fragrantly spiced bread, laced with raisins, is delicious anytime—for brunch, lunch, or dinner.

makes 1 loaf

216

2 1/2 cups all-purpose flour
2 tablespoons light brown sugar
2 teaspoons baking soda
3/4 teaspoon salt
1/2 teaspoon baking powder
1 1/4 teaspoons ground cumin
1/2 teaspoon ground cinnamon
2 teaspoons finely grated fresh
   orange zest
1 1/4 cups golden raisins
1 1/4 cups buttermilk
1/4 cup vegetable oil
1 large egg, lightly beaten

1 Preheat the oven to 350°. Lightly grease a 9 × 5-inch loaf pan and set aside.

2 In a medium bowl, combine the flour, brown sugar, baking soda, salt, baking powder, cumin, cinnamon, and orange zest. Stir in the raisins.

3 In a large liquid measuring cup, combine the buttermilk, vegetable oil, and egg.

4 Make a well in the center of the dry ingredients. Slowly pour in the liquid ingredients, and stir with a wooden spoon until just blended. Do not overmix. Pour the batter into the prepared pan.

5 Bake for 40 to 50 minutes or until a toothpick inserted in the center comes out clean. Leave in the pan until cool enough to handle, then transfer to a rack to finish cooling.

note *This bread can be made several hours ahead, and it freezes well. If wrapped in plastic wrap, it can be kept at room temperature 3 to 4 days.*

Lemon Scallion Soda Bread

SODA BREADS HAVE A LOVELY TEXTURE, more delicate than that of yeast breads. The most famous, Irish soda bread, is made with whole wheat flour, which provides its characteristic color and taste. This recipe calls for unbleached white flour, and the bread is scented with scallions and lemon zest. As a variation, feel free to replace 1 cup of unbleached flour with 1 cup of whole wheat flour.

217

m a k e s   2   s m a l l   r o u n d   l o a v e s

1 Preheat the oven to 350°. Lightly dust a baking sheet with cornmeal and set aside.

2 In a medium bowl, combine the flour, salt, baking powder, baking soda, lemon zest, and scallions.

3 In a large liquid measuring cup, combine the buttermilk and vegetable oil.

4 Make a well in the center of the dry ingredients. Slowly pour in the liquid ingredients, and stir with a wooden spoon until a soft dough forms. Transfer the dough to a lightly floured work surface. Lightly knead the dough until it is smooth, about 2 minutes.

5 Divide the dough in half and form it into two balls. Place them onto the prepared baking sheet. With a sharp paring knife, slash the tops in an X. Dust the tops lightly with flour.

6 Bake until the bread sounds hollow when tapped on the bottom and the top is lightly browned, about 35 to 40 minutes.

cornmeal for dusting the baking
    sheet
4 cups unbleached all-purpose flour
1 1/4 teaspoons salt
1 teaspoon baking powder
1 teaspoon baking soda
1 tablespoon finely grated fresh
    lemon zest
5 to 6 scallions, white and green
    part, thinly sliced
1 1/2 cups buttermilk
1/3 cup vegetable oil

note *This bread can be made several hours ahead, and it freezes well.*

Herbed Dijon Beer Bread

HERBS, MUSTARD, AND BEER—this bread has plenty of gusto. Make sure you do not use a beer with a strong taste that will overpower the other ingredients. A mild-flavored domestic beer will work very well. Leftovers are wonderful when toasted or used for grilled sandwiches.

makes 1 loaf

218

3 cups all-purpose flour

4 teaspoons baking powder
   (1 tablespoon plus 1 teaspoon)

1 teaspoon salt

1/4 cup chopped fresh parsley

1 1/2 tablespoons chopped fresh dill
   or chives

1 1/2 cups (one 12-ounce bottle)
   mild-flavored domestic beer, at
   room temperature

1 1/2 tablespoons brown sugar

2 teaspoons coarse-grain Dijon
   mustard

1 Preheat the oven to 350°. Lightly grease a 9 × 5-inch loaf pan. Dust the pan with cornmeal and set aside.

2 In a medium bowl, combine the flour, baking powder, salt, parsley, and chives.

3 In a large liquid measuring cup, combine the beer, sugar, and mustard.

4 Make a well in the center of the dry ingredients. Slowly pour in the liquid ingredients, and stir with a wooden spoon until just blended.

5 Pour the batter into the prepared pan. Bake for 50 to 60 minutes or until a toothpick inserted in the center comes out clean. The top will have a textured appearance and be a very light brown.

note *This bread can be made several hours ahead, and it freezes well. If wrapped in plastic wrap, it can be kept at room temperature for 3 to 4 days.*

Buttermilk Cornbread & Variations

I'VE ALWAYS LOVED CORNBREAD, but many recipes are high in fat and cholesterol. I came up with this version using vegetable oil, egg whites, and buttermilk so I could eat it with a little less guilt.

makes 1 square loaf

219

1 Preheat the oven to 400°. Lightly grease an 8- or 9-inch square baking pan.

2 In a medium bowl, combine the cornmeal, flour, sugar, baking powder, salt, and baking soda.

3 Add the vegetable oil and stir.

4 In a 2-cup measuring cup, combine the egg whites with the buttermilk. Pour the buttermilk mixture into the dry ingredients, stirring quickly with a wooden spoon until just blended. Do not overmix. The batter should be lumpy.

5 Spread the batter evenly in the prepared baking pan. Bake for 20 to 25 minutes until the top is golden and a toothpick inserted in the center comes out clean. Cool on a rack until serving.

1 cup yellow or white cornmeal, preferably stone-ground
1 cup all-purpose flour
1 1/2 tablespoons sugar
2 1/2 teaspoons baking powder
1 teaspoon salt
1/2 teaspoon baking soda
1/4 cup vegetable oil
2 egg whites, lightly beaten
1 cup buttermilk

note This bread can be made an hour or two ahead, and it freezes well.

VARIATIONS

Bacon Chive: Add 1 recipe Lardons (*page 274*), and 2 tablespoons chopped chives to the dry ingredients in step 2. Proceed with the directions.

Chili Cheese: In step 2, add 1/2 cup grated cheddar or Monterey Jack cheese, 1/4 cup canned, drained, chopped jalapenos, and 1 1/2 tablespoons chopped fresh cilantro to the dry ingredients. Proceed with the directions.

Onion Flat Bread

THIS WHOLE WHEAT FOCCACCIA-STYLE BREAD is topped with onions and lightly scented with rosemary. The onions are salted, squeezed, and rinsed to remove any bitter juices. Although I make a rectangular bread, feel free to form the dough into a circle and bake it on a round pizza pan.

220

makes 1 flat bread

3/4 cup lukewarm water (105° to 115°)

1 tablespoon dry yeast (not rapid rise)

1 teaspoon sugar

2 cups unbleached all-purpose flour

1 cup whole wheat flour

1 1/2 teaspoons salt

6 tablespoons extra virgin olive oil

1 medium onion, very thinly sliced

1 tablespoon kosher salt

1 teaspoon chopped fresh rosemary leaves (optional)

freshly ground black pepper to taste

1 Put the water in a 2-cup liquid measuring cup and sprinkle the yeast and sugar on top. Don't stir—let the mixture stand for about 5 to 8 minutes until the yeast is proofed. If the yeast is good and the water is the right temperature, the yeast will be bubbly and quite foamy. If it isn't, discard the mixture and repeat the procedure with yeast from a new package.

2 In a large bowl, combine both flours and the salt. Make a well in the center of the dry ingredients and pour in the yeast mixture. With a wooden spoon, stir to blend. Add 3 tablespoons of the olive oil, and stir well with the wooden spoon until a soft dough forms.

3 Turn the dough out onto a lightly floured work surface. With the palm of your hand, knead the dough until it is smooth and satiny. Form the dough into a ball. Place the dough in a lightly oiled bowl, turning it to coat evenly. Cover the bowl with a damp kitchen towel and let the dough rise in a warm place until it doubles in size, about 1 hour.

4 Put the onion in a colander and with your fingers rub it with the kosher salt. Gently squeeze the onions to remove the juices that form. Rinse well under cold running water, drain, and pat dry. In a small bowl, combine the onions, the remaining 3 tablespoons of olive oil, and the rosemary and set aside.

5 Meanwhile, preheat the oven to 400°. Lightly coat a baking sheet or jelly roll pan with olive oil and set aside.

6 Punch the dough down and knead it briefly while it is still in the bowl. Turn the dough out onto a lightly floured work surface. Knead the dough until it is smooth, about 5 minutes.

7 Roll the dough into a 10 × 12 inch rectangle about 1/2 to 3/4 inch thick. Place the dough on the prepared baking sheet. Cover the dough with the damp kitchen towel and let it rise for an additional 50 to 60 minutes.

8 Using your fingertips, make several shallow indentations on the surface of the dough, leaving a 1/2-inch border around the edges. Lightly press the onion topping onto the dough. Season with pepper.

9 Bake until lightly golden around the edges and lightly browned on the bottom, about 15 to 20 minutes. Let the bread cool slightly on a rack before cutting into squares. Serve warm.

note This bread can be made several hours ahead and reheated, and it freezes well.

Anna's Crusty French Loaf & Variations

ANNA, A WOMAN I KNOW FROM DENMARK, makes what she calls Danish baguettes. She rattled off the recipe in metric measurements, which I converted for use in American kitchens. It's a simple version of French bread which is a perfect accompaniment to many stews.

Like Anna, you can make the dough the night before and refrigerate it, letting it slowly rise overnight and develop additional flavor. The next day, bake it—and *voila!* There's bread. I've given directions for both "Refrigerator Make-Ahead" and "Traditional Rise" methods.

makes 3 long, narrow, French-style loaves

2 cups warm water (105° to 115°)

1 tablespoon dry yeast (not rapid rise)

1 teaspoon sugar

5^1/2 to 6^1/2 cups unbleached all-purpose flour

2 teaspoons salt

3 to 4 tablespoons extra virgin olive oil

1 egg white, lightly beaten, or 1 tablespoon water for glazing the dough

cornmeal for dusting the baking sheet

1 Put the water in a 4-cup liquid measuring cup and sprinkle the yeast and sugar on top. Don't stir—let the mixture stand for about 5 to 8 minutes until the yeast is proofed. If the yeast is good and the water is the right temperature, the yeast will be bubbly and quite foamy. If it is not bubbly and foamy, discard the mixture and repeat the procedure with yeast from a new package. Add the olive oil to the yeast mixture.

2 Meanwhile, in a large bowl, mix 5^1/2 cups of the flour and the salt. Make a well in the center of the dry ingredients. Gradually pour in the yeast mixture, stirring with a wooden spoon until the dough is quite firm and very sticky to the touch.

3 Turn the dough out onto a lightly floured work surface. Lightly dust your hands with flour and knead the dough, adding as much of the remaining flour—in small amounts—as necessary so the dough is no longer sticky. Knead until the dough is smooth and satiny, about 10 minutes.

4 Place the dough in a lightly oiled bowl, turning it to coat evenly. Cover the bowl with a damp kitchen towel or plastic wrap. At this point, you may refrigerate the dough overnight and follow the "Refrigerator Make-Ahead" method the next day, or proceed with the "Traditional Rise" method.

5 *Refrigerator Make-Ahead Method:* The day after the dough is made, lightly dust a baking sheet with corn-meal and set aside. Remove the dough from the bowl and place on a lightly floured surface. Shape it into 2 French breads or 3 slender baguettes, about the length of the baking sheet. Roll the loaves slightly into a cylinder so they are uniformly shaped. Place them onto the prepared baking sheet. Cover the loaves with a damp kitchen towel and let them rise for 30 to 40 minutes. (Proceed with step 7.)

6 *Traditional Rise Method:* Place the dough in a warm place and let it rise until doubled, about 1 to 1 1/2 hours. Lightly dust a baking sheet with cornmeal and set it aside. Remove the dough from the bowl and place on a lightly floured surface. Punch the dough down and shape into 2 French breads or 3 slender baguettes, about the length of the baking sheet. Roll the loaves slightly into a cylinder so they are uniformly shaped. Place them onto the prepared baking sheet. Cover the loaves with a damp kitchen towel and let them rise for an additional 25 to 30 minutes. (Proceed with step 7.)

7 Preheat the oven to 425°. With a very sharp paring knife, slash the top of each loaf lengthwise, slightly off center, or slash diagonally in 2 or 3 places. Brush the tops with egg white or water. Bake for 15 minutes.

8 Reduce the oven temperature to 375°. Bake until the bread sounds hollow when it is tapped on the bottom and the top is nicely browned, about 12 to 15 minutes longer.

note *This bread is best if eaten on the same day it is made. It freezes well.*

VARIATIONS

Whole Wheat: Replace 1 1/2 cups of the unbleached all-purpose flour with whole wheat flour.

Seeded: After glazing with the egg white, gently press sesame seeds into the tops.

223

Round Country Loaf & Variations

THIS BREAD HAS AN APPEALING RUSTIC LOOK—its top is lightly dusted with flour. I've made it for years because it is extremely versatile. It is terrific warm or toasted, and leftovers are wonderful for sandwiches.

makes 1 loaf

³/4 cup warm water (105° to 115°)
1 tablespoon dry yeast (not rapid rise)
1 teaspoon sugar
3 cups unbleached all-purpose flour
1 teaspoon salt
2 egg whites, lightly beaten
2 tablespoons butter, melted
Cornmeal for dusting the baking sheet
Additional flour for dusting bread

1 Put the water in a 1-cup liquid measuring cup and sprinkle the yeast and sugar on top. Don't stir—let the mixture stand for about 5 to 8 minutes until the yeast is proofed. If the yeast is good and the water is the right temperature, the yeast will be bubbly and quite foamy. If it is not bubbly and foamy, discard the mixture and repeat the procedure with yeast from a new package.

2 Meanwhile, in a large bowl, combine 2¹/2 cups of the flour and the salt. Combine the egg whites and butter and stir them into the flour mixture. Make a well in the center of the flour mixture, and with a wooden spoon, stir in the yeast mixture. Add as much of the remaining ¹/2 cup of flour to form a dough that is sticky but not wet. Stir until the dough pulls away from the sides of the bowl.

3 Turn the dough out onto a lightly floured work surface. Lightly dust your hands with flour. Knead the dough until it is no longer sticky and is smooth and satiny, about 10 minutes.

4 Place the dough in a lightly oiled bowl, turning it to coat evenly. Cover the bowl with a damp kitchen towel or with plastic wrap. Place the dough in a warm place and let it rise until doubled, about 1¹/2 hours.

5   Preheat the oven to 375°. Lightly dust a baking sheet with cornmeal and set aside. Punch the dough down, flattening it slightly, and knead briefly. Pinch the ends of the dough together to form a round ball. Place the dough seam side down onto the baking sheet. Cover the loaf with the damp kitchen towel. Let the dough rise for 30 minutes.

6   With a sharp paring knife, slash an X in the top. Cover with the towel and let rise for 10 to 15 minutes longer.

7   Lightly dust the top of the loaf with flour. Bake until the bread sounds hollow when tapped on the bottom and the top is lightly browned, about 30 to 35 minutes.

VARIATIONS

Whole Wheat: Use 1 cup of whole wheat flour and 2 cups of unbleached all-purpose flour.

Orange Herb: In step 3, sprinkle the dough with 2 teaspoons finely grated fresh orange zest and 2 teaspoons chopped fresh thyme leaves or 1 1/2 teaspoons chopped fresh rosemary leaves and 1/3 cup chopped fresh parsley and knead the ingredients into the dough.

note   *This bread can be made several hours ahead, and it freezes well.*

South African Garlic, Herb, & Cheese Pot Bread

MY NEIGHBOR, ANSA, FIRST TAUGHT ME how to make pot bread or potbrood. It is a South African bread, served at barbecues known as *braais*, that is baked in a cast iron pot.

Traditionally, the bread was cooked over a fire. The dough-filled, covered pot was placed in the hot coals and baked for 30 minutes. More coals were then placed on the lid and the bread continued to bake for an additional 30 minutes or until a knife came out clean. Today, most people bake the bread in a conventional oven.

This potbread is made from a basic bread dough that is rolled out and filled with garlic, herbs, and cheese, and then rolled into a cylinder, sliced, and arranged in a decorative manner in the pot. For variation, sprinkle some pitted, chopped, imported black olives on the cheese.

makes 1 large loaf

2 cups warm water (105° to 115°)

1 tablespoon dry yeast (not rapid rise)

1 tablespoon sugar

2^1/2 tablespoons olive oil

5^3/4 cups unbleached all-purpose flour

2 teaspoons salt

1^1/2 tablespoons minced fresh garlic (about 6 cloves)

2/3 cup minced fresh flat-leaf parsley

3 tablespoons finely minced scallion greens or chives

2^1/2 teaspoons minced fresh rosemary

1^1/2 cups finely grated sharp cheddar or Swiss cheese

1 Put the water in a 4-cup liquid measuring cup and sprinkle the yeast and sugar on top. Don't stir—let the mixture stand for about 5 to 8 minutes until the yeast is proofed. If the yeast is good and the water is the right temperature, the yeast will be bubbly and quite foamy. If it is not bubbly and foamy, discard the mixture and repeat the procedure with yeast from a new package. Add 2 tablespoons of the olive oil to the yeast mixture.

2 In a large bowl, combine the flour and salt. Make a well in the center of the dry ingredients. Pour in the yeast mixture and stir well with a wooden spoon.

3 Turn the dough out onto a lightly floured work surface. Knead the dough until it is smooth and satiny, about 7 minutes, then form it into a ball. Place the dough in a lightly oiled bowl, turning it to coat evenly. Cover the bowl with a damp kitchen towel and let the dough stand in a warm place until it doubles in size, about 1 1/2 hours.

4 Meanwhile, in a small skillet over medium heat, heat the remaining 1/2 tablespoon of the olive oil. Add the garlic and cook, stirring occasionally, for about 1 to 2 minutes. Do not let the garlic brown. Transfer the garlic to a small dish and set aside.

5 In a small bowl, combine the parsley, scallion greens, and rosemary, and set aside.

6 Generously grease the interior of a 2 1/2-quart round cast iron or enamel-coated cast iron stewpot, about 8 to 9 inches in diameter and 3 to 3 1/2 inches high.

7 Punch down the dough and knead it briefly while it is still in the bowl. Turn the dough out onto a lightly floured work surface. Knead the dough again about 7 minutes.

8 Cut off a small piece of the dough. With a lightly floured rolling pin on the lightly floured work surface, roll the small piece into a 9 1/2- to 10-inch circle. Place the circle in the bottom of the prepared pot, allowing the dough to reach about 1 inch up the sides.

9 With the lightly floured rolling pin on the lightly-floured work surface, roll out the remaining dough to about a 15 × 22-inch rectangle. With a sharp knife, trim the dough so the edges are even. Discard the excess dough.

Continued

10 Leaving a 1-inch border around all the edges, evenly spread the cooked garlic onto the dough. Evenly sprinkle the mixed herbs onto the garlic, and then sprinkle the cheese on top of the herbs.

11 Starting with a long side, roll the dough up into a log that is approximately 3 inches in diameter and 22 inches long. Cut approximately 1 to 1 1/2 inches of the dough off each end so that the ends are even. Discard the excess.

12 Slice the dough into 8 equal slices. Place 1 slice in the center of the prepared pot and arrange the remaining 7 slices in a circle around the center slice. Let the dough rise until it almost reaches the top of the pot, about 1 to 1 1/2 hours.

13 Meanwhile, preheat the oven to 350°. When the dough is finished rising, bake it in the pot for 50 to 60 minutes.

14 Run a knife around the edges of the pot to loosen the bread. Carefully invert the pot onto a cooling rack, allowing the bread to slip out. While holding the hot bread with a clean kitchen towel, turn it over so the side showing the rolled cylinders is on top. Let the bread cool on the cooling rack for 10 to 15 minutes before slicing.

note *This bread can be made several hours ahead. It freezes well.*

Herbed Corn Biscuits

CORNMEAL BOOSTS THE TEXTURE and flavor of the biscuits. These are a pleasant alternative to both cornbread and standard biscuits and can be substituted for either. You can omit the herbs and cayenne to create a corn biscuit that is also good with jam for breakfast.

makes about 12 biscuits

229

1 Preheat the oven to 400°. Lightly grease a baking sheet and set aside.

2 In a bowl, combine the flour, cornmeal, sugar, baking powder, salt, cayenne, chives, and parsley. With your fingertips or a pastry blender, cut in the butter until the mixture resembles coarse crumbs.

3 Stir in the milk until a soft dough forms. If the dough is slightly dry, add a little more milk, 1 tablespoon at a time.

4 Turn the dough out onto a lightly floured work surface and gently knead it for 1 to 2 minutes. Roll out the dough into rectangle about 1/2 to 3/4 inch thick. Cut it into 12 equal squares, or into 12 rounds with a biscuit cutter. Place the squares onto the prepared baking sheet. Bake for 10 to 15 minutes until lightly golden. Cool on a rack and serve warm.

1 1/2 cups all-purpose flour

3/4 cup yellow or white cornmeal, preferably stone-ground

1 tablespoon sugar

1 1/2 tablespoons baking powder

1/2 teaspoon salt

1/8 to 1/4 teaspoon cayenne, to taste

1 tablespoon chopped chives

1 tablespoon chopped fresh flat-leaf parsley

5 tablespoons butter or margarine

3/4 cup regular or 2% milk

note These biscuits can be made an hour or two ahead and reheated, and they freeze well.

Biscuits Any Which Way

THE LATE JAMES BEARD PUBLISHED a recipe for cream biscuits, upon which this one is based. I've made these foolproof biscuits, with variations for savory or sweet, for years because they're quick, easy, and always good.

makes about 12 biscuits

230

Basic Savory Mix
2 cups unbleached all-purpose flour
1 tablespoon baking powder
1/2 to 1 teaspoon salt*
1 1/4 cups half and half

1 Preheat the oven to 425°. Lightly butter a baking sheet.

2 In a medium bowl combine the flour, baking powder, and salt.

3 With a wooden spoon, stir in the half and half until a dough forms.

4 Turn the dough out onto a lightly floured work surface. Knead the dough gently with your fingertips 3 or 4 times until it just holds together. Pat the dough into a rectangle about 3/4 inch thick.

5 Cut the dough with a 2 to 2 1/2-inch round biscuit cutter and place the biscuits onto the prepared baking sheet. Bake for 12 to 15 minutes until lightly browned on the bottom.

*If you are making the bacon variation or the sweet variation, use only 1/2 teaspoon salt.

VARIATIONS

To make a very light biscuit, use 1 cup all-purpose flour and 1 cup cake flour (not self-rising), such as Swan's Down brand.

Herb Biscuits: Add ¼ cup mixed fresh chopped herbs such as parsley and chives; or parsley and dill; or parsley, thyme, and chives to the dry ingredients and proceed with the recipe.

Bacon Biscuits: Add 1 recipe Lardons (*page 274*) to the dry ingredients and proceed with the recipe.

Sweet Biscuits: Add 2 tablespoons of sugar to the dry ingredients and proceed with the recipe. Dust the top lightly with sugar before baking.

note   *These biscuits can be made an hour or two ahead and frozen. Reheat the biscuits, wrapped in aluminum foil, in a 325° oven until they are warm.*

231

root vegetables and grains

Great Potato Pancakes

THE MOST MARVELOUS FRAGRANCE USED to waft from my German neighbors' apartment. I found out it was their potato pancakes, or *Reibekuchen*. One day, they brought some to me and were kind enough to teach me how to make them. Now my apartment is also graced with that wonderful aroma. These are fabulous served alongside stews of European origin.

232

makes 10 to 12

1 pound, about 3, medium potatoes, peeled
1 small onion
2 eggs, lightly beaten
3/4 teaspoon salt
pinch freshly grated nutmeg
1 to 2 tablespoons vegetable oil for frying

1 Into a colander set over a bowl, coarsely grate a little of the potato. Grate a little of the onion, then more potato. Continue until all the potato and onion are grated.

2 Using your hands, gently squeeze any excess liquid from the potato and onion and discard the liquid.

3 Put the potatoes in a medium bowl. Stir in the eggs, salt, and nutmeg.

4 Heat a medium nonstick skillet or griddle over medium-high heat. Add a little of the vegetable oil and let it get hot. Spoon a heaping tablespoon (about 1 1/2 tablespoons) of the potato batter into the skillet. You should be able to fit enough batter for 3 to 4 pancakes in a 10-inch skillet.

5 Fry the pancakes until their bottoms are lightly golden; with a spatula, flip the pancakes over. Fry the other side of each pancake until it is lightly golden. Transfer to a plate and cover to keep warm or place them on a baking sheet in a low oven (about 250°). Repeat until all the batter is used. Serve immediately.

note *These are best served immediately. However, in a pinch, you can reheat them in an oven or by quickly frying them again on both sides in a lightly greased hot skillet or griddle. You can use nonstick cooking spray in place of the vegetable oil.*

Creamy Potato Gratin

POTATO GRATIN COULD BE MY DOWNFALL. There are many renditions of this traditional potato dish: some with onions, some sprinkled with grated Parmesan, and Sweden's famous Jansson's Temptation in which a tin of chopped anchovies are added to the cream. I find this version—lightly scented with bay leaf and topped with Swiss or cheddar cheese—hard to resist.

serves 6

1 Preheat the oven to 350°. Lightly butter a shallow 2-quart baking dish.

2 In a small saucepan over medium heat, heat the cream with the bay leaf for about 3 minutes. Do not let the cream boil. Remove from the heat and let stand while preparing the rest of the recipe.

3 In a skillet over medium heat, melt the butter. Add the onion and cook, stirring occasionally, until it is tender and lightly golden, about 15 minutes. Season the onion with 1/4 teaspoon of the salt and a pinch of the pepper and set aside.

4 Arrange half of the potatoes in an overlapping layer in the prepared baking dish. Season them with half of the remaining salt and pepper. Place the onion on top of the potatoes. Arrange the remaining potatoes on top of the onion and season with the remaining salt and pepper.

5 Remove the bay leaf from the cream, and pour the cream over the potatoes. Evenly sprinkle the cheese on top. Bake until the cheese is browned and the potatoes are tender, about 50 minutes. Let stand for 5 minutes before serving.

3/4 cup cream or half and half
1 bay leaf
2 teaspoons butter
1 medium onion, thinly sliced
1 teaspoon salt
1/2 teaspoon freshly ground black pepper
1 1/4 pounds, about 3 to 4, medium potatoes, peeled and thinly sliced
2/3 cup grated Swiss or cheddar cheese

note *Leftovers can be reheated in a 325° oven, but cover the top loosely with aluminum foil.*

Oven-Roasted Red Potatoes with Rosemary

I LOVE THE SMELL OF THESE POTATOES when they are roasting. They are a fabulous alternative to boiled potatoes or French fries. Try to get potatoes that are of similar size. If some are larger, cut them so all the potato pieces are about equal; this way the cooking time will be the same.

serves 6

234

1 pound baby red potatoes, about 1 inch in diameter, halved

2 tablespoons extra virgin olive oil

2 teaspoons finely chopped fresh rosemary or crumbled dry rosemary

3/4 teaspoon salt

1/4 teaspoon freshly ground black pepper

1　Preheat the oven to 400°. With a paper towel dipped in some olive oil, lightly coat a heavy metal baking sheet or 15 × 10-inch metal roasting pan and set aside.

2　In a medium bowl, toss the potatoes with the extra virgin olive oil. Add the rosemary, salt, and pepper and toss to mix evenly.

3　Arrange the potatoes cut side down on the prepared baking tray. Bake until the potatoes are tender and lightly golden on the cut side, about 25 to 30 minutes. Turn the potatoes over and bake for 10 to 15 minutes longer.

note　*Although not ideal, these potatoes can be made a few hours before they are being served. The cooked potatoes should be covered loosely, kept at room temperature, and then reheated in a 200° to 250° oven until hot, about 10 to 15 minutes.*

Garlic & Herb Mashed Potatoes

EVER SINCE GARLIC MASHED POTATOES made a splash on the culinary scene a few years back, I can't seem to get enough of them. I've added some fresh herbs, which makes them even better.

serves 6

1 Put the potatoes in a large saucepan and cover with plenty of cold water. Place the pan over medium-high heat and boil the potatoes until they are quite tender and can be pierced easily with a paring knife, about 15 to 20 minutes. Drain well in a colander.

2 Meanwhile, in a small skillet over medium-low heat, melt the butter. Add the garlic and cook, stirring often, for 2 minutes. Do not let the garlic turn brown. Set aside.

3 Press the potatoes through a potato ricer or a food mill into a large bowl or place the potatoes in a large bowl and mash thoroughly with a potato masher. Add the garlic butter and as much of the warmed milk as necessary to form a smooth yet firm consistency. Stir in the basil and season with salt and pepper to taste.

note *Although mashed potatoes are best served when freshly made, they can be reheated successfully in a microwave or in a double boiler over gently simmering water. Add a little extra milk if they are too stiff when reheating.*

2 pounds medium potatoes, about 5 to 6, peeled and cut into chunks

2 tablespoons butter

3 plump cloves garlic, minced

1/2 to 3/4 cup milk, heated

2 1/2 tablespoons chopped fresh basil or chives

salt and pepper to taste

235

Mashed Potatoes with Cucumber

CUCUMBERS ADD A SUBTLE, gentle flavor to these mashed potatoes. They are a marvelous companion to stews and roasts that have a rich gravy. This recipe can easily be doubled.

serves 4 to 6

236

1 pound medium potatoes, about 3, peeled and cut into chunks

2 1/2 tablespoons butter

1 medium cucumber, peeled, seeded, and coarsely chopped, about 1 cup

1/3 to 1/2 cup milk, heated

3/4 teaspoon salt

1/8 teaspoon white pepper

1 Put the potatoes in a large saucepan and cover them with plenty of cold water. Place the pan over medium-high heat and boil the potatoes until they are quite tender and can be pierced easily with a paring knife, about 15 to 20 minutes. Drain well in a colander.

2 Meanwhile, in a medium skillet over medium-low heat, melt 1 1/2 tablespoons of the butter. Add the cucumber and cook, stirring occasionally, until tender, about 10 minutes. Transfer the cooked cucumber to a food processor fitted with the metal blade. Add 1 tablespoon of the warmed milk. Pulse until a puree forms.

3 Press the potatoes through a potato ricer or a food mill into a large bowl or place the potatoes in a large bowl and mash thoroughly with a potato masher. Add the cucumber puree, the remaining tablespoon of butter and as much of the warmed milk as necessary to form a smooth yet firm consistency. Season with salt and pepper.

note *Although mashed potatoes are best served when freshly made, they can be reheated successfully in a microwave or in a double boiler over gently simmering water. Add a little extra milk if they are too stiff when reheating.*

Spiced Mashed Sweet Potatoes

THE ORDINARY SWEET POTATO becomes special with a bit of fresh ginger and vanilla. Many people, myself included, like side dishes that can be prepared in advance, and this one fits the bill.

serves 6

1   Preheat the oven to 400°. Bake the sweet potatoes for 50 to 60 minutes or until the potatoes are cooked through and can be pierced easily with a paring knife.

2   Scoop the pulp out of the potatoes and discard the skins. Press the sweet potato pulp through a potato ricer or a food mill into a large bowl or place the flesh in a large bowl and mash it thoroughly with a potato masher.

3   Add the butter, milk, ginger, vanilla bean, and salt. Stir until smooth.

note   *These can be made ahead and placed in a baking dish, covered with aluminum foil, and reheated in a 350° oven until hot, about 15 to 25 minutes; or they can be reheated in a double boiler or a microwave.*

2^1/2 pounds sweet potatoes

3 tablespoons butter

^{1}/3 to ^{1}/2 cup milk, heated

1-inch piece fresh ginger, peeled and finely grated

^{1}/4 of a vanilla bean, split and seeds scraped out (optional)

^{3}/4 teaspoon salt

237

Mashed Turnips & Apples

THE TURNIP ENTHUSIASTS IN MY FAMILY begged me not to remove turnips from the Thanksgiving menu. I created this dish for them. On their own, turnips can have quite a sharp taste, but when subdued by apples, they become sweeter and more delicate.

serves 6

238

1 pound white turnips, peeled and cut into cubes

2 teaspoons butter

2 MacIntosh apples, peeled, cored, and chopped

1 teaspoon sugar

pinch of cinnamon or freshly grated nutmeg

3/4 teaspoon salt

3 tablespoons cream or half and half, heated (optional)

1 Put the turnips in a large saucepan and cover them with plenty of cold water. Over medium-high heat, bring the water to a boil and boil them for 10 to 15 minutes or until they are very tender and can be pierced easily with a fork. Drain well in a colander.

2 Meanwhile, in a small skillet over medium heat, melt the butter. Add the apples, sugar, and cinnamon and cook, stirring occasionally, until the apples are very tender.

3 In a food processor or blender fitted with the metal blade, combine the turnips and apples. Pulse until a smooth puree forms.

4 Transfer the puree to a bowl, and season with salt. Stir in the half and half.

note *This is a good make-ahead dish. Place the puree in an ovenproof serving dish, season with salt, and stir in the cream. Cover with plastic wrap and refrigerate for up to 2 days before serving. To reheat, cover with aluminum foil and bake in a 350° oven until heated through, about 15 to 20 minutes, or place the puree in a microwave dish and follow your microwave's instructions for reheating.*

Lemon or Orange Couscous

CITRUS ZEST ENLIVENS THIS OTHERWISE MILD GRAIN, a form of semolina. This recipe, which takes only about 5 minutes to make, can be easily doubled or cut in half. Use any leftovers in a cold grain-and-vegetable salad the following day.

serves 6

239

In a medium bowl, combine the couscous and salt. Pour the boiling water over the couscous. Add the butter and stir briefly. Let the mixture stand for 5 minutes. With a fork, stir in the grated zest. Fluff with a fork and serve.

VARIATION
Top with Spiced Nuts using slivered almonds (*page* 273), or stir in a few toasted sliced almonds or currants.

1 cup instant couscous
$^1/_2$ teaspoon salt
1 cup boiling water or chicken broth
1 teaspoon butter
2 teaspoons finely grated fresh lemon or orange zest

Basic Polenta & Variations

POLENTA, ONCE UNPRETENTIOUS FARE that graced the tables of Italy, crossed the Atlantic and landed on menus of some of America's best restaurants. This simple dish, which can be dressed up with herbs or mushrooms, is a fine accompaniment to many stews.

serves 6

4¹/2 to 5¹/2 cups boiling water
1 teaspoon salt
1¹/2 cups polenta

1 In a large saucepan over medium-high heat, bring 4¹/2 cups of water and salt to a boil. In a gradual but steady stream, pour the polenta into the center of the pot while stirring constantly with a wooden spoon to prevent lumps from forming. For softer polenta, use more water.

2 Reduce the heat to medium to keep a gentle boil. Cook, stirring frequently, for about 30 to 35 minutes until the polenta begins to pull away from the sides of the pan and is very thick. Serve immediately or follow instructions for Polenta Squares.

VARIATIONS

Herbed Polenta: In step 2, add 2 tablespoons each of chopped fresh basil, flat-leaf parsley, and chives to the polenta after it has cooked for about 25 minutes. Stir well to mix evenly.

Mushroom Polenta: In step 2, add ¹/2 pound sliced mushrooms that have been cooked in a little butter or olive oil. Stir well to mix evenly.

Make-Ahead Polenta Squares: With olive oil, lightly oil a 10 × 15 × 2-inch jelly roll pan or cookie sheet and set it aside. Prepare the polenta as directed. When the polenta has finished cooking, pour it onto the prepared pan. Using a moistened rubber or icing spatula, spread it in an even layer, about $1/2$ inch thick. Let the polenta cool at room temperature. When it is cool and firm, cut it into 2 to 3-inch squares and set aside. To serve as a side dish, heat a medium or large skillet or grill skillet over medium heat, and lightly coat the pan with a little olive oil. Working in batches, fry the polenta, turning the squares until they are lightly browned on top and bottom.

Basic Risotto & Variations

RISOTTO, THE CLASSIC ITALIAN PREPARATION, is an elegant complement to stews and grilled or roasted meat; it also works well on its own as a starter. I've also turned a batch of this, served with salad and dessert, into a light meal for 3 to 4 people.

Authentic risotto takes time and patience; in my opinion, the result is well worth the effort. See the note below to find out how to cheat a little by preparing it partially in advance, just as many restaurants do.

serves 6

2 tablespoons olive oil
1 teaspoon butter
1 small onion, finely diced
1 1/2 cups arborio rice
2 tablespoons dry white wine or vermouth
5 to 6 cups chicken broth, heated
3/4 teaspoon salt
freshly ground black pepper to taste

1 In a medium saucepan over medium heat, heat the olive oil and the butter. Add the onion and cook, stirring occasionally, until the onion begins to soften, about 3 to 5 minutes.

2 Add the arborio rice and stir constantly so that the grains are completely coated with the olive oil and butter mixture. Add the wine and cook, stirring occasionally, until the wine is absorbed completely.

3 Add one cup of the heated broth and cook, stirring often. When the broth is almost completely absorbed by the rice, gradually add more broth, 1 cup at a time. Cook after each addition, stirring often, until the rice has almost absorbed the liquid. The risotto is finished when the rice is tender but still firm and the liquid has been absorbed. It should have a creamy texture. This should take between 20 to 25 minutes in total. Add the salt and pepper and serve.

VARIATIONS

Parmesan Herb: When the risotto is finished, add 2 tablespoons chopped fresh flat-leaf parsley or 1 tablespoon finely minced basil. Do not season the risotto with the salt and pepper, but stir in 1/3 cup freshly grated Parmesan cheese.

Saffron: When the final addition of broth is almost absorbed, stir in 1/2 to 1 teaspoon saffron threads. Then season the risotto with the salt and pepper.

Wild Mushroom: Place 1 ounce dried porcini in a small bowl and pour 1 cup boiling water over them. Let stand for 20 to 30 minutes. Pour the liquid through a strainer lined with a paper coffee filter, and reserve. Rinse the porcini with a little bit of water to remove any lingering grit, and gently squeeze them dry. Chop them or use a scissors to cut them into small pieces. Set aside. Add the reconstituted mushrooms and reserved mushroom liquid during the final addition of broth, after the risotto has been cooking about 18 to 20 minutes. (Use a little less chicken broth.)

note To prepare risotto ahead of time, follow the recipe and cook the risotto three quarters of the way through, about 13 minutes. Reserve the broth that hasn't been used. The rice should still be somewhat firm, only slightly tender. Spread the risotto in a thin, even layer on a baking sheet or in a large flat baking dish. Chill it in the refrigerator. Once it is chilled, you can cover it with plastic wrap. It will keep for at least a day if covered.

To finish cooking the risotto, heat the reserved broth plus 1 to 1 1/2 cups extra in case you need it. In a large saucepan over medium heat, melt 1 tablespoon of olive oil. Add the risotto and cook for 1 minute, stirring constantly. Gradually add the broth, 1/2 cup at a time, and cook, stirring constantly. When the broth is almost completely absorbed by the rice, add more broth, 1/2 cup at a time. The risotto is finished when the rice is tender, but still firm and the liquid has been absorbed. This should take about 5 to 7 minutes.

243

Spiced Rice & Variations

THIS WONDERFULLY AROMATIC AND FLAVORFUL RICE is a pleasing support to curries and other spiced stews from the Caribbean, India, Indonesia, Malaysia, and South Africa. It is also good with grilled, baked, or sautéed fish and poultry.

serves 6

1 1/2 tablespoons vegetable oil

2 medium onions, quartered and thinly sliced

2 cinnamon sticks

4 cardamom pods

4 cloves

2 allspice berries

1 1/2 cups basmati or long-grain white rice

3 1/2 to 4 cups water

1 In a medium saucepan over medium heat, heat the vegetable oil. Add the onions, cinnamon sticks, cardamom pods, cloves, and allspice berries. Cook, stirring occasionally, until the onions are tender and lightly golden, about 15 minutes.

2 Add the rice and cook, stirring constantly, for 1 to 2 minutes. Add 3 1/2 cups of the water. Cover the pot and cook for 20 to 25 minutes. Once the water comes to a boil, reduce the heat slightly so the water is gently bubbling, not rolling. If the water boils out before the rice is tender, add a little extra water. Before serving, remove the whole spices, if desired.

VARIATIONS

Yellow Spiced Rice: Add ³/₄ teaspoon turmeric or a pinch of saffron after adding the water to the rice in step 2.

Yellow Spiced Rice Variation: After adding the turmeric to the water, add ¹/₃ cup raisins, sliced almonds, or grated coconut. Do not add coconut if you are serving the rice with a dish prepared with coconut milk.

245

salads

Rujak

THIS UNIQUE, SOMEWHAT EXOTIC Indonesian fruit salad is marvelous paired with spiced stews like those with a Southeast Asian, Malaysian, or Indonesian flair. It also goes well with grilled fish, meat, or poultry.

Choose mangos and pears that are not fully ripe so that they don't disintegrate. Make this salad up to half an hour before serving. If you can't get some of the fruit, substitute more of other fruit in the recipe.

serves 6 to 8

Salad

1 large or 2 small ruby red or pink grapefruit, peeled and sectioned*

1 underripe mango, diced

4 ounces jicama, peeled and diced, or 1 pear, peeled, cored, and diced

1 slightly underripe medium pineapple, peeled, cored, and diced

1/2 European seedless cucumber, peeled and diced

1 Granny Smith apple, peeled, cored, and diced

2 tablespoons fresh chopped mint

Dressing

1 1/2 tablespoons fresh lime juice

1/2 cup brown sugar

1/4 teaspoon salt

1/4 to 1/2 teaspoon cayenne, to taste

1/2 to 1 tablespoon warm water, if necessary

1 In a medium bowl, combine the grapefruit, mango, jicama, pineapple, cucumber and apple and set aside.

2 *To prepare the dressing:* In a small bowl, mash together the lime juice, brown sugar, salt, and cayenne using the back of a soup spoon. Stir in as much of the warm water as necessary to form a very thick, syrupy liquid.

3 Add the dressing to the fruit and stir to mix well. Stir in the mint before serving.

*To section a grapefruit: Slice a thin piece off the top and bottom so the flesh is exposed. Place the grapefruit, one cut side down, on a cutting board, and use a sharp paring knife to cut off the rind, following the curvature of the fruit. Remove the membrane, and then cut between each section with the paring knife to remove the sections.

Roasted Beet & Onion Salad on Watercress

ROASTING IS A SUPERB TECHNIQUE that concentrates and enhances the natural sweetness of beets and onions. Together, they make an extraordinary salad, offset by tender but strongly flavored greens.

serves 6

247

1　Preheat the oven to 400°. Lightly coat the beets and onions in olive oil and season with salt. Place them in a single layer on a baking sheet. Bake for 30 minutes, then turn them over.

2　Continue baking for a total baking time of about 1 hour, until the beets are tender and can be pierced easily with a paring knife. There should be no resistance. The onions should be easily pierced with a paring knife and be lightly golden in color. Because the sizes of beets and onions vary, check the vegetables after 40 minutes. Remove those that are cooked and continue cooking those that are still a bit hard.

3　Meanwhile, prepare the dressing. In a small bowl, whisk together the vinegar, salt, and pepper. Slowly whisk in the olive oil. Set aside.

4　When the beets are cool enough to handle, peel off the skin with a sharp paring knife. It should slip off easily if they are cooked through. Quarter or thinly slice the beets and the onions.

5　In a medium bowl, combine the beets, onions, parsley, mint, and dressing, tossing well until the vegetables are evenly coated. Serve on a bed of watercress or arugula.

Salad

1 pound medium beets

$1/2$ pound medium onions, peeled

1 tablespoon olive oil

$1/2$ teaspoon salt

1 tablespoon chopped fresh parsley or chives

1 tablespoon chopped fresh mint or basil

1 large bunch watercress or arugula, long stems trimmed

Dressing

3 tablespoons balsamic or red wine vinegar

$1/2$ teaspoon salt

freshly ground black pepper to taste

1 tablespoon extra virgin olive oil

Jicama Mango Salad

JICAMA, ALSO KNOWN AS YAM BEAN, is a delightfully crisp tuber with a mild but sweet taste. Long popular in Mexico as well as parts of Asia and the South Pacific, it is now available in many American supermarkets and specialty produce stores.

serves 6 to 8

248

1/4 cup fresh orange juice

1 tablespoon fresh lime juice

1/2 teaspoon salt

1 small (about 1 pound) jicama, peeled and cut into thin strips

3 radishes, cut into thin strips

1 1/2 tablespoons peanut or canola oil

1 mango, diced

1 bunch watercress, washed and trimmed

pinch of cayenne

chopped fresh cilantro

1 In a medium bowl, combine the orange juice, lime juice, salt, jicama, and radishes. Let the mixture stand at room temperature for 30 minutes. Strain and reserve the juice from the jicama and radishes.

2 *To prepare the dressing:* In a small bowl, whisk the peanut oil into the reserved juice.

3 In the medium bowl, combine the jicama, radishes, mango, and watercress. Add the dressing and toss gently. Garnish with cayenne and chopped fresh cilantro.

VARIATION

For *Jicama Orange Salad,* substitute diced fresh orange segments*, membranes removed, from 2 small oranges for the mango.

*To section an orange: Slice a thin piece off the top and bottom so the flesh is exposed. Place the orange, one cut side down, on a cutting board. With a sharp paring knife, cut off the rind, following the curvature of the fruit. Remove the membrane, and then cut between each section with the paring knife to remove the sections.

Sugar Snap Peas with Orange & Herbs

THIS SPLENDID SALAD IS CRISP, refreshing, and sweet. To add color, I like to garnish it with a few fresh berries when they are in season. If you can't find sugar snap peas, substitute snow peas.

serves 6

1 Have a medium bowl of ice cold water ready. In a large saucepan of lightly salted boiling water, cook the peas until tender but still crisp, about 1 to 1½ minutes. Drain the peas in a colander and immediately plunge them into the ice cold water to stop the cooking process. When they are cold, drain them well and put them in a salad bowl.

2 In a small bowl, combine the orange juice, orange zest, salt, pepper, and olive oil.

3 Pour the orange dressing and parsley or mint over the sugar snap peas and toss. Garnish each portion with the berries before serving. Do not toss with the berries or they will break.

VARIATION
Replace the raspberries with ¼ cup Spiced Nuts using slivered almonds (*page 273*).

1⅓ pounds sugar snap or snow peas, ends cut off and strings removed

⅓ cup freshly squeezed orange juice

1 teaspoon finely grated fresh orange zest

½ teaspoon salt

¼ teaspoon freshly ground black pepper

3 tablespoons olive oil

1 tablespoon chopped fresh flat-leaf parsley or mint leaves

½ cup fresh blackberries or raspberries for garnish, optional

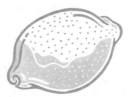

Tomato & Sautéed Mushroom Salad

FLAVORFUL AND LIGHT, this is an appetizing alternative to a green or tossed salad. It can be served either as a starter or alongside the main course.

serves 6

Dressing

2 tablespoons red wine vinegar

1 plump clove garlic, minced

¹/₂ teaspoon salt

¹/₄ teaspoon freshly ground black pepper

4 tablespoons extra virgin olive oil

Salad

1 tablespoon olive oil

¹/₄ pound shiitake, cremini, or white mushrooms, sliced

¹/₄ teaspoon salt

2 tablespoons chopped fresh flat-leaf parsley

3 to 4 ripe medium tomatoes, cored and cut into wedges

2 scallions, white and green part, thinly sliced

1 To prepare the dressing: In a small bowl, combine the vinegar, garlic, salt, and pepper. Slowly whisk in the olive oil and set aside.

2 In a medium skillet over medium heat, heat the olive oil. Add the mushrooms and cook, stirring occasionally, until the mushrooms are cooked through, about 3 to 4 minutes. Add the salt and parsley. Whisk the dressing lightly with a fork to mix it evenly, then add half of the dressing to the mushrooms and toss. Set aside.

3 In a medium bowl, toss the tomatoes in the remaining half of the dressing. Arrange the tomatoes on salad plates. Top with the mushrooms. Garnish with sliced scallions.

Warm Greens

COOKED GREENS ARE A FAVORITE in the American South, the Caribbean, and Africa. These sharp greens, packed with vitamins, are terrific when served with Hot Pepper Vinegar or a few dashes of Tabasco. Southerners, who like their greens well-done, will probably want to cook the greens longer than I do here. If you find these greens too strong or bitter for your taste, substitute spinach or escarole and cook in a small amount of water until just tender.

251

serves 6

/ Remove any tough stems from the greens, then wash them well in several changes of water. Chop the greens coarsely into strips.

2 In a large stewpot over medium-high heat, combine the greens, onion, sugar, and as much water as necessary to barely cover the greens. When the water comes to a boil, reduce the heat to medium-low. Partially cover the pot and cook, adding additional water as necessary, until the greens are tender, about 30 minutes. Cook them longer if you prefer them very soft.

3 Season with salt and serve warm with Hot Pepper Vinegar on the side.

3 pounds collard, turnip, or mustard greens, or kale
1 large Spanish onion, thinly sliced
2 tablespoons sugar
1/2 teaspoon salt
Hot Pepper Vinegar (page 271)

Herbed Vegetable Slaw

GARDENS ALWAYS SEEM TO PRODUCE too much summer squash—both yellow and zucchini. We used to plant them every year and hope that some of the plants would die. They always flourished. In an effort to figure out new ways to use the abundant crop, this light and tasty slaw was born.

252

serves 6

Dressing
2¹/₂ tablespoons white wine vinegar
¹/₄ teaspoon Dijon mustard
³/₄ teaspoon salt
¹/₄ teaspoon freshly ground pepper
6 tablespoons extra virgin olive oil

Salad
1 medium red bell pepper, sliced into very thin strips
2 medium zucchini, shredded
2 medium yellow squash, shredded
1 large carrot, shredded
1 medium onion, cut in half and thinly sliced
2 medium tomatoes, seeded and diced
2 tablespoons chopped fresh basil
2 tablespoons chopped fresh flat-leaf parsley
1 tablespoon chopped fresh tarragon or chives

1 To prepare the dressing: In a small bowl, whisk together the vinegar, mustard, salt, and pepper. Slowly whisk in the olive oil and set aside.

2 To prepare the salad: In a salad bowl, toss together the red bell pepper, zucchini, yellow squash, carrot, onion, tomatoes, basil, parsley, and tarragon.

3 Pour the dressing over the vegetables and refrigerate for at least 1 hour before serving.

VARIATION
In step 2, add ¹/₃ cup chopped, pitted, imported black olives, such as Nicoise, oil-cured, or Calamata.

note This salad can be made up to a day ahead and refrigerated.

Colorful Crunchy Slaw

THIS VERSATILE SLAW COMPLEMENTS the food of many nations with minor adjustments or substitutions. If you are making an Asian or Mexican dish, use the peanuts, substitute diced papaya or mango for the currants, and substitute chopped cilantro for the parsley. For a Mediterranean, Northern European, or American dish, use the currants and walnuts.

serves 6 to 8

253

1 In a large bowl, combine the red and green cabbage, carrots, scallions, currants, and nuts.

2 In a small bowl, whisk together with a fork the vinegar, sugar, salt, pepper, and peanut oil.

3 Pour the dressing over the cabbage mixture. Stir in the herbs and refrigerate for at least 1 hour before serving.

note *If you have the time, make this slaw up to a day ahead and refrigerate it to let the flavors develop fully.*

2 cups shredded red cabbage, about $1/2$ pound

2 cups shredded green cabbage, about $1/2$ pound

2 medium carrots, grated

5 to 6 scallions, white and green part, thinly sliced

$1/2$ cup currants or raisins

$1/2$ cup chopped walnuts or peanuts

$1/2$ cup raspberry, blackberry, or red wine vinegar

3 tablespoons sugar

$1 1/4$ teaspoons salt

$1/2$ teaspoon freshly ground black pepper

$1/3$ cup walnut or peanut oil

3 tablespoons chopped flat-leaf parsley

2 tablespoons chopped chives

Spicy Green Bean Sambal

I LOVE THIS SALAD. It's tangy, lively, and light. It harmonizes with many curries and stews from Southeast Asia, Indonesia, Malaysia, the Caribbean, South America, and South Africa. It is also a perfect sidekick to grilled chicken, meat, and fish. If you like it hot, use the larger amount of *sambal ulek.*

254

serves 6

1 pound green beans, sliced on an angle

3 scallions, white and green part, thinly sliced

2 cloves garlic, minced

1 1/2 tablespoons lime juice

1 1/2 tablespoons peanut or vegetable oil

2 cloves garlic, minced

1/2 to 1 teaspoon *sambal ulek* (page 276) or 1/2 teaspoon crushed red pepper flakes

2 tablespoons chopped fresh cilantro

2 tablespoons chopped fresh mint or parsley

1/2 teaspoon salt

1   Have a medium bowl of ice water ready. In a large saucepan over high heat, cook the green beans in plenty of lightly salted boiling water until they are tender but still crisp, about 5 minutes. Drain the beans in a colander and immediately plunge them into the ice water to stop the cooking. When they are cool, transfer the beans to a medium bowl.

2   Add the scallions, garlic, lime juice, peanut oil, garlic, sambal ulek, cilantro, mint, and salt. Toss to mix well and serve.

VARIATION
Garnish with chopped peanuts or toasted sesame seeds.

note   This salad can be made up to 4 hours ahead and refrigerated.

Lemony Asparagus or Green Beans with Nuts

FRESH ASPARAGUS USED TO BE AVAILABLE for such a short time in the spring that it was something to look forward to and savor. Although it now can be purchased almost year 'round, it can be very costly out of season, and is not always as flavorful. Consequently, in the off-season, I prefer to substitute green beans. Either vegetable can be cooked ahead, held in the refrigerator, and tossed with the dressing just before serving.

serves 6

1   *To prepare the dressing:* In a small bowl, combine the lemon juice, salt, pepper, and lemon zest. Slowly whisk in the olive oil and set aside.

2   Have a medium bowl of ice water ready. Bring a shallow skillet of lightly salted water to a boil, and add the asparagus or green beans. Cook until tender, about 5 minutes. Drain the vegetables in a colander, and then immediately plunge them into the ice water to stop the cooking. When cool, remove the vegetables from the ice water and set aside.

3   In a large shallow bowl, toss the asparagus or green beans with the dressing. Serve garnished with chopped nuts and parsley.

Dressing

1 1/2 tablespoons fresh lemon juice

1/2 teaspoon salt

1/4 teaspoon freshly ground black pepper

2 teaspoons freshly grated lemon zest

4 to 5 tablespoons hazelnut, walnut, or olive oil,* depending on the sharpness of the lemon juice

Salad

1 pound fresh asparagus, preferably thin stalks, washed

and ends trimmed, or green beans, sliced on an angle

1/4 cup chopped hazelnuts or walnuts, preferably toasted

2 tablespoons chopped fresh flat-leaf parsley

*Use hazelnut oil if garnishing with hazelnuts or walnut oil if garnishing with walnuts. Extra virgin olive oil can be used with either nut.

Carrot Orange Sambal

A SAMBAL IS AN ACCOMPANIMENT served throughout Indonesia, Malaysia, and South Africa. It is a refreshing and tangy side dish for spicy food. Similarly prepared salads are found in Northern Africa. The rules for making a sambal are simple: shred, grate, or thinly slice the vegetable, quickly marinate it in an acidic liquid such as citrus juice or vinegar, and season it. It is quite acceptable to add one finely minced, seeded jalapeno or serrano if you want to create a sambal with its own balance of cool and hot.

serves 6

5 to 6 medium carrots, peeled and shredded, about 2 1/2 cups

3 tablespoons fresh lemon juice

3 tablespoons fresh orange juice

1 1/2 tablespoons sugar

1/2 teaspoon salt

1 large navel orange, membranes removed, cut into sections and coarsely diced*

2 tablespoons chopped fresh cilantro

pinch of ground coriander, preferably freshly ground

Place the carrots, lemon juice, orange juice, sugar, and salt in a small bowl; stir to mix thoroughly. Stir in the orange and cilantro. Let the mixture stand at room temperature for 30 minutes. Before serving sprinkle on the ground coriander.

*To section an orange: Slice a thin piece off the top and bottom so the flesh is exposed. Place the orange, one cut side down, on a cutting board. With a sharp paring knife, cut off the rind, following the curvature of the fruit. Remove the membrane, and then cut between each section with the paring knife to remove the sections.

Raita

I'VE EATEN THIS INDIAN ACCOMPANIMENT for years. It is the perfect complement to curries. I've seen it made with the cucumbers sliced, diced, or shredded—so do what suits you best. I've also eaten a few different versions; thus, the variation section below. Make this salad a few hours ahead and refrigerate it so the ingredients have time to blend.

In a medium bowl, combine the cucumbers, yogurt, and salt. Add one of the flavor boosting variations and serve chilled.

VARIATIONS
Feel free to combine these by adding herbs to the garlic version.

Mint or Cilantro: 1 tablespoon minced fresh mint or cilantro, 1 tablespoon fresh lemon juice, pinch of cayenne or ground cumin

Garlic: 1 tablespoon fresh lemon juice, 1 to 2 plump cloves garlic, minced, to your taste

257

Basic Raita

1 European or English cucumber, peeled and thinly sliced or diced into 1/2-inch cubes or shredded

1 1/2 cups plain low-fat yogurt

1/2 teaspoon salt or to taste

Pickled Cucumber Salad

CUCUMBERS ARE ONE OF THE MOST VERSATILE, frequently used salad ingredients. With simple modifications, cucumber salads adorn the tables of many nations, providing a refreshing balance to both savory and spicy dishes. Use either version as indicated in the menu suggestion.

serves 6

258

Basic Recipe

1 large European or English cucumber, peeled (See Variations for preparation.)

1/3 cup white wine, or cider or rice wine vinegar

2 tablespoons water

1 to 2 tablespoons sugar, to taste

1/2 teaspoon salt

In a medium bowl, combine the cucumber, vinegar, water, sugar, and salt. Add the flavorings for either savory or spicy dishes. Stir thoroughly. Refrigerate until serving.

VARIATIONS

For mild savory dishes: Thinly slice the cucumber and add 1 1/2 tablespoons chopped fresh parsley or dill and 1 tablespoon chopped fresh chives.

For spicy dishes such as curries and chili: Coarsely grate or thinly slice the cucumber and add 2 to 3 tablespoons chopped fresh cilantro or mint and 1 jalapeno or serrano, seeded and minced (optional).

note   This can be made up to 1 day ahead and refrigerated.

Pickled Beets

PICKLED BEETS ARE EATEN AROUND THE WORLD—Scandinavia, Germany, Russia, Eastern Europe, the United Kingdom, South Africa, and the United States, to name a few places. They are a perfect partner to many stews.

serves 6

259

1 Place the beets in a saucepan of cold water. Bring to boil and cook until tender. Drain them in a colander. Let the beets sit until they are cool enough to handle, then peel them.

2 Slice the beets thinly. In a medium mixing bowl, layer the beets and onion.

3 In a measuring cup combine the vinegar, sugar, salt, and pepper. Pour the vinegar mixture over the beets and onions. Cover and chill until ready to serve.

VARIATION
If serving alongside spiced dishes, you might want to add 1 jalapeno or serrano, seeded and minced, to the vinegar mixture in step 3.

note This can be made up to 2 days ahead and refrigerated. It is best if it is made at least 4 hours ahead.

10 ounces small beets, trimmed
1 small onion, sliced thinly
$1/2$ cup cider vinegar
$1 1/2$ tablespoons sugar
$1/4$ teaspoon salt
$1/8$ teaspoon freshly ground black pepper

Avocado Salad

AVOCADOS, LIKE CHILI PEPPERS, mangoes, and papayas, have found permanent homes in several warm weather regions—Southeast Asia and the Pacific, South Africa, South America, the Caribbean, Mexico, Florida, and California. Salads featuring avocados are adaptable to the cuisine of the nations in which they grow.

260

serves 6

2 ripe avocados, diced

1 tablespoon lime or lemon juice

3 scallions, white and green part, thinly sliced

3 ripe tomatoes, diced

2 tablespoons chopped fresh cilantro or parsley

$^1/_2$ teaspoon salt

$^1/_4$ teaspoon freshly ground black pepper

$^1/_4$ teaspoon or more cayenne, to taste (optional)

1 In a medium bowl, toss the diced avocado with the lime juice.

2 Add the scallions, tomatoes, cilantro, salt, pepper, and cayenne. Stir thoroughly but gently, and serve.

VARIATIONS

Avocado Corn Salad: Add $^3/_4$ cup chilled cooked corn kernels in step 2.

Avocado Olive Salad: Add $^1/_2$ cup chopped pitted black olives in step 2.

note *Even when the avocado is tossed with lime juice, it can still discolor slightly. Add the avocado pit to the bowl to help prevent the salad from discoloring too much if making the salad more than a few minutes in advance.*

Cucumber Tomato Salsa

THIS SIMPLE, VERSATILE SALSA can be made several hours ahead and goes with many Mexican, American, South American, Caribbean, South African, and Indonesian dishes.

serves 6

At least 1 hour before serving, combine in a medium bowl the cucumber, scallions, bell pepper, tomatoes, salt, black pepper, and cilantro. Stir to mix well. Cover and refrigerate until serving.

VARIATION
Hot and Spicy: Add 1 plump clove garlic, chopped; and 1 jalapeno or serrano, seeded and minced.

note *This can be made up to several hours ahead and refrigerated.*

1 European or English cucumber, peeled and diced

4 scallions, white and green part, thinly sliced

1 medium bell pepper (green, red, yellow or orange), diced

3 to 4 plum tomatoes, seeded and diced

1/2 teaspoon salt

1/4 teaspoon freshly ground black pepper

1 1/2 tablespoon chopped fresh cilantro, basil or flat-leaf parsley

261

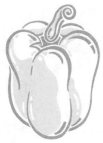

Mesclun Salad with Goat Cheese

MESCLUN, A MIXTURE OF BABY LETTUCES, is comparatively expensive, but the marvelous salad that results is worth the price. Once relatively unknown in this country, this special salad of Provence, was made popular by Alice Waters of Chez Panisse in Berkeley, California.

serves 6

7 cups mesclun or baby lettuce mix (about 6 generous handfuls)

1 medium Belgian endive, thinly sliced

6 red or yellow cherry tomatoes, halved

Basic Vinaigrette using raspberry or balsamic vinegar, garlic, and minced herbs such as fresh chives, tarragon, or basil (page 266)

1 small log plain or herbed goat cheese or chevre, sliced into 6 pieces

Lardons (page 274) or Crispy Shallots (page 272) for garnish, optional

1 In a salad bowl, combine the mesclun, endive, and tomatoes. Add enough of the dressing to coat the salad lightly and toss gently to mix. Do not overdress. Save any extra dressing for another use.

2 Arrange the salad on chilled salad plates and put 1 piece of goat cheese on each. Garnish with Lardons or Crispy Shallots, if desired.

Make-Ahead Herbed Garden Salad

SOMETIMES YOU NEED TO PREPARE everything in advance. What a relief it was for me to make this tasty herb-laced salad, pull it from the fridge, and take it to a neighbor's potluck with only a few finishing touches. Toss the greens with the dressing right before serving.

serves 6

1 *To prepare the dressing:* In a small bowl, combine the orange juice, vinegar, garlic, salt, and pepper. Slowly whisk in the olive oil. Cover and set aside at room temperature.

2 *To prepare the salad:* In a large salad bowl, layer the torn lettuces, watercress, and endive. Put the herbs on top of the greens. Do not toss, but cover the bowl with plastic wrap and refrigerate for up to 6 hours.

3 Just before serving, add the tomatoes to the salad. Peel and chop the avocado and add it to the salad. Add the dressing and toss well to combine.

Dressing
- 2 tablespoons fresh orange juice
- 1 tablespoon red wine or balsamic vinegar
- 1 clove garlic, minced
- 1/2 teaspoon salt
- 1/4 teaspoon freshly ground black pepper
- 5 to 6 tablespoons olive oil

Salad
- 1 small head red leaf lettuce, washed, dried, and torn into pieces, about 2 1/2 cups
- 1 small head Boston lettuce, washed, dried, and torn into pieces, about 2 1/2 cups
- 1 small bunch watercress, stems discarded, about 1 1/2 cups
- 6 leaves, Belgian endive, sliced
- 2 tablespoons chopped fresh chives
- 2 tablespoons chopped fresh flat-leaf parsley leaves
- 2 tablespoons chopped fresh basil leaves or mint leaves
- 1 tablespoon chopped fresh thyme or lemon thyme leaves
- 12 red or yellow cherry tomatoes, halved
- 1 medium avocado, optional

A Good & Simple Salad

I ADORE THE CRISPNESS and character of Romaine lettuce and think it is at its best when tossed in a lemony-garlic dressing with a hint of Parmesan. This salad is really a no-egg, no-anchovy Caesar salad that both kids and adults will enjoy.

serves 4 to 6

264

Dressing

2 tablespoons fresh lemon juice

1/2 teaspoon Dijon mustard

1 to 2 plump cloves garlic, minced or put through a garlic press

1/4 teaspoon salt

1/8 teaspoon freshly ground black pepper

2 1/2 tablespoons freshly grated Parmesan or Romano cheese

6 to 7 tablespoons extra virgin olive oil, depending on the sharpness of the lemon juice

Salad

1 medium head Romaine lettuce, washed, dried, and torn in small pieces, about 7 cups

generous handful of croutons, preferably freshly made, optional

1 or 2 very ripe tomatoes, sliced, diced, or quartered, optional

Lardons (page 274), optional

Crispy Shallots (page 272) for garnish

freshly ground black pepper

1 To prepare the dressing: Place the lemon juice, mustard, garlic, salt, pepper, Parmesan, and olive oil in the jar of a blender. Process until smooth. (This will take only a few seconds.) The dressing can also be whisked together in a small bowl. Transfer the dressing to another container.

2 Dip a piece of the lettuce in the dressing and taste for salt. Sometimes the cheese is very salty, although you may want to add salt. If the dressing is too acidic—some lemons can be more acidic than others—whisk in a little extra olive oil.

3 To prepare the salad: Place the lettuce in a salad bowl and add optional ingredients, if desired. Toss with enough of the dressing to coat the lettuce lightly. Do not overdress the salad.

Garnish with Crispy Shallots, if using. Shake on pepper when serving.

note The dressing will not keep, as fresh lemon juice goes "off" if refrigerated overnight.

Arugula Salad

MY DAD USED TO GROW PLENTY of arugula in his garden, so I fortunately was able to eat it often. This recipe is not new, but is a tried-and-true Italian salad that has found a home on many American tables. The strong greens offset by the sweet oranges are always sensational. If you wish, substitute wedges of the ripest summer tomatoes for the oranges. The size of arugula bunches sold in stores can vary quite a bit; judge the amount by eye so that each person will have a generous serving.

265

s e r v e s   6

In a salad bowl, combine the arugula, red onion, orange sections, and olives. Add enough of the vinaigrette to lightly coat the salad and toss gently. Do not overdress the salad. Save any extra dressing for another use.

2 large or 3 small bunches arugula, washed and ends trimmed
1 small red onion, thinly sliced
2 small oranges, sectioned*
18 imported black olives, such as Calamata, Nicoise, or Italian
Basic Vinaigrette using red wine vinegar (page 266)

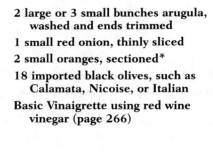

*To section an orange: Slice a thin piece off the top and bottom so the flesh is exposed. Place the orange, one cut side down, on a cutting board. With a sharp paring knife, cut off the rind, following the curvature of the fruit. Remove the membrane, and then cut in between each section with the paring knife to remove the sections.

Basic Vinaigrette

OSCAR WILDE SAID, "To make a good salad is to be a brilliant diplomatist—the problem is entirely the same in both cases. To know exactly how much oil one must put with one's vinegar." Homemade vinaigrette is absolutely delicious and can be prepared with a variety of vinegars, juices, and oils, as listed below. This dressing is easy to make, but do taste it with a piece of lettuce to ensure you have the diplomatic balance right. It will keep for a week or two in a covered container in the refrigerator. The recipe can easily be doubled or tripled.

makes about $1/2$ cup

1 to 2 tablespoons your choice of vinegar or juice, as listed below

$1/4$ teaspoon Dijon mustard

$1/4$ teaspoon salt or to taste

freshly ground black pepper to taste

flavorings of your choice as listed below, optional

4 to 6 tablespoons your choice of oil, as listed below

1 By hand: In a small bowl, combine the vinegar and/or juice, mustard, salt, pepper, and flavorings. Slowly whisk in the oil until a smooth dressing forms. Dip a lettuce leaf in the dressing to taste for salt and pepper and to see if a little extra oil is needed. (Some vinegars or the juice of some lemons may be more acidic than others, requiring a bit more oil.) Adjust to your taste.

2 Blender method (for larger quantities): Put the vinegar and/or juice, mustard, salt, pepper, and flavorings in the blender jar. Cover and pulse once or twice. Remove the plastic knob from the center of the cover, and replace the cover on the blender. (Do not stick your finger or a utensil into the hole at any time.) With the machine running, gradually pour the oil through the hole in the cover. The dressing will become thick and the ingredients will be blended. Turn off the machine, remove the cover, pour the dressing into another container. Taste, and adjust the seasonings.

Vinegar and Juices

Strong flavor: sherry wine vinegar, lemon juice, lime juice

Moderate flavor: balsamic vinegar, red wine vinegar, white wine vinegar, tarragon vinegar, cider vinegar, raspberry or other fruit vinegar

Mild flavor: rice wine vinegar; orange juice or apple cider

Combinations: 1 tablespoon of any of the strong or moderate vinegars or juices with 1 tablespoon of orange juice or apple cider

Oils

Very flavorful: sesame, mustard (Use only a few drops in combination with other oils.)

Flavorful: Extra virgin olive, walnut, hazelnut, virgin olive

Mild: safflower, canola, peanut, sunflower

Flavorings

These will suit the basic quantity; adjust if you are making a larger amount.

- 1 to 2 cloves finely minced garlic
- $1/4$ to $1/2$ finely minced shallot or 1 to 2 teaspoons finely grated onion
- $1/2$ to 1 chili pepper, seeded and finely minced
- $1/2$ to 1 teaspoon minced fresh ginger
- 1 to 2 tablespoons of any (or a combination of) minced fresh herbs: flat-leaf parsley, chives, basil, thyme, lemon thyme, dill, or mint
- 1 tablespoon poppy seeds or toasted sesame seeds

nine ESSENTIALS

Fresh Mango Chutney

Hot Pepper Vinegar

Crispy Shallots

Spiced Nuts

Lardons

Roasted Garlic Puree

Sambal Ulek

Homemade Chicken Broth

Quick Beef Broth

Basic Vegetable Broth

Basic Fish Broth

Faking It: The Doctored-Up
      Canned Broth

Fresh Mango Chutney

ALTHOUGH MANY CHUTNEYS ARE COOKED, this one is meant to be eaten raw. It is excellent with most Indian, Caribbean, or South African curries, but do not serve it with Thai curries. Make the chutney a few hours to a day ahead of time so that the flavor in the various ingredients have some time to blend.

270

serves 6

1 1/4 to 1 1/2 pounds ripe mangos, about 2 medium

1/2 cup sugar

1/2 teaspoon salt

1/2 to 1 teaspoon cayenne or other ground red chili pepper, to taste

1/2 teaspoon ground cumin

1/4 teaspoon turmeric

1 clove garlic, very finely minced or pressed through a garlic press

1/2-inch piece fresh ginger, peeled and grated

1 1/2 to 2 tablespoons cider, cane, or rice wine vinegar

1 Remove the flesh from the mangos and coarsely chop it. Discard the peel.

2 Put the sugar in the bowl of a food processor fitted with the metal blade and pulse for 30 to 60 seconds. Add the mango flesh, salt, cayenne, cumin, turmeric, garlic, ginger, and vinegar to the food processor. Pulse until a slightly chunky puree forms.

3 Transfer the mixture to a bowl. Cover and store in the refrigerator until serving.

note This recipe or its leftovers can be frozen in a covered container for about 1 month. Thaw in the refrigerator. It will last in the refrigerator for 3 to 5 days.

Hot Pepper Vinegar

COMMERCIAL HOT PEPPER VINEGAR is now available in some groceries, but it is quite easy to make your own. Usually served as a condiment with warm greens, this spicy vinegar adds spark when lightly sprinkled on many steamed vegetables or vegetable salads, or sparingly added to marinades for grilled meat and seafood.

271

Place the chilis in a clean, large bottle or jar with a screw cap. Pour in the vinegar so chilis are completely immersed. Cover the bottle and place in a dark cabinet for at least 3 weeks so the flavor develops.

8 to 10 whole jalapeño, bird's-eye, or serrano chili peppers

16-ounce bottle cider or white vinegar

note *Refrigerate the hot pepper vinegar after opening. If you don't use the vinegar within a week, make sure the chilis are completely covered in vinegar or they may turn moldy, and both the chilis and vinegar will have to be discarded. You can also strain the vinegar and put it in another container once the flavor develops.*

Crispy Shallots

THESE FRIED SHALLOTS ARE A MARVELOUS garnish for many stews, pureed or mashed vegetables, potatoes, or salads. This recipe can easily be doubled or tripled. The shallots will last in a sealed container for about 1 week. Do not refrigerate them—they will get soggy.

¹/4 pound shallots, about 8 to 10, thinly sliced
peanut oil for frying

1   Line a large strainer or colander with paper towels and set it over a bowl. In a large, deep skillet over medium heat, heat the peanut oil until it is hot, about 350°. The oil should be about 1 inch deep. Place a shallot slice in the pan—if the oil sizzles, it is ready. Working in batches if necessary, fry the shallots until they are lightly golden and crispy.

2   With a slotted spoon, transfer the shallots to the prepared strainer or colander and drain the excess oil. Place the shallots on a paper towel and blot off any remaining excess.

3   Let the shallots cool completely. Serve immediately or place in an airtight container.

Spiced Nuts

THESE TASTY NUTS ARE GOOD for snacking, but they are also a nice garnish for salads or fruit stews. You can use slivered almonds, cashews, peanuts, or pecan or walnut halves. This recipe can be doubled or tripled as you wish. The nuts will keep in a closed container in the refrigerator for about 1 month, although they will be eaten long before then.

1 cup nuts of your choice: slivered almonds, cashews, peanuts, pecans, or walnuts

1 1/2 tablespoons sugar

1/4 teaspoon crushed red pepper flakes

peanut oil for frying

1/4 teaspoon cumin, or to taste

1/4 teaspoon salt, or to taste

1/8 to 1/4 teaspoon cayenne, or to taste

pinch to 1/8 teaspoon white pepper

1 In a saucepan over medium heat, bring 2 cups of water to a boil. Add the nuts. Bring the water to a boil again and cook approximately 30 seconds for slivered almonds, 1 minute for cashews and peanuts, and 1 to 2 minutes for pecans and walnuts. Drain well in a colander.

2 While the nuts are still hot, toss them with the sugar and crushed red pepper flakes.

3 In a small bowl, combine the cumin, cayenne, salt, and white pepper.

4 In a medium skillet over medium heat, heat the peanut oil until it is hot, about 350°. The oil should be about 3/4 to 1 inch deep. Place a nut in the pan—if the oil sizzles, it is ready. Working in batches if necessary, fry the nuts until they are lightly golden.

5 With a slotted spoon, transfer the cooked nuts to a large strainer or colander set over a bowl. Drain and discard the excess oil.

6 Put the nuts into a bowl and toss them with the spice mixture. Taste and adjust the seasonings.

Lardons

LARDONS ARE FRESHLY COOKED bacon bits that are a necessary addition to several stews. They can also garnish salads, potatoes, and vegetables or be added to cornbread and biscuits.

8 thick-cut slices of bacon or 8 slices of slab bacon, rind removed

274

Cut the bacon slices crosswise into $1/2$-inch-wide strips. Place them in a medium skillet over medium-low heat. Cook, stirring occasionally, until they begin to brown. With a slotted spoon, transfer the bacon to a paper towel-lined plate and blot off the excess fat.

Roasted Garlic Puree

ROASTED GARLIC ADDS A GENTLER garlic flavor when used in place of fresh garlic. Taste what you are making to determine how much you need. I've used it in hummus, white bean puree, soups, and mashed potatoes. Because the garlic becomes sweet, it is wonderful spread on sliced, grilled, or toasted French or Italian bread. You can roast as few as one, or several heads at a time.

1 Preheat the oven to 350°. Slice about ⅛ inch off the top of a whole head of garlic to expose the cloves.

2 Place the garlic on a baking sheet. Lightly season with salt, pepper, and if using, thyme or rosemary. Drizzle a little olive oil on the garlic.

3 Bake about 1½ hours, or until the cloves are very tender and can be easily pierced with a paring knife.

4 Let the garlic cool. Squeeze the pulp from the paper-like exterior. Mash the pulp with a spoon or puree it in a mini- or regular food processor. Add a little olive oil to the puree if you wish.

whole heads of garlic, as many as you want to roast
salt
freshly ground black pepper
freshly chopped thyme or rosemary
extra virgin olive oil

275

Sambal Ulek

SAMBAL ULEK OR *OELEK* IS available commercially, imported from Thailand or the Netherlands, but it is quite simple to prepare. It will keep in an airtight container in the refrigerator for up to 2 weeks.

The recipe can be doubled or tripled. Red bird's-eye or cayenne or other red chili peppers can be used. Wear thin rubber or plastic gloves when preparing this recipe or your fingers may get burned from the heat of the chilis, a very unpleasant tingling sensation that can last for 1 or 2 days.

276

1/2 pound red chilis, either red bird's-eye, cayenne, or long red chili, stems removed and coarsely chopped

1 1/2 cups water

1 1/2 teaspoons salt

1/2 teaspoon sugar, optional

1 1/2 tablespoons white or rice wine vinegar

1 tablespoon peanut oil

3 to 4 tablespoons hot water

1 In a medium saucepan over high heat, combine the chilis and water. When the water comes to a boil, reduce the heat to medium and simmer for 15 minutes. Drain the chilis in a strainer.

2 In a food processor fitted with the metal blade, combine the chilis, salt, sugar (optional), and vinegar and pulse until a puree forms. Add the peanut oil and 3 to 4 tablespoons of hot water and process until the puree is smooth.

note *It is easier to cut a large amount of chilis with scissors rather than to chop them with a knife; either way, you should still wear gloves!*

Homemade Chicken Broth

THIS BASIC CHICKEN BROTH can be used in stews and soups, and can be frozen for up to 6 months. This recipe can be cut in half or doubled, per your need and the size of your freezer.

makes about 2 1/2 quarts

1 In a large (about 8 quarts) stockpot, combine the chicken parts, carrots, onions, celery, peppercorns, bay leaf, parsley, and water to cover.

2 Over medium-high heat, bring the liquid to a boil. Skim off any foam that forms. Reduce the heat to medium-low and simmer for 3 to 4 hours, skimming the fat and foam every half hour or so. Do not let the liquid boil.

3 Strain the broth and discard the solid ingredients. Cool at room temperature by stirring and placing the pot in a sink partially filled with ice water. When the broth is cool, refrigerate it for several hours or overnight. Remove any fat that solidifies on the surface. Use within 2 to 3 days or freeze.

VARIATION
You can use this recipe as a basic guide for turkey and duck broth, too.

note If the heat was slightly too high, you may need to replace some of the water that evaporated during step 2. For a stronger broth: Once the broth is strained and cooled and the fat has been removed, return it to a saucepan over medium heat and reduce the broth by half.

5 pounds chicken parts (bones, necks, backs, thighs)
2 medium carrots, cut into chunks
2 medium onions, peeled and halved
3 to 4 stalks celery with leaves attached, cut into chunks
2 teaspoons black peppercorns
1 bay leaf
3 sprigs parsley
5 quarts water

Quick Beef Broth

UNLIKE THE CANNED PRODUCT, this basic beef broth has no salt. It can be used in stews and soups and can be frozen for up to 6 months.

makes about 2 quarts

278

3 pounds beef bottom round or rump roast

2 medium carrots, cut into chunks

2 medium onions, peeled and halved

3 stalks celery with leaves attached, cut into chunks

3 to 4 plum tomatoes, halved and seeded

3 sprigs parsley

1 bay leaf

3¹/2 quarts water

1 In a large stockpot, combine the beef, carrots, onions, celery, tomatoes, parsley, bay leaf, and water to cover.

2 Over medium-high heat, bring the liquid to a boil. Skim off any foam that forms. Reduce the heat to medium-low and simmer for 1¹/2 to 2 hours, skimming the fat and foam every half hour or so. Do not let the liquid boil. Add more water during the cooking time if too much has evaporated.

3 Strain the broth, reserve the meat, and discard the remaining solid ingredients. Cool at room temperature by stirring and placing the pot in a sink partially filled with ice water. When the broth is cool, refrigerate it for several hours or overnight. Remove any fat that solidifies on the surface. Use within 2 to 3 days or freeze.

note *The meat can be sliced and served as pot roast. For a stronger broth: Once the broth is strained and cooled and the fat has been removed, return it to a saucepan over medium heat and reduce the broth by half.*

Basic Vegetable Broth

THIS VEGETABLE BROTH CAN BE MADE with any combination of mildly flavored vegetables. Add a few dried mushrooms if you wish. Do not use broccoli, cabbage, turnips, or beets because they will discolor the broth and impart too strong a taste. The broth can be used in stews and soups and can be frozen for up to 6 months.

makes about 2 quarts ·

1 In a large stockpot, combine the potato, carrots, parsnips, celery, leeks, onion, mushroom stems, parsley, bay leaf, peppercorns, and water to cover.

2 Over medium-high heat, bring the liquid to a boil and then reduce the heat to medium-low and simmer for about 50 to 60 minutes, adding more water if too much has evaporated.

3 Strain the broth and discard the solid ingredients. Use immediately or cool at room temperature by stirring and placing the pot in a sink partially filled with ice water. When the broth is cool, refrigerate it. Use within 3 days or freeze.

1 large potato or sweet potato, cut into chunks

2 medium carrots, cut into chunks

2 small parsnips, cut into chunks

1 stalk celery with leaves attached, cut into chunks

2 medium leeks, washed and cut into chunks

1 medium onion, peeled and halved

1 1/2 cups mushroom stems (not shiitake), optional

4 sprigs parsley

1 bay leaf

1 teaspoon black peppercorns

2 1/2 to 3 quarts water

Basic Fish Broth

THIS BROTH IS QUICK AND EASY to make. Ask your grocer's fish counter for bones. If you are making a recipe with shrimp, add the shells to the brew. The trick is not to let the liquid boil. Use the broth in stews or soups. The broth can be doubled, and can be frozen for up to 2 months.

makes about 1 1/2 quarts

1 1/2 pounds bones from mild fish such as sea bass, cod, grouper, monkfish, sole, snapper, or scrod

2 celery stalks with leaves attached, cut into chunks

1 small onion, peeled and halved

1 leek, washed and cut into chunks

1 bay leaf

shells from shrimp, optional

4 1/2 cups water

1 1/2 cups white wine or additional water

1   In a medium stockpot (about 4 quarts), combine the bones, celery, onion, leek, bay leaf, shrimp shells (if using), and water and wine to cover.

2   Over medium-high heat, bring the liquid to a gentle boil, and then reduce the heat to medium-low and simmer for 20 to 30 minutes. Do not allow the liquid to boil.

3   Strain the broth and discard the solid ingredients. Use immediately or cool, uncovered, at room temperature. When the broth is cool, refrigerate it. Use within 2 days or freeze.

Faking It: The Doctored-Up Canned Broth

WE DON'T ALWAYS HAVE TIME to make broth from scratch, so here are a few tips on improving the canned variety. Use low-sodium canned product; chicken is most readily available.

makes about 1 to 1 1/2 quarts

Chicken

6 cups canned low-sodium chicken broth

1/2 pound boneless skinless chicken, cut into strips

1 celery stalk, coarsely chopped

1 small carrot, coarsley chopped

1 medium onion, peeled and halved

Beef

6 cups canned low-sodium chicken broth

1/2 pound beef bottom round or round, cut into small cubes

1 celery stalk, coarsely chopped

1 small carrot, coarsely chopped

1 medium onion, peeled and halved

Mushroom

6 cups canned low-sodium chicken broth

6 to 8 dried mushrooms such as porcini, shiitake or chanterelle

1 celery stalk, coarsely chopped

1 small carrot, coarsely chopped

1 medium onion, peeled and halved

Shellfish

6 cups canned low-sodium chicken broth

shells from 1 1/2 pounds shrimp

1 celery stalk, coarsely chopped

1 small carrot, coarsely chopped

1 medium onion, peeled and halved

Fish

equal amounts clam juice and water to fit recipe, such as 1 cup clam juice and 1 cup water

To enrich broth: In a large saucepan over medium heat, combine the ingredients for each type of broth. Bring the liquid to a boil, and then reduce the heat to medium-low so the liquid barely bubbles. Cover partially and simmer for 20 to 30 minutes. Strain the solids, and use immediately or cool at room temperature by stirring and placing the pot in a sink partially filled with ice water and refrigerate. The broth must be used within 2 to 3 days or frozen.

INDEX

282

283

285